Democracy without Associations

Interests, Identities, and Institutions in Comparative Politics

Series Editor:
Mark I. Lichbach, University of California, Riverside

Editorial Advisory Board:
Barbara Geddes, University of California, Los Angeles
James C. Scott, Yale University
Sven Steinmo, University of Colorado
Kathleen Thelen, Northwestern University
Alan Zuckerman, Brown University

The post–Cold War world faces a series of defining global challenges: virulent forms of conflict, the resurgence of the market as the basis for economic organization, and the construction of democratic institutions.

The books in this series take advantage of the rich development of different approaches to comparative politics in order to offer new perspectives on these problems. The books explore the emerging theoretical and methodological synergisms and controversies about social conflict, political economy, and institutional development.

Democracy without Associations: Transformation of the Party System and Social Cleavages in India
Pradeep K. Chhibber

Gendering Politics: Women in Israel
Hanna Herzog

Democracy without Associations

———

*Transformation of the Party System
and Social Cleavages in India*

Pradeep K. Chhibber

Ann Arbor
THE UNIVERSITY OF MICHIGAN PRESS

2002   2001   2000   1999   4   3   2   1

A CIP catalog record for this book is available from the British Library.

Library of Congress Cataloging-in-Publication Data

Chhibber, Pradeep K., 1956–
    Democracy without associations : transformation of the party
system and social cleavages in India / Pradeep K. Chhibber.
        p.   cm. — (Interests, identities, and institutions in
comparative politics)
    Includes bibliographical references and index.
    ISBN 0-472-10962-6 (cloth : acid-free paper)
1. Political parties—India.   2. India—Politics and
government—1977–   I. Title.   II. Series.
JQ298.A1   C48   1998
324.253—ddc21   98-25511
                                                            CIP

To my parents Kanta and Opinder Chhibber

Contents

Acknowledgments

This book is a small beginning in my attempt to understand why some social divisions are more salient than others. The particular angle this enterprise focuses on is the role that political parties can play in exacerbating some differences while muting others. The book also represents an effort to understand Indian party politics. As I developed an interest in party politics, especially the role of political parties in Indian politics, the question that intrigued me then and this book purports to provide some answer to is—how similar and different are Indian parties from parties in other parts of the world? Indian political parties look different only because some institutional conditions, the role and structure of the state and the nature of social relations, constrain an Indian politician.

John Petrocik and Richard Sisson share the credit for sustaining and encouraging my interest in political parties and Indian politics. The project was brought to fruition by a number of people. In India, an unusual assortment of individuals have helped sharpen my understanding of Indian politics and the debt to them is both intellectual and personal. Dr. G. V. S. Murthy taught me about winning elections, staying in power, and retaining popularity. Preet Bedi showed me the importance of pragmatism, clear thinking, yet without losing sight of the passion for doing the right thing. Discussions with Shakti Sinha were always insightful and professional courtesies never intruded into the friendship. Rupak Vaish helped me better understand the shifting sands of right-wing politics while conversations with Anil Kapur stressed the significance of nationalism. Rajiv Chhibber introduced me to the politics of the street. Subhash Misra was always there as a friend and, sometimes, as a colleague. Subhash not only made operationalizing the surveys easier but he also never lost faith in me and provided consistent encouragement. His friendship has proved invaluable through this process.

In the academic community in Delhi the late Frank Thakurdas introduced me to Plato, Gian Singh Sandhu brought home the value of intellectual integrity, and M. P. Singh and Subrata Mukherjee were always supportive. In Ann Arbor, conversations with Samuel Eldersveld, especially his prodding and insightful criticisms, were more than immensely useful. Mark Brandon, Ann Lin, Bob Pahre, and Michael Ross read some chapters and gave very thoughtful suggestions and criticisms. Ravinder Bhavnani, David Backer, and Ken Kollman read the entire manuscript and provide keen insights for revision. This work is better for their efforts. Research assistance provided by Caroline Arnold, Shiela Malkani, and Dulcey Simpkins at key points proved invaluable. And finally, Doug Dion kept me honest while smelling the roses.

In addition to my colleagues at Michigan a number of other people read and commented on parts of the manuscript and their efforts were helpful. Felipe Aguero and Mariano Torcal made helpful remarks on the ideas as did Lori Gronich and Dennis Patterson, who read parts of it carefully. A final reading by Hans Blomkvist and P. Dasgupta helped sort out some of the remaining inconsistencies. Cherie Steele read the entire manuscript carefully and gave great suggestions for improving many parts of the book. This book is much improved because of her help and suggestions. Frieda read the entire manuscript many times and heard the ideas often enough. Her intellectual input was vital to this book.

I also gratefully acknowledge Cambridge University Press for permission to reproduce parts of "Who Voted for the Bharatiya Janata Party?" *British Journal of Political Science* 27:631–39 (October 1997), reprinted with the permission of Cambridge University Press; Sage Publications, for use of segments from Pradeep Chhibber and Mariano Torcal, "Elite Strategy, Social Cleavages, and Party Systems in a New Democracy: Spain," *Comparative Political Studies* 30:27–54 (February 1997), copyright © 1997, reprinted by permission of Sage Publications, Inc.; the University of Texas Press for permission to reproduce large parts of "State Policy, Rent Seeking, and the Electoral Success of a Religious Party in Algeria," *Journal of Politics* 58:126–48 (February 1996); and to the *Journal of Development Studies* for "Political Parties, Electoral Competition, Government Expenditures, and Economic Reform in India," *Journal of Development Studies* 32, no. 1: 74–76, reprinted by permission.

Figures

Tables

Chapter 1

State Structures, Associational Life, and the Social Basis of Party Systems

A dramatic shift took place in Indian party politics during the elections of 1996 and 1998, when the Bharatiya Janata Party (BJP), a right wing religious party, emerged as the largest party in parliament. Even more surprising was the composition of the ruling coalitions. Regional political parties governed India after the 1996 elections and are key elements of the coalition that brought the BJP to power in 1998. Caste-based parties were key elements of the 1996 United Front government. For the first time since independence in 1947, the Indian party system, which had been dominated by the catchall Congress Party, is fractured along regional, caste, and religious lines.

These changes in India's party system raise a series of questions that are of general interest to political scientists. What are the conditions under which a party system comes to be based on social cleavages? Is the relationship between social cleavages and the party system axiomatic or can political parties influence the links they have to social cleavages? More specifically, are there particular state structures and societal conditions under which parties can more readily exploit certain social differences rather than others? How is a catchall party system transformed into one rooted in social cleavages?

Nation-states in which the state plays a large role in their economic life and are also marked by weak associational life, party strategy and electoral competition can determine which social cleavages come to form the basis of the party system. Party competition can also determine which cleavages are politicized, the issues around which these cleavages coalesce, and whether the cleavages find expression at the national, regional, or local level. Although this book focuses on explaining the emergence of a cleavage-based party system and the attendant electoral decline of the Congress Party in India, the argument has implications for other settings as well. The framework offered can be used to explain the transformation

of a catchall party system into a cleavage-based party system in a variety
of settings. The formation of a class-based party system in Spain and the
emergence of religious cleavages as a basis of party support in Algeria, two
countries characterized by a state that played a large role in the economy
and weak associational life, is a result of party competition. The concluding chapter offers a reflection on how the relationship between social
cleavages and party systems comes to be formed.

The End of the Congress System

From the first elections in independent India in 1952 until 1967, the Congress Party was electorally dominant. It controlled not only the Lok Sabha
but all of the state assemblies—the Vidhan Sabhas.[1] Since 1967, the Indian
party system has seen nominal changes as Congress's electoral fortunes
fluctuated. By 1998, however, the proportion of seats held by Congress in
the Lok Sabha declined to less than 30 percent (see fig. 1). The Congress's
vote share also dropped to 25 percent in 1998, compared to an average of
over 40 percent in elections over the four previous decades.[2]

The 1998 general elections were a watershed for Indian party politics
for a number of other reasons: the Congress Party not only failed to
muster a plurality in the Lok Sabha but found itself out of power in many
Indian states.[3] For the first time in Indian politics, a right-wing Hindu
party, the BJP, in a pre- and postelectoral coalition with state-based parties constitutes the government at the center;[4] and regional and caste-
based parties have conclusively demonstrated their electoral strength.

A fragmentation of the Indian party system has accompanied the electoral decline of the Congress Party. The effective number of parties in the
Lok Sabha has increased from less than two during the 1950s and 1960s,
the period of one-party dominance, to more than five in 1998 (see fig. 2).[5]
This change is largely due to the emergence of state-based parties. The
United Front Government, which came to govern India in 1996, was constituted primarily by parties that are based in and limited to particular
states, including the Telugu Desam (Andhra Pradesh), Dravida Munnetra
Kazhagam (Tamil Nadu), the Tamil Maanila Congress (Tamil Nadu), and
the Assam Gano Parishad (Assam). Even the BJP, in 1998, relied on
regional parties to stay in power at the center. Party competition in the
states is now between different sets of parties (see table 1). This is in sharp
contrast to much of the period after independence, when the Congress was
the dominant party in all of the states. While the Congress is still in power

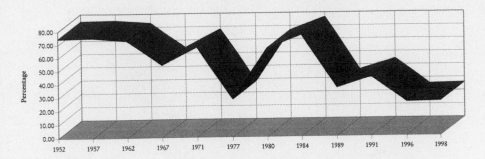

Fig. 1. Percentage of Lok Sabha seats held by Congress, 1952–98. (Data from Butler, Roy, and Lahiri 1996; Election Commission 1996.)

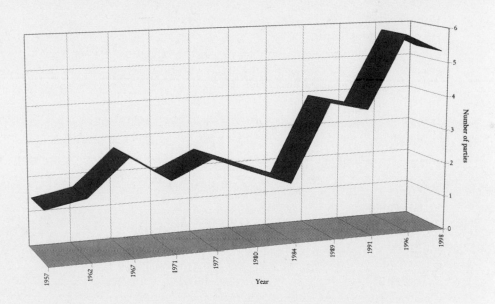

Fig. 2. Effective number of parties in the Lok Sabha, 1957–98. See text for details on the calculation of the effective number of parties. (Data from Butler, Roy, and Lahiri 1996; Election Commission 1996.)

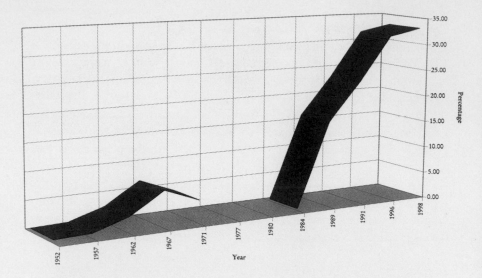

Fig. 3. Percentage of Lok Sabha seats held by the BJP, 1952–98. The BJP participated in the 1977 and 1980 elections as part of the Janata coalition. (Data from Butler, Roy, and Lahiri 1996; Election Commission 1996.)

TABLE 1. Party Competition in the Major States

State	Major Parties
Andhra Pradesh	Telugu Desam, Congress
Assam	Asam Gano Parishad, Congress
Bihar	Janata Dal, BJP, Congress
Gujarat	BJP, Congress
Haryana	Haryana Vikas Party, BJP, Congress
Karnataka	Janata Dal, BJP, Congress
Kerala	United Front, Left Front
Madhya Pradesh	Congress, BJP
Maharashtra	BJP, Shiv Sena, Congress
Orissa	Congress, Janata Dal, Biju Janata Dal
Punjab	Akali Dal, BJP, Congress
Rajasthan	BJP, Congress
Tamil Nadu	Dravida Munnetra Kazhagam, All-India Dravida Munnetra Kazhagam, Tamil Maanila Congress
Uttar Pradesh	BJP, Samjawadi Party, Bahujan Samaj Party
West Bengal	Communist Party of India (Marxist), Congress

in some states, it is no longer in power in a majority of states and in some Congress is not even the third largest party.

In addition, the BJP, whose predecessor the Jana Sangh was formed in 1951, emerged, after four decades of poor showings at the hustings, as the largest party in the Lok Sabha in 1996. The number of seats held by the BJP increased from 10 in 1989 to 161 in 1996 to 178 in 1998, bringing its share of seats to a third (see fig. 3).[6] Alongside the BJP, caste-based parties have emerged in parts of India.[7] In the Northern Indian state of Uttar Pradesh, for instance, a party system rooted in caste cleavages has emerged, with the forward castes supporting the BJP, the backward castes favoring the Samajwadi Party (SP), and the scheduled castes voting for the Bahujan Samaj Party (BSP).[8] The emergence of parties whose social basis is rooted either in a specific religious ideology or a particular caste signals the emergence of a cleavage-based party system in India.

Social Cleavages and Party Systems

Most accounts of these changes in the Indian party system have focused on the electoral decline of the Congress Party and the end of the Congress system. The party's electoral success over the years has been attributed to its ability to represent and, more importantly, to contain the various social divisions that pervade Indian society (Kothari 1964; Manor 1990; Rudolph 1987). Not surprisingly, then, most explanations of the party's decline have focused on why the Congress could no longer contain within its fold the various social divisions that characterize Indian society, thereby rendering the Congress system unviable. The rise of the BJP and caste-based parties is, therefore, explained through the social cleavage theory of party systems.[9]

The success of the BJP, for example, is attributed to successful mobilization of the Hindu vote, as the party played on the historic tensions between Hindus and Muslims. It has been argued that the vote for the BJP is then directly related to either the proportion of Muslims residing in an area (Brass 1993); economic competition between Hindus and Muslims, which is determined by the occupational patterns of Muslims (Rudolph and Rudolph 1993); or a religious nationalist ideology under which Hindus perceive India to be a Hindu nation-state (Varshney 1993).

Similarly, the emergence of a caste-based party system—whose clearest manifestation is in Uttar Pradesh—is ascribed to the inherent conflict between backward and forward castes, a conflict whose roots lie in the different position occupied by the castes in an economic and social hierarchy (Frankel 1987). The replacement of a one-party dominant system by state-specific parties has also been explained as resulting from preexisting social cleavages that are state specific; in essence, since the cleavages are state specific, only state-based parties could emerge (Chhibber and Petrocik 1989).

The social cleavage theory of party systems, on which these arguments are based, has had a significant influence on the study of party politics and party systems not only in India but elsewhere. In its theoretical conceptualization, links between cleavages and the party system arose as a consequence of the political mobilization and organization of sectors of society affected by the transformative national and industrial revolutions that took place during the formation of contemporary political societies (Lipset and Rokkan 1967; Lipset 1994).[10]

Over time, however, the concept of cleavage has become a vague and ambiguous category that is used to classify any political conflict. Bartolini and Mair propose that all cleavages are constituted by the combination of "social stratification, corresponding cultural systems and sociopolitical organizational forms—not only political parties, but also the network of social, professional, and other organizations which are expressive of the cleavage" (213). According to this interpretation, social differences associated with the process of economic development and state formation exist but only become cleavages as a result of electoral mobilization. For these social cleavages to come into existence, not only are social differences necessary but these differences should be institutionalized, developing their own "autonomous strength" and "acting as an influence on social, cultural and political life" (218).[11]

For this theory to be applicable to the Indian case, social divisions such as caste could influence party politics only when they exist as organizations with their own autonomous strength. Numerous interpretations of Indian electoral politics have argued that this is the case. Rudolph and Rudolph (1960), for instance, note that caste associations were indeed significant players in Indian electoral politics during the period immediately following independence. They argued that, though well-articulated voluntary associations were confined to the urban educated, caste remained an important channel of interaction in traditional society. Caste associations emerged under British rule with the expansion of communication, which, especially during the first half of the twentieth century, linked various subcastes. The newly formed castes pressed for political and economic mobility. These associations were not natural, and membership in them was not purely ascriptive (8). These caste associations were "moving . . . towards the manifest structure characteristic of the voluntary association," and hence they brought "political democracy to Indian villages" (9). Thus, formal caste associations, where they exist, can be expected to provide the formative basis for a social cleavage.

The well-documented influence of caste and religion in Indian party politics does not, however, rest on the presence of voluntary associations. Few Indians profess membership in religious or caste associations.[12] Membership in other associations, such as trade unions, is also limited. That notwithstanding, it could be argued that an informal organization of caste is a sufficient basis for establishing links between political parties and social cleavages.[13] Yet each caste, especially each *jati,* is not large enough to provide a political party with either the organizational or numerical support necessary to win a plurality in an election.[14] Since *jatis* are local, they may have political influence at the local level but little significance at the state or national levels (Brass 1990). Why should caste come to structure the party system at the state level in the 1990s?

There is an additional problem. Given the local manifestation of *jati,* why should the various *jatis* in parts of North India coalesce into three broad political alliances, forward, backward, and scheduled castes, with each group supporting a different party? Additionally, even though the economic and social position of backward and forward castes has been modified since independence, why do these divisions provide a basis for the party system in Uttar Pradesh only in the 1990s and not earlier? Further, if Hindus and Muslims have been historically at odds with each other, why does the BJP gain support when it does? The reasons for these omissions are fairly simple. The social cleavage framework ignores the role of agency. It simply derives interests from extant social cleavages, without asking why particular cleavages should be politicized when they do. Even when social cleavages are politicized it is not clear whether they will come to structure the party system. Cox (1997) puts the problem succinctly, "[a] given set of social cleavages does not imply a unique set of politically activated cleavages, and hence does not imply a unique party system" (16).

This development is especially intriguing as, in an electoral system such as India's—single member simple plurality (SMSP)—voters are mobilized locally.[15] Further, if caste as *jati* only influences local politics, why should statewide social cleavages come to structure the party system? (Brass 1993). Why should *jatis,* which are local and still seek to maintain their distinct identities, form political alliances with other *jatis* and create larger caste-based political alliances such as forward and backward castes in 1991? Moreover, why do these cleavages form the basis of the party system at the state level? A focus on political parties can resolve these concerns. Parties provide one vehicle for the politicization of cleavages. Like secondary associations, such as trade unions, they can act as the *formateurs* of the links between social cleavages and party systems. Political parties, however, cannot do so in all circumstances. Their ability to create links with social cleavages is constrained by the role of the state, institutional structures such as federalism and electoral laws, and by the existence of competing political bodies, namely secondary associations.

The State, Associational Life, Party Systems, and Social Cleavages

While there are any number of discussions on the role of political parties in particular nations, and on whether parties are important or not, there is little theoretical delineation of conditions under which parties may be able to play a greater role in creating links between social cleavages and the party system. A reason for the poverty of theory in this area is that the literature on party formation, party system change, and party organization does not explicitly address either the role of the state or associational life.[16]

The Role of the State, Federalism, and Party Systems

The omission of the role played by the state is especially surprising given the paradigm used by most party theorists, who see politicians as seekers of votes, office, and policy. As continuous reelection is the only way to attain these ends, politicians necessarily engage in constituency service and respond to the demands of pressure groups. To this end, they also logroll and seek pork barrel legislation. The ability of politicians to meet the demands of constituents and pressure groups is, at any given moment, dependent upon different state arrangements, each of which clearly offer different sets of incentives.[17] Put simply, politicians do indeed seek office, votes, and policy, but are constrained both by the role played by the state in the economy and state institutions.[18]

In rentier states, such as Algeria, the state is the owner of and distributor of most resources to society. Access to state office in the rentier state then provides an opportunity to politicians to distribute and accumulate state revenue. In other countries, such as the United States, politicians have not been able to avail themselves of such opportunities, since the rise of what Coleman (1996) calls the "fiscal state" placed some policies in the hands of the civil service and limited the influence of politicians to appropriate and distribute resources. In both kinds of states, politicians do seek office, but once in office they perform very different tasks. In a similar vein, some states have independent central banks, which place monetary policy off limits for politicians. Nelson Mandela in South Africa and Eduardo Frei in Chile have little ability to influence monetary policy, which is controlled by an autonomous central bank. Politicians seeking reelection in either system would therefore have to develop strategies that do not include changing monetary policy. In India, on the other hand, this is not the case, and Indian politicians who control the central bank can manipulate monetary policy to suit political ends.

Federalism, especially fiscal federalism, introduces opportunities and constraints for politicians. In federal systems, allocation decisions are assigned to subnational levels of government, which means that subnational governments, too, can distribute resources and set policy. Politicians respond to this division of authority and make appropriate adjustments. Spain began its new democracy with a process of decentralization that resulted in 17 different regional governments (*comunidades autonomas*), each of which has heterogeneous levels of wealth, social composition, and political competition (Vallès 1987; Montero and Torcal 1990). The regional governments, however, are not responsible to the electorate for most taxes, which are instead administered by central authorities. Since regional politicians do not have to concern themselves with how to pay for social services, they yield to "persistently strong demand for more and better [social] services" (Organization for Economic Cooperation and Development 1992–93, 63). Since regional politicians can mobilize support through social expenditures, social spending at the regional level has become excessive. The same luxury is not available to national leaders, who are faced with the fact that in endeavoring to raise resources through taxation they have to deal with budgetary restrictions imposed by the European Exchange Rate Mechanism and the approaching European monetary union deadline. In more centralized states, such as Venezuela, the influence of regional politicians is more limited (Levine 1973).

Federalism can also influence a party's organization.[19] In Spain, the Franco regime had centralized power. At the time of the transition to democracy, the government in Madrid was more powerful than the Spanish provincial governments. The political parties that developed in the posttransition period mirrored this imbalance: the national unit of the party dominated provincial units. The Unión de Centro Democrático (UCD), which governed Spain immediately after the transition, was a centralized party in which provincial offices were under central control. The centralization of power enabled the national leader to draw up "candidate lists" (Hopkin 1995). Similarly, the Partido Socialista Obrero Español (PSOE) developed first at the national level and then developed regional roots. As a consequence, Felipe Gonzalez, the leader of the socialists and prime minister from 1982 to 1996, ran the provincial socialist parties as adjuncts of the national party (Gunther et al. 1986). On the other hand, in the United States, because the national state developed well after the establishment of political parties, parties developed reasonably independent local organizations and are decentralized relative to parties in other countries (Eldersveld 1982).

Associational Life and Party Systems

Associational life also affects the role that parties play in the political process. In nations where associational life is weak, there are no intermediate organizations between society and the state. As a result, individuals look directly to the state to resolve their concerns.[20] An analysis of data drawn from the World Values Survey, carried out in 40 countries during 1990–91, demonstrates this phenomenon quite clearly. Respondents were asked whether they saw the provision of basic necessities as an individual responsibility or whether the state was more responsible for providing basic necessities; answers were arrayed on a 10-point scale, with 1 representing individual responsibility and 10 state responsibility. Respondents were also queried on their membership in secondary associations. This membership was recoded to form three categories of people—those who were not members of any association; those who belonged to one association; and those who were members of more than one association. Membership in a secondary association had a significant influence on where respondents looked for the provision of basic necessities (see table 2). The level of membership in secondary associations had this impact even after controlling for a number of competing explanations. The ideological orientation (self-placement on a left-right scale) of the respondents was introduced as a control on the assumption that respondents closer to the left would favor a greater role for the government. Reported family income (low to high) could influence perceptions of the role of the government, with wealthier respondents opting for greater individual responsibility.

Individuals' trust in their government and opinions on whether the government was run by a few vested interests were included as measures of individual perceptions of the government on the presumption that those who did not trust the government were less likely to see it as the provider of basic necessities. Two additional controls, gender and the respondent's place of residence, were also introduced as controls. The negative coefficient of membership in secondary associations demonstrates that those who do not belong to secondary associations are more likely to suggest that the state provide basic necessities.

The impact of the state being perceived as having a primary responsibility in nations where associational life is weak enables political parties to play a large role. In Venezuela, for instance, the authoritarian phase left behind a fragmented society and weak secondary associations (Levine 1973). With the emergence of democracy, parties came to be the major political force because they were able to incorporate a full range of social interests and the "mobilization [of social groups] was utterly channeled and controlled by political parties" (Levine 1995, 11), leading some to characterize the Venezuelan system as a "partyarchy" (Coppedge 1994). Similarly, the authoritarian legacy in Spain was that of a strong centralized state and a society with few independent associations apart from the

TABLE 2. Belonging to Secondary Associations and the Role of the State
(OLS estimates)

Variable	Coefficient	Standard Error
Country run by a few vested interests	0.178*	0.320
Trust in government	0.074*	0.017
Gender	0.294*	0.028
Income	0.001*	0.001
Size of town	0.035*	0.005
Left-right self-placement	−0.006*	0.001
Membership in a secondary association	−0.280*	0.018
Constant	4.395	0.051

Source: The World Values Survey, 1991
*Significant to 0.05
$N = 46,616$
$F = 99.136$
$R^2 = 0.02$
Standard error = 2.98

Catholic Church. The weak associational dimension of society, in turn, allowed political parties to exert tremendous influence on the nature of the transition to democracy (Aguero 1995; Higley and Gunther 1992; Gunther et al. 1995). The success of the Spanish transition is attributed solely to the ability of party elites to make and remake social coalitions out of the relatively weakly organized society in all areas except religion, where a well-organized church set the agenda.[21] Similarly, in Chile, where associational life outside the church is not well developed, political parties set the public policy agenda in most areas (Valenzuela 1978).

In Italy, the relationship of social movements to the state is also mediated through the party and the political system. This is more true in southern Italy than it is in northern Italy. Though Putnam's (1993) description of the differences between northern and southern Italy focuses mostly on social capital, the absence of secondary associations in the south has had its impact on the party system as well. Weak associational life made room for patronage politics in the region, which in turn helped the Christian Democrats dominate southern Italian politics. In the south, party was the central agent linking state to society (LaPalombara 1987; Tarrow 1989). Because there were competing associations in the north, no political party could establish a central place in the political process to quite the same extent as the Christian Democrats did in the south. Likewise, the destruction of voluntary associations after the Civil War in the American South allowed most politics to be channeled through the single dominant Democratic Party (Key 1949).

States, Associational Life, and Political Parties

As argued, the role of political parties cannot be examined outside the institutional framework within which they have to work. This framework includes both state institutions, such as federalism, and social institutions, such as associational life, which together lay down the nature of the interaction between social cleavages and the party system.[22] To determine the influence of a party, then, an analysis of the role played by the state in the economy, state institutions such as federalism and electoral laws, and the extent of associational life, is critical.[23]

Political parties can play a more important role in creating links between social cleavages and the party system in contexts in which the state plays a large role in setting economic and social policy and associational life is weak.[24] In situations in which there are well-developed associations, on the other hand, political parties have to compete with those associations and are therefore less central. Spain is a case in point. While associational life in Spain is not well developed and political parties could exercise influence in most areas, parties were not as effective in the domain of religion due to the fact that they had to deal with a long-established church. This is also true for political parties in many parts of Latin America, such as Chile, where parties have played a large role in setting policy in most areas except religion, which is dominated by the Catholic Church.

State, Associational Life, Party Systems, and Party System
Change in India

The influence exercised by the state over economic and social policy gave the Congress Party, which controlled the state at independence, significant influence over setting policy. As the state so dominated other social, political, and economic institutions, politicians' incentives centered around capturing the state. The federal structure, by assigning power to subnational (state) governments, provided politicians with incentives to control state governments and constrained political parties to mobilize support on a state by state basis. Indian society, on the other hand, though stratified, is composed of numerous castes, none of which by itself has the numerical strength to determine electoral outcomes in most electoral constituencies. Additionally, associational life in India is weak, as most Indians do not belong to formal associations and many of the associations that do exist are either tied to political parties or, if autonomous, are either transitory phenomena or are ineffective politically. The predominant role assigned to the state and the lack of well-developed associational life imparted political parties in India with a larger role than in societies with more associations and a less dominant state. Placing parties in the context of the large role played by the state and the nature of associational life provides us an account for the transformation of the party system, from one dominated by the catchall Congress Party to one rooted in social cleavages. It also provides an explanation for how particular social cleavages, region, caste, and religion come to be linked to the party system.

Not every possible social division is translatable into a cleavage that can structure a party system. History undoubtedly plays an important role in determining which social differences can be made politically salient. In India, caste is one such distinguishing characteristic and language and religion are others, whereas race is not. In electoral democracies, in addition, numbers play an important role in determining which cleavages are politicized. The social division a party mobilizes has to be neither too small nor too large. Take for instance *jati* (*jatis* are very small in numbers). *Jatis* cannot emerge as a mainstay for the party system insofar as they cannot provide any political party with sufficient electoral support. Political parties, insofar as they rely on caste as a basis for building support, have to engage a more expansive notion of caste. Such a conception would attempt to build coalitions across *jatis* but still on a reconceptualized understanding of caste. The idea of a backward caste, a multi-*jati* grouping, is one example of the reordering of caste into a larger social entity.

If a group is too large, such as the poor, that too can prove to be a disadvantage. No political party, if it seeks to win elections, can afford to be actively anti-poor. Not surprisingly, all political parties in India advocate pro-poor policies. This lowers the probability that poverty, by itself, can provide a social basis to the party system. Further, it is in the interest of the political parties to divide such a group along lines other than those that make this group a majority. Similarly with caste. If a caste group is a majority, such as in some southern Indian states (e.g., Karnataka) where there is an overwhelming majority of backward castes, no party can afford to be anti-backward caste.

Developmental Policies of the Indian State

The Indian state, since independence, has played a key role in transforming economic and social life in India. The "developmental ideology . . . was a constituent part of the self-definition of the post-colonial state," which "acquired its representativeness by directing a programme of economic development on behalf of the nation" (Chatterjee 1994, 55). The role of the state in economic change became clear with the adoption of the second Five Year Plan, which stressed state-controlled, heavy-industry-led economic development.

When India was granted independence in 1947, the Congress Party was handed the reins of power by the British. The party thus came to control the most powerful institution in postindependence India—the state—and was therefore immediately at the center of the political process. National leaders at independence felt that Congress was not only a political party but simultaneously an agent of development and social change.[25] As Kothari (1964) notes, when Congress "came to power, [it] assigned a positive and overwhelming role to government and politics in the development of society" (1164). The Congress Party also introduced national legitimacy as a "principal issue of politics and gave to the government and the ruling party an importance of great symbolic value . . . [and] the Congress in power made for a concentration of resources, a monopoly of patronage and a control of economic power which crystallized the structure of its power and made competition with it a difficult proposition." (1167)

Federalism

The other facet of the Indian state that influenced the role that political parties were to play was its institutional framework, especially the federal system. In India's federal system, the major players are the central and state governments, not local governments. The center and the states are responsible for the allocation of resources and the provision of services, even at the local level. An immediate consequence of this arrangement is that political parties, above all the Congress, organized themselves in such a way as to dominate the center and/or the states. This outcome is not surprising if one considers the fact that the local governments in India have little independent authority, much less the capability to decide how resources are to be allocated. Local governments merely spend the money that is allocated by the center and the states, which in the process also determines the spending priorities of local governments.[26]

Electoral Laws

Meanwhile, the electoral law, single member simple plurality, ensured that support had to be mobilized locally, which requires building constituency-specific coalitions. These are often multicaste coalitions.[27] The joint effect of electoral laws and social institutions is that mobilization for votes was rarely, if ever, national. The impact of these electoral laws is, however, mediated by state structures. As state governments, not local ones, are resource centers, voters develop preferences over policies adopted by the state governments. This response, in turn, influences their vote—whether they vote for candidates or parties and whether they choose locally competitive or statewide competitive political parties. An example may perhaps clarify this line of thinking. In the United States, it was only with the centralization of economic decision making (or fiscal centralization) in Washington after the implementation of the New Deal in the 1930s that the federal government acquired a large role in local economies, leading voters finally to abandon locally competitive for nationally competitive parties. Voters did so as they developed preferences over national policy. They had no reason to develop these preferences as long as the national government did not play a role in local economies. Absent this influence from the center, local issues dominated voters' electoral preferences (Chhibber and Kollman 1998).

Associational Life

A popular interpretation of Indian society sees it as divided into many small caste, linguistic, religious, and class divisions; these divisions, in turn, are the lines along which political parties mobilize support. A key element of Indian society that is often overlooked, however, is its weak associational life. In 1991, only 13 percent of all Indians belonged to an organization, the lowest figure for all of the democracies on which comparable data is available (see table 3). In sharp contrast, in countries such as Iceland, Sweden, the Netherlands, Norway, and Denmark, over 80 percent of the respondents belong to at least one association. Spain, after India, registers the second lowest level of associational membership (23 percent).[28]

The Catchall Party and Party System Change

The Congress Party came to dominate the Indian electoral system because it carried a national mandate as the party that had brought independence. Electoral laws and weak associational life enabled the Congress Party to emerge as a catchall party. As discussed earlier, the SMSP system forces political parties to mobilize support locally, and in India this entailed building multicaste coalitions at the local level. These alliances, and the electoral predominance of the party, were sustained through a mix of policies and selective allocations of the resources available within the Indian state.[29]

The catchall nature of the Congress Party, especially when the relationship between the party and social cleavages is viewed at the state level, may then be attributed to the electoral system and the local nature of social cleavages in India. The absence of associational life further enabled the Congress Party to retain its catchall nature, as the party was not required to adopt a policy that represented a particular opinion in the state. Associations, especially naional associations, have forced political parties in other SMSP systems, notably those of the United States and Britain, to adopt positions other than those required to sustain local alliances.[30] Patronage politics associated with the extensive dispersal of state resources, insofar as it let Congress maintain its multicaste coalition at the local level, led to the continuation of the catchall system.

These structural features, which led to the creation and maintenance of a catchall party system, also constrained the nature of party system change. To win a plurality, an opposition political party had two options. It could, first, engage in the catchall politics similar to that associated with the Congress Party. In other words, a party could win an election and then

TABLE 3.   "Global" Associational Membership

Country	Percentage belonging to at Least One Association
Iceland	90
Sweden	85
Netherlands	84
Norway	82
Denmark	81
Finland	77
United States	71
South Korea	71
West Germany	67
Canada	64
Belgium	57
Great Britain	52
Hungary	50
Ireland	49
Switzerland	43
Brazil	43
Slovenia	39
France	38
Mexico	36
Italy	34
Japan	30
Romania	30
Argentina	24
Spain	23
India	13

Note: India data are drawn from a 1991 postelection survey. The question asked whether respondents were members of an association. All other data are from the World Values Survey, 1991.

retain the support of a multicaste coalition at the local level much the same way the Congress did—that is, through the instruments of the state. If a party, or a collection of parties, followed this strategy, the resulting politics would resemble that of the Congress and a catchall party system would be sustained (in that this party, too, would not be rooted in statewide social cleavages) except that the party in power would be a party other than the Congress. This, to a large extent, was the politics associated with the Janata Party, which came to power in the late 1970s.

An alternative strategy for an opposition party would be to raise an issue that creates a coalition of voters that spans electoral constituencies. With the introduction of such an issue, voters from across the various constituencies could be mobilized to vote for a particular party. If the basis on which these voters are mobilized is linked to a social characteristic such as caste, the party system would come to be based on statewide social cleavages. At the state level, then, the party system would be tied to social cleavages. Given the predominant role ascribed to the state in India, such a statewide coalition could be formed by adopting a policy that would be of concern to most voters such as quotas in government jobs and educational institutions.[31]

An instance in which the introduction of particular policies, especially those that could sever the Congress's local multicaste coalition, transformed the party system and proved to be problematic for the party was the adoption of the report of the Mandal Commission, which had recommended quotas for backward classes in government jobs and educational institutions.[32] The introduction of this issue, since it signaled a reallocation of state jobs, structured voter preferences across electoral constituencies. This policy, not local issues, came to dominate future elections. The Congress Party could neither openly support nor explicitly oppose the adoption of the policy, since that would imply that it was taking a stand in favor of either the forward or backward castes, both of which were in the Congress coalition.[33] Other political parties capitalized on the dilemma faced by the Congress Party.[34] In Uttar Pradesh, for instance, when the BJP made overt gestures toward the forward castes, the SP actively recruited the backward castes and the Muslims, and the BSP projected itself as the only party capable of representing the interests of the scheduled castes, Congress's vote share dropped.[35] The introduction of an issue that influenced the preference orderings of voters statewide led to the transformation of the party system from one dominated by a catchall party to one in which the major political parties were clearly tied to social cleavages statewide. Links between social cleavages and party systems, then, were created by party competition and state policy.[36]

Implications

The argument developed here suggests, first, that theories of party system change developed in the context of well-developed associational life may not be applicable in all cases. Instead, party system change can, in some cases, only be understood in the context of state structures, social institutions, and the role of parties therein. This interpretation suggests that socially based explanations of party decline—that is, explanations that rest on the role of social groups and parties as responding to exogenous social changes (Kitschelt 1992; Inglehart 1995)—are phenomena limited to certain contexts.

Second, it suggests that if institutions are to be taken seriously the number of parties and the nature of electoral competition are influenced not only by electoral rules but by the rules of the game imposed by state structures and social institutions. To this end, the influence political parties have, particularly their impact on social and economic policy, cannot be attributed to partisan positions alone but depends crucially on the place occupied by a party in relation to both state structures and social institutions.

This issue is especially salient in the context of the influence of electoral laws. Research in this area has examined the links between party systems (often defined as the effective number of parties) and electoral laws and social structures. Party systems are seen as resulting from the interaction of electoral laws and social structures. The argument developed in this book, however, questions whether electoral laws are as influential in determining the nature of the party system as has commonly been assumed. In India, the party system has moved from a single-party-dominant to a multiparty system. This shift has been accompanied by the transformation of a catchall party system to one in which links between social cleavages and party systems are clearly defined. This transformation has occurred independently of the electoral laws, which have remained constant in this period. Similarly, in Spain there is the move from a catchall to a cleavage-based party system, despite the fact that the electoral laws have not changed. In both India and Spain, then, electoral laws have remained the same but the relationship of party system to social cleavages has changed dramatically. This outcome, however, is not surprising if one considers that voters choose between candidates based on policy preferences; assuming that the state plays a large role in society, voters develop preferences over state policy and then begin to choose among candidates and parties based on those sets of preferences independent of the influence exerted by electoral laws.

The Argument and Its Generalizability

The central argument developed in this book is that in electoral democracies in which an activist state dominates political life and associational life is weak the emergence of a cleavage-based party system can result primarily from party strategy and competition. The bulk of the book focuses on explaining the emergence of a cleavage-based party system in India. It then endeavors to determine whether the hypotheses developed are limited to India or are replicable in other contexts. The validity of the argument is tested in Spain, an economically developed Western European nation, and in Algeria, a North African postcolonial society with vast reserves of and revenues derived from oil. Not only do these two countries differ from each other, but they both differ from India in terms of their social organization, cultural makeup, and economic life. Like India, however, Spain and Algeria are characterized by activist states and weak associational life. Similarly to India, in both countries the emergence of links between social cleavages and party systems is attributable to party competition. Insofar as the theoretical findings are replicable in such diverse settings, the book "pushes scholars to discover new explanations that might not have emerged from a more homogeneous set of cases" (Collier 1993, 112).

Some might argue that these findings are not generalizable since the book focuses solely on cases in which there is weak associational life and an activist state. Yet the argument presented here is largely applicable for a number of reasons. First, present research on the relationship between social cleavages and party systems, because of its explicit focus on Western Europe, is limited to cases in which strong associational life exists independent of political parties. In other words, the Lipset and Rokkan thesis has dealt adequately with the relationship between party systems and social cleavages in the context of strong associations. This analysis is explicitly concerned with those cases in which there is little associational life.

Second, the analysis suggests that the Lipset and Rokkan thesis, which has largely been accepted as a theory for the links between social cleavages and party systems, is limited to a specific set of cases. A more general theory of the link between social cleavages and party systems can only emerge once we place parties within the context of state structures and the nature of civil society. In principle, such a framework would enable us to explain a larger variety of cases. Seen in this light, the Indian, Algerian, and Spanish cases offer the most in terms of a clear, comprehensive, theoretical statement (Caporaso 1995, 458).

Third, and most important, the Indian, Spanish, and Algerian cases, insofar as they demonstrate novel ways in which parties can make cleavages, offer a serious empirical challenge to the widely accepted social cleavages theory of party systems.[37] The argument developed not only, *pace* Rogowski (1995), focuses on anomalies that are "too pronounced to be accidental," but it also offers a clear alternative formulation.

The Chapters

This book examines the impact of state institutions and the absence of associational life on party politics in India. Chapter 2 addresses the organization of the state and the nature of associational life in India. It begins with an analysis of the federal relationship in India. While ties between the center and the states are well documented, what is less well understood is the relationship between the center/state and the locality. It therefore focuses attention on local government, especially its relationship with state and central governments. The argument developed is that local governments have little political and economic power, and the analysis is substantiated by empirical evidence from local elite surveys of 1966 and 1996, a comparison of the 64th and 73rd Amendments to the Indian Constitution, and an examination of local government initiatives in Karnataka, which, after introducing radical local government reform in the 1980s, withdrew the reforms a few years later and concentrated power in the hands of the state government.

Chapter 3 discusses the nature of the Indian party system. It argues that because of the role played by the state governments and the attachment of political parties to state governments the Indian party system is a state-based system. Electoral rules, especially the SMSP system and weak associational life, led to the emergence of a catchall party system. Attitudes of Congress Party activists and elites show that the party was an office-seeking party whose activists were less concerned with party organization than with gaining access to state resources. Congress, it will be argued, had little organization to speak of at the local level, even in the districts. Whatever organization did exist was mostly at the state level.

The office-seeking nature of the party system and the strong party-state linkage that existed in India in the immediate postindependence period also structured the strategy of opposition parties. The emergence of opposition to Congress in 1967 was clearly over access to state office, and the Congress Party's defeat can clearly be attributed to defections from the party over access to state office. The 1967 election is examined in some detail in chapter 4, concentrating on the nature of the opposition to the Congress, the opposition's raison d'être, and the Congress's response to that opposition. As the emergence of opposition to Congress in the mid-1960s was state specific, this led to two responses by the national party: an increased role of the center in the states and a general expansion of the role of the state with this in mind. Chapter 4 also discusses the political considerations that entered into the distribution of national resources to the states by the central government and a general expansion of the role of the state.

Chapter 5 continues this line of reasoning. Using aggregate and survey data, it argues that opposition to Congress was not a result of the mobilization of new groups but rather was due largely to the elements of its coalition that had once supported it but now opted for different parties. The intra- and interparty competition that has characterized Indian politics since 1967 is over access to the state. As party competition became more intense, state office also increasingly became the focus of this conflict. The resulting increase in cabinet size—in some cases by over 50 percent—and cabinet instability are a direct consequence of this competition. Data on cabinet sizes and cabinet instability for the major Indian states (15) demonstrate this quite clearly.

Chapter 6 discusses the implications of the increased role of the state for party system change. It notes that party system change, especially the anchoring of political parties in social cleavages, is not due to exogenous social changes, such as demographic shifts or the emergence of new issues, but rather is endogenous to party politics. The decline of the Congress Party and the emergence of a cleavage-based party system in Uttar Pradesh (UP) is a direct result of party competition. In UP, until 1989, the Congress was a catchall party whose electoral success was based on its reliance on multicaste coalitions at the local level. By 1993, however, a party system rooted in backward and forward castes had emerged in UP. The emergence of this caste-based party system is linked to perceptions of the state government's policies and party competition.

Chapter 7 makes the case that the electoral success of the BJP is also endogenous to party politics. The electoral success of the BJP is attributed to its ability to forge a coalition between religious groups, the middle classes (in terms of economic interests), the forward castes, and those who had an interest in national politics. This alliance was made possible because of the politics of the Congress Party. State policy formulated by the Congress-led developmental state—secularism and economic intervention—provided the political opportunity for religious parties to build coalitions between religious groups and the middle classes. Policy responses by the developmental state to fiscal and political crises provided the catalyst for elites of religious parties to cement a coalition of religious groups and more laissez-faire economic interests. The identification of the Congress Party with the state that began in 1971 opened the door for the BJP to capitalize on its nationalist message. Chapter 8 uses the argument offered in the book to provide some perspective on why parties are considered so central to Indian politics, the nature and extent of current economic reforms, the paradox of the coexistence of democracy and collective violence, and the electoral decline of the Congress Party.

Chapter 9 explores the comparative implications of this line of reasoning for explaining party system change and the emergence of social cleavages. The Spanish and Algerian cases are used to demonstrate the generalizability of the ideas put forth for India. In Spain, the party system was characterized by the dominance of the catchall Unión de Centro Democrático and the Partido Socialista Obrero Español. By 1993, however, a cleavage-based party system had emerged, with the PSOE and the Partido Popular (PP) drawing support from different classes. In Algeria, where there was no real religious association, the Front de Islamique Salut, (FIS) was able to mobilize both religious and class cleavages. The ability of the FIS to do so was less a result of exogenous social forces than it was a consequence of the policies pursued by the ruling Front de Liberation Nationale (FLN). The concluding chapter offers a discussion of the relationship between party systems and social cleavages.

Chapter 2

Central, State, and Local Governments in India

The dominant paradigm in Indian politics at independence was that the government would be the engine of economic and social transformation. Most of this change would be carried out by the national government. State governments were made partners in this process, while local governments were not incorporated into the enterprise of nation building and economic and social change. The distribution of responsibilities mirrors the federal structure in India, which is heavily skewed toward the central and state governments. Local governments are dependent on the state government both politically and economically and function more as agencies of the state government than as independent levels of government. Attempts to provide local governments with independent authority and power have been scuttled by state governments. Karnataka, for example, which made significant progress toward empowering local governments in the mid-1980s, reasserted the primacy of the state government in 1993. Similarly, the 73rd Amendment to the Constitution, ostensibly modeled after the 64th Amendment, which devolved power to local authorities, made changes to the latter so that the authority of state governments would not be usurped. This chapter details the role played by the state as a central actor in restructuring the Indian economy and discusses the nature of federalism in India. It begins with a portrayal of the position ascribed to the state in restructuring the Indian economy and society. It then discusses in depth the federal structure of the Indian state.

The Role of the Indian State at Independence

The directive principles of state policy, enumerated in part IV of the Indian Constitution (Arts. 36–51), made the Constitution a policy document and assigned an extensive role to the state.[1] The directive principles state that "the State shall strive to promote the welfare of the people by

securing a social order permeated by social, economic and political justice" (Art. 38).[2] The state was also supposed to ensure a decent standard of
living (Art. 43); seek a more equitable distribution of wealth (Art. 39); and
try to raise the level of nutrition and improve public health (Art. 47). These
directive principles, which are nonjusticiable, were seen as economic ideals
that the state was supposed to strive for and as directions to the legislature
and the executive branch on how the state was to exercise its legislative and
administrative authority. The state was also seen as the agent of economic
change and therefore expected to follow a path of planned development.

Planning for Economic Development and the State

At independence, there was general consensus among Indian policymakers that the nation-state was to be the engine of social and economic development. "Even before the planning system was established, the center
took full control over the industrial sector by legislation, as permitted by
the Constitution, since it was agreed on all sides that industrialisation
would be at the heart of development and the necessary thrust could only
be provided by the state operating through the central government"
(Mozoomdar 1994, 99). The state was able to play such a large role without any contestation because of its historical role, which arose out of the
independence movement. As Chatterjee notes, the emphasis on the nation-
state emerged as a result of nationalism, and "the economic critique of
colonialism . . . was the foundation from which a positive content was supplied for the independent national state: the new state represented the only
legitimate form of exercise of power because it was a necessary condition
for the development of the nation" (1994, 55).

About the time India became independent, there was also a worldwide
ideological consensus that the state should be the engine of economic
transformation. Several factors helped generate this intellectual climate,
including acceptance of the Keynesian paradigm, in which the state plays
an active role in the economy, at the end of World War II throughout most
of the industrialized world (Hall 1986); an acknowledgment of the general
validity of Arthur Lewis's thesis on the extraction of resources from agriculture and their redirection toward industry as a sine qua non of development (Lewis 1954); and the generally favorable reaction to Gerschenkeron's (1962) thesis concerning the key role played by the state in the
economic advancement made by "late developers." The geopolitical situation at the end of World War II also encouraged this line of thinking. The

key assumption was that national independence could be maintained through the attainment of economic power. In an industrial world, economic power could be achieved through heavy-industry-led industrialization. The rapid rise of the Soviet Union as an industrial and political power provided a model for policymakers in many developing countries.

State-led industrialization was seen as necessary for a number of reasons particular to the Indian economy as well. First, large amounts of capital were needed to establish the industrial base required for sustained and diversified growth. These resources could only be mobilized by the state, especially given the low rate of private saving in India. Second, public investment could create an industrial structure more easily without having to rely on higher levels of corporate profitability, which would increase income disparities. Third, reliance on public rather than private enterprise would foster growth of the metal, mineral, machine-building, and chemical industries. Economic power, in this way, would not be rooted in industrial houses (Mozoomdar 1994).

Support for this expansive role of the state came from across the political spectrum. The Left wanted all-India plans led by a National Planning Committee and "the National Planning Committee . . . [would be] the first real experience of the emerging state leadership of the Congress . . . with working out the idea of 'national planning.'" The more centrist Congress, too, felt that "planning was not only a part of the anticipation of power by the state leadership of the Congress, it was also an anticipation of the concrete forms in which that power would be exercised within a national state" (Chatterjee 1994, 53). Meanwhile, the Bombay Plan, devised by leading industrialists, relied on planning by the state (Byres 1994). Hence, at independence and in the decade that followed independence there was widespread political support for the notion that the Indian state was to be the architect and arbiter of economic development (Paranjape 1964; Hanson 1966; Rudolph and Rudolph 1987; Kaviraj 1996; Chakravarty 1987).

Responsibility for the economic transformation of India was placed in the hands of the Planning Commission, an extraconstitutional body answerable only to the national government. While the national government exercised control over the sphere of economic policy, its agent, the Planning Commission, "remained outside the formal constitutional framework" (Kaviraj 1996, 88). The significance of the commission was obvious from the fact that initially the prime minister was its chairman; since Prime Minister Jawaharlal Nehru was also India's undisputed national leader at that point, it imparted a personal and institutional significance to the commission. Nehru supported the Planning Commission, and "under Nehru, the Secretary of the Planning Commission also served as Cabinet Secretary, which gave the Commission a unique position in the bureaucracy" (Varshney 1993, 51). Planning consequently came to depend "increasingly on the monological instruments of the state and its bureaucracy" (Kaviraj 1996, 90), and the program of modernity adopted by the central government led to a continuous expansion of the state as it "went in a frenetic search of alibis to control ever larger areas of social life" (91).

That search is readily apparent in the area of social policy. The central government decided to take an extremely proactive role in the uplifting of the scheduled castes and tribes. Apart from setting up quotas for both of these social categories in appointments to government jobs and admission to educational institutions, the central government also decided to set up Scheduled Caste Development Corporations and a Scheduled Tribe Finance and Development Corporation.[3] The express aim of these corporations was to provide resources for the economic advancement of these groups. Educational policy, too, is set by the central government, which plays a large role in both devising curricula and establishing schools by means of instruments such as the National Policy on Education and educational television programs whose content is determined by central organizations like the Central Institute of Educational Technology. Both the central and state governments have also begun to play a role in attempting to meet the nutritional needs of children in schools. The state has extensive programs to deal with rural unemployment and rural development, most notably the Jawahar Rozgar Yojana (Jawahar Employment Plan) and the Integrated Rural Development Program.[4]

The Indian state, then, for historical reasons associated with the experience of colonialism, the international geopolitical situation, the ideological orientation of its policymakers, and the economic realities of India, was seen as *the* agent of social and economic transformation.[5]

Federalism

The political realities associated with building support across a vast nation with many different interests led Congress to adopt a federal system with a fair measure of provincial autonomy.[6] Federalism as an institution is characterized by a division of authority among governmental units; each unit is constitutionally recognized as having its own clearly demarcated sphere(s) of authority.[7] In India, there are three widely recognized levels of government: central, state, and local. Local government, especially popular local government, is a multitiered system that extends from the village to the district, called *panchayati raj.* In most states, *panchayati raj* is largely a three-tiered arrangement: the district (*zilla parishad*), the village (*gram panchayat*), and an intermediate level (the *samiti*). The nature and name of the arrangement differs across states (Ministry of Rural Development 1991). The federal relationship in India may be understood in terms of two dyads: the relationship between the center and the states and the relationship between the states and the localities. Both dyads have a political as well as a fiscal dimension.

Center-State

The relationship between the central and state governments is mediated by constitutional provisions as well as by administrative and financial relations that tend to tip the balance of power in favor of the center.[8] The formal relationship between the center and the states will be examined briefly in terms of three aspects: the constitutional distribution of political powers between the center and the states, the union's powers under emergency laws to intervene in the affairs of states, and the overriding power of the center with respect to the states as far as financial matters are concerned.[9]

Constitutional Provisions
Article 1 of the of the Indian Constitution states that "India, that is Bharat, shall be a Union of States." The term *union of states* was used because the federation was not the result of an agreement by units but was imposed from above. The component units have no freedom to secede.[10] Moreover, the national Parliament can change a state's boundaries by a simple majority—for instance when the Indian Parliament adopted the States Reorganization Act of 1956, reducing the number of states from 27 to 14.

The Distribution of Powers
The basic principles governing the distribution of power between the center and the states are laid out in Part XI of the Indian Constitution. Part XI is itself divided into two chapters: one governing legislative relations, which establishes the constitutional division of powers over policy areas between the center and the states; and one covering administrative rela-

tions. The respective jurisdictions of the center and the states are spelled out in three lists. The union list, consisting of 97 items, is the longest of the three and provides control to the center over issue areas such as defense, foreign affairs, income tax, and even interstate trade and commerce and state high courts. The state list consists of 66 entries that deal with issues of more local interest such as law and order, education, and agriculture. The concurrent list consists of 47 items that are under the joint jurisdiction of the center and the states such as economic and social policies, monopolies, and price control. As far as the concurrent list is concerned, a law passed by the national Parliament takes precedence over a state law in cases in which the two are in conflict. Moreover, residual powers (those not specified in the Constitution) are also vested in the central government, unlike federal systems such as that of the United States in which residual powers rest with the states.

Emergency Powers of the Center
While the division of power appears to give the state governments a measure of autonomy, this does not carry over into periods of crisis, when the national Parliament can pass legislation on any matter it deems necessary. The power of the center under these emergency rules therefore covers even those issues that are under the jurisdiction of states. These emergency provisions have given the central government considerable leverage over state politics. Another provision that directly affects the states is Article 356 of the Constitution, which stipulates that if the president (actually the prime minister) is satisfied with a governor's claim (state governors are not elected but are appointed by the central government) that the state cannot be governed according to the provisions of the Constitution then the president can assume executive power over all facets of the state's administration and Parliament can legislate on behalf of the state assembly.[11]

Financial Relations between the Center and the States
The Indian Constitution clearly delineates the financial jurisdictions of the center and the states. This elaborate division of power, however, does not imply that the authority of the center and the states is coequal. In fact, states have limited opportunities to raise resources, especially since most of them are unwilling to tax agricultural income.[12] The center's control over economic policy—especially the planning process—also has left the states dependent upon the center. Most of the funds transferred from the center to the states have been in the "form of non-statutory Plan and dis-

cretionary assistance" (Gulati 1987, 4), which has no legal basis in the Constitution but is allocated at the discretion of the central government. The central government also played an active role in determining the industrial development of a state. The central government was responsible for granting industrial licenses, which gave permission to establish an industry and dictated its size, location, and scope.

Further, the center often has the final voice in determining the rate and levels of taxation, even if these taxes affect the states in critical ways. For instance, the center decides whether and at what rate to levy any of the taxes under Articles 268 and 269 of the Constitution, the proceeds of which go entirely to the states (Lakdawala 1991, 11).[13] The center also levies important taxes such as the income tax, corporate income tax, customs duties, and excise duties on most goods. Of these, only income taxes, especially personal income taxes, are shared by the states based on a formula determined by a constitutionally mandated body—the finance commission—which is constituted every five years to examine center-state financial relations. States still retain some important taxes such as those based on land and agricultural income (taxes that the states have been very reluctant to levy), excise duties on alcohol and certain other goods, sales taxes on all goods but newspapers, taxes on mineral rights, taxes on vehicles, taxes on the sale of electricity, and luxury taxes. Apart from taxes on the sale of liquor, however, the instruments over which the state governments have control are not very elastic. Consequently, state government revenues are not very buoyant. As "growth-responsive taxes can largely be levied only by the Centre and since the Centre has the dominant right to borrow in the domestic market as well as from abroad, a greater part of the financial resources accrue to the Centre" (Khatkhate and Bhatt 1987, 41).[14]

State government finances are also affected by the fact that states are restricted from raising their own resources by taking on debt. Constitutionally, as long as they are indebted to the central government, states can borrow from the market only with the central government's approval. Even if states are not indebted, they have only a limited ability to borrow in the financial markets, sell special treasury bills to raise money, and obtain loans from foreign governments (Rao and Chelliah 1991).[15] Not surprisingly, then, the fiscal balance during most of the period since independence has favored the central government, which has been able to "borrow virtually unlimited sums, particularly from the Reserve Bank of India, and the limitation placed on the state's power to borrow even from the market when they are indebted to the Centre has tended to cause a very high degree of centralisation in the capacity to raise financial resources and with it, the States' heavy fiscal dependence upon the Centre" (19). As a result, states have had to provide social and economic services that have a high income elasticity of demand, and thus the gap "between [their] own resources and needs has been continuously increasing over the years" (22).

Despite this political and fiscal centralization, states still have a large measure of autonomy in deciding how the monies distributed by the central government will be spent. Together with the national government, states are responsible for building the infrastructure. State governments also have "major responsibilities in the fields of education, public health and social services; they have considerable regulatory authority over industrial enterprises, small businesses and shops . . . land ownership, land use and land taxation [and] they play a key role in agriculture and rural development" (Weiner 1996, 1).[16] While state governments do indeed have less autonomy as far as raising money is concerned, they are able to set their own spending priorities. The per capita expenditures of the state in the areas of social policy (education and public health) and economics (agriculture and industry) vary significantly. As figure 4 indicates, while Kerala spends more than the other states per capita on education (as a proportion of the per capita tax revenues of the state) Haryana's expenditures on education are the lowest. Bengal and Assam devote similar amount of resources to education, whereas developed states such as Gujarat and Maharashtra spend far less. Differences among the states may also be seen in expenditures made by the states on industry and agriculture (see Fig. 5). Orissa and Bihar are two states that spend the resources on these policy areas, whereas Tamil Nadu and Bengal are among the lowest spenders.

Local Government in India

In contrast, the third tier of Indian federalism, local government, has very limited financial resources, is politically and administratively controlled by the state governments, and has virtually no autonomy even in terms of spending the money it receives from the state governments. Despite Mohandas Gandhi's emphasis on local government, the first draft of the Indian Constitution did not even include a provision for *panchayats,* and the final version says little about local bodies, urban or rural. The only reference to local government and *panchayats* is in the directive principles of state policy. There, too, local governments are not accorded any independent status; instead their existence as well as any power they may exercise

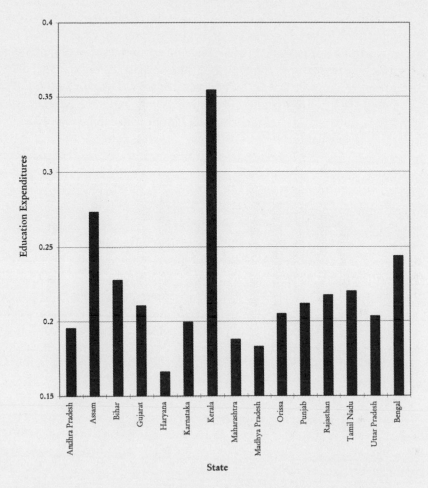

Fig. 4.   Per capita educational expenditures by state governments, 1969–91. (Data from *Reserve Bank of India Bulletin,* various issues.)

is dependent upon the state governments. The Constitution expects the state "to organize village *Panchayats* and endow them with such powers and authority as may be necessary to enable them to function as units of self-government," but it is state governments that are empowered in all matters of "local government, that is to say, the construction and powers of municipal corporations, improvement trusts, district boards, mining settlements authorities and other local authorities for the purpose of local self-government or village administration" (Bagchi 1991, 99).[17]

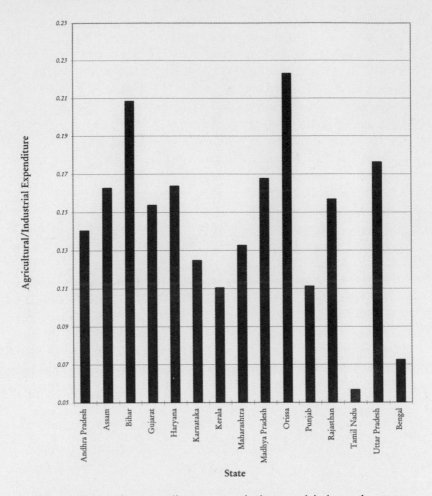

Fig. 5.   Per capita expenditures on agriculture and industry by state governments, 1969–91. (Data from *Reserve Bank of India Bulletin,* various issues.)

For almost a decade after independence, there was little effort to introduce local government. It was the central government, not the state governments, that stressed decentralization. The constitution of a national committee led by Balwantrai Mehta, a member of Parliament, and its recommendations favoring decentralization led the states to adopt acts addressing the formation of *panchayats.* By 1959, all of the states had passed *panchayat* acts, and by the mid-1960s *panchayats* were in all parts of

the country. While the center was, on the one hand, legislating the formation of *panchayats,* on the other hand its actions in the sphere of development undermined the *panchayats'* independent authority. In 1960, in keeping with its development imperative, the central government launched an
intensive agricultural district program (IADP) that bypassed local communities. Soon other schemes such as the Small Farmers Development Agency
(SFDA), the Drought Prone Areas Programme (DPAP), and the Intensive
Tribal Development Programme (ITDP) were introduced. The policies
promulgated by these programs were, however, outside the purview of the
elected local governments. In 1967, the status of the Ministry of Community Development was reduced to that of a department and subsumed
under the Ministry of Food and Agriculture. The end of the idea of community development was signaled in 1971, when the title "Community
Development" was dropped from the department's name and replaced
with "Rural Development."[18] This "marked the end of both the 'community' and 'panchayats' as agents of change and agencies of development"
(Matthew 1995, 7). Thus, local governments have little independent constitutional authority, and what authority they possess has been circumscribed
by the actions of the state government as an agent of the center. Local elites
are cognizant of the limits of their power and authority.

Local Elites and the Power of Local Government

Local elites, who are well aware of local governments' lack of power and
authority, also see the central and state governments as having primary
responsibility for solving local problems. Local elites were interviewed in
three states, Maharashtra, Gujarat, and Uttar Pradesh, in 1966.[19] Respondents included officeholders of block offices, other local influential
bureaucrats and politicians, block development officers, village extension
officers, and leaders of parties and other influential organizations. Almost
half of the local elites saw the local government as lacking sufficient power
and autonomy to deal with matters of health and to solve the problems
affecting youths such as juvenile delinquency. About 70 percent of the
local elites saw the local government's authority as inadequate in the areas
of housing, employment, and the provision of services such as electricity.
The only area in which a majority felt that the local government had some
influence was school construction.

Respondents were also asked who, in their opinion, has primary
responsibility for solving housing problems, seeing that everyone has a
job, building schools, establishing health clinics, ensuring electric supply,

solving the problems affecting youth, and supporting cultural activities. Their responses to these seven questions, identifying central, state, or local governments as responsible for each, were aggregated and recoded to generate a scale from 1 to 7, with higher numbers representing more mentions of either central and state or local governments. A higher proportion of those interviewed identified the central and state governments as taking greater responsibility than local governments. The average number of times the central and state governments were mentioned was 3.31, whereas the local government was referred to only 2.46 times.[20]

Local elites were also asked whether they had undertaken any action in various areas of economic and social development. Apart from agricultural development, in which 40 percent of the local elites had undertaken some independent action, most had played virtually no role at all. In housing, 13 percent had undertaken some independent action, in industrial development 17 percent, and in social welfare 23 percent.

This study was repeated in 1996 in the same blocks in Gujarat, Maharashtra, and Uttar Pradesh, and similar patterns were discovered.[21] Only 28 percent of the 450 respondents felt they had enough power to solve the problems in their block. Respondents were also asked whether they had undertaken any projects or initiated independent actions. Seventy percent said that they either did not have the autonomy or did not take the initiative to undertake actions for the development of their block. Moreover, 46 percent said that they had never participated in discussions with senior officials or leaders about economic policy or economic development. When asked who made decisions about the programs to be implemented in their area, fewer than 20 percent mentioned the district government, either alone or in conjunction with the state and central governments, and almost 80 percent referred exclusively to the state or central government.

The two sets of interviews reveal startling similarities. Local elites have little power or authority in most issue areas and have few discussions with central or state officials on local matters. Their attitude, insofar as they see higher levels of government as key in local issues, is understandable given the minimal financial and political autonomy they have with respect to the state government.

Local Government Finance

While attempts have been made to resurrect the status of local government, most notably by the 64th and 73rd Amendments to the Indian Constitution, the financial position of local governments in India is poor.

Across developed countries, the share of local government expenditures in total government spending varies between 20 and 29 percent. India, "is well below the norm, with local government accounting for only 8.6 percent of total government expenditure in 1976–77 and 6.4 per cent in 1986–87" (Datta 1993, 146).

Urban governments in India also expend minimal resources on their residents, with Gujarat and Maharashtra being the only states in which urban governments have an income of more than Rs 50 for every resident in an urban area (see table 4). The resources of rural governments are even more limited. "Sixty percent of the *panchayats* of the country have a per capita income below Rs 0.50" (Jain 1993, 182). The resources raised by the *panchayat samitis* (the intermediate levels of rural local government) were "Rs 0.49, Rs 0.25 and Rs 1.28 *per capita* in Andhra Pradesh, Rajasthan and Madras respectively in 1961–62" (220). In Bihar, "the annual income of panchayats . . . was less than one rupee per capita per annum" (Sinha 1995, 49). An analysis of a report of the Ministry of Rural Development on *panchayati raj* institutions (PRIs) shows that the per capita revenue of village *panchayats* ranged from Rs 28.56 in Kerala to less than half a rupee in Orissa (see table 5).

TABLE 4.   Per Capita Revenue of Urban Governments (in rupees)

State	Per Capita Revenue
Andhra Pradesh	30
Assam	11
Bihar	7
Gujarat	55
Haryana	24
Karnataka	23
Kerala	24
Madhya Pradesh	23
Maharashtra	76
Orissa	21
Punjab	37
Rajasthan	16
Tamil Nadu	27
Uttar Pradesh	19
West Bengal	25

Source: National Institute of Urban Affairs, 1983

Note: Urban revenue is the reported per capita income of a sample of municipal authorities from 1971 to 1980 at 1970–71 prices.

Rural areas are almost completely dependent upon the state governments for whatever revenues they have at their disposal.[22] The "zilla parishads (district governments) also have no power to reappropriate the funds for any project which they might feel is necessary in the area" (Haragopal and Sudarshanan 1995, 23–24). In Gujarat, for example, as much as 90 percent of the funds of *panchayati raj* institutions come from the state government and "even in matters relating to village approach road, money was allocated in the state budget. In the mid-seventies, out of the total budget of Rs 9,552,000 for all the district panchayats only 872,000 came from their own sources while Rs 8,679,000 was in the nature of government grants for specific activities" (69). A study of local government finances by the Institute of Public Finance and Policy reiterates the poor financial position of rural local governments. The three districts in Maharashtra that were analyzed had budgets of Rs 103 crores, Rs 87 crores, and Rs 40 crores.[23] Of these, the districts directly raised only Rs 4 crores, Rs 1.44 crores, and Rs 1.14 crores, respectively. In Gujarat, the two districts whose finances were analyzed mustered only Rs 2.71 crores and R 1.44 crores by themselves out of total incomes of Rs 69.2 crores and Rs 89.6 crores, respectively.

While state governments complain about the center not allowing them to raise money directly from the market, state governments themselves do not usually allow local urban bodies to take on direct loans (Bagchi 1991,

TABLE 5.   Per Capita Revenue of Village *Panchayats,* 1991 (in rupees at current prices)

State	Per Capita Revenue
Andhra Pradesh	10.35
Gujarat	18.74
Haryana	13.14
Kerala	28.56
Maharashtra	10.65
Orissa	0.41
Punjab	15.27
Rajasthan	2.55
Tamil Nadu	2.30
Uttar Pradesh	8.46

Source: Indian Ministry of Rural Development, 1996
Note: Figures were calculated by the author; data for other states were not reported and exclude government grants.

117). Like state governments, which are not willing to tax agriculture, local bodies are not willing to impose property taxes, which in principle could be a major source of independent revenue for them (117).[24] As a result, the financial position of the *panchayats* in general is not satisfactory, and "in most panchayats the ratio of administrative expenditure to the total expenditure is high and a little amount is left for obligatory and discretionary functions, which have direct bearing on the satisfaction of the needs of the people" (Jain 1993, 217).

Local governments also lack the authority to make independent decisions about how to spend the resources coming from the state governments: as "funds transferred by the State government either for carrying on development activities or activities under agency basis are specifically designated . . . [and] the controlling officers and the concerned administrative departments continue to supervise the Zilla Parishad . . . they monitor the utilisation of the grants and exercise budgetary control over the expenditure" (Barnabas and Bohra 1995, 16). In other words, resources that are granted to local governments are often tied to programs initiated by the central or state governments. Local bodies have to spend these grants on "predesignated items" (Bagchi 1991, 117), and local governments in India function mostly as "mere departments of government" (Jain 1993, 226).

In Bihar, for instance, "gram panchayats had a very weak financial base right from their inception . . . [and] these institutions [have] not emerged as financially viable and effective units." A provision allotting 6.25 percent or more of land revenue to *panchayats* was carried out, and "the panchayats had been resorting to filing writ petitions against the state government to secure their share." All functions relating to development and planning, including cottage industries, poverty eradication, welfare, adult and primary education, minor irrigation, and agricultural extension, were assigned by the state government, and there was no clear demarcation between *panchayat* and state functions. The rest of the functions were local, and "there was no clear indication as to which of these were obligatory and which discretionary" (Sinha 1995, 49). Even when the central government introduces programs that may be implemented locally, such as the Jawahar Rozgar Yojana (JRY), which are ostensibly assigned directly to the *mukhiya* (village head) by the central government, the work of the *mukhiya* is conducted under the supervision of the District Rural Development Agency (DRDA) and the block.[25]

Another indicator of the low importance accorded by state governments to local governments is the loans granted by the state governments to *panchayati raj* institutions. From 1972 to 1992, about 4 percent of the state's total nondevelopmental expenditure was provided to the *panchayati raj* institutions as loans (see fig. 6). This number drops to about 1 percent of the states' total expenditures. The average amount of loans provided by the state governments varies across the states, with some states, such as Tamil Nadu and West Bengal, allocating a larger share of their total nondevelopmental expenditures as loans in contrast to states like Haryana, which provided less than half a percent in the form of loans to local institutions (see fig. 7).[26]

The Political Relationship between State and Local Governments

Local governments also have limited political autonomy. All local bodies are established by the state legislature. The state can change the boundaries of localities and had the power to dissolve local bodies until the 74th Amendment was adopted in 1993. Administratively, the state government must approve any bylaws and rules that are framed by municipal bodies. Nor do local governments have the right to recruit and control their own staffs. Most persons working for local bodies are state employees, and local representatives, even if elected, cannot appoint local administrators.

State governments also control *panchayats* by endowing each with the right to determine the areas in which it can exercise authority. Article 243, Section G of the Constitution says that "legislature of a State may, by law, endow the Panchayats with such power and authority as may be necessary to enable them to function as institutions of self-government." Aside from Bihar and Punjab, the states have carefully avoided any reference to *panchayats* as institutions of self-government (Singh 1994, 20). Some states, such as Haryana, went to the other extreme. The *Panchayati Raj* Act of Haryana permits the state government to cancel any resolution of a *panchayat* that it deems not in the public interest. In Kerala and Punjab, the state government can, with a simple notification, take away any of the *panchayat's* functions; it can also call for information and reports from local bodies, review local actions, provide conditional grants-in-aid, and annul decisions made at the local level. State governments can even suspend and dissolve local councils.

In Andhra Pradesh, the Vengala Rao Committee identified several factors contributing to public dissatisfaction with the *panchayati raj,* chief among them the fact that this level of government "suffered from lack of

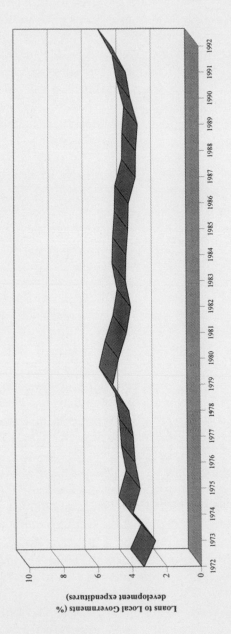

Fig. 6. Loans to local governments by state governments as a percentage of total development expenditures. (Data from *Reserve Bank of India Bulletin*, various issues.)

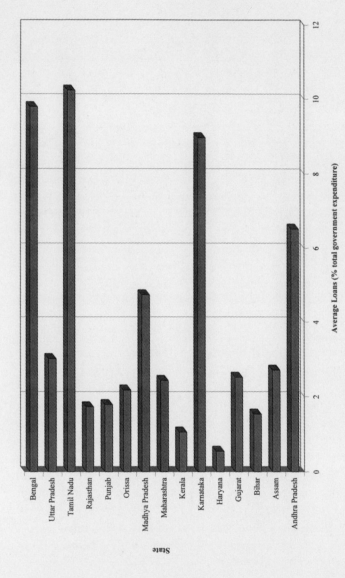

Fig. 7. Average loans granted by state governments to local governments, 1972–92, as a percentage of total government expenditures. (Data from *Reserve Bank of India Bulletin*, various issues.)

functional freedom," as state bureaucrats retained enormous influence over panchayati raj institutions (Haragopal and Sudarshanan 1995, 20). Also the state government can change or modify the budgets of *zilla parishads*. In Bihar, community development projects, even though "the local tiers, essentially the zilla and block units, acquired new functions and allotments under the various poverty eradication schemes of the higher governments [and] were run by the district development officers (D.D.Os) and the block development officers (B.D.Os) . . . the bureaucratic system was implementing development schemes under guidelines from above, with no local inputs" (Sinha 1995, 48).

In Kerala, "over the years, however, while the panchayats could exercise most of their mandatory duties, only very few, if any, of the development functions were given to them and none of the responsibilities contemplated in the act [Kerala Panchayat Act, 1960] were entrusted to them by any of the governments that followed." A *panchayati raj* bill was introduced in the Kerala Assembly in 1967 but lapsed before it could become law; the state government tried unsuccessfully to implement the act in 1970 and 1971 (Ramachandran 1995, 108). "A fear had taken root in the state that there was voodoo about decentralisation in Kerala as every government which had attempted it had fallen." Despite the efforts to decentralize, the Kerala government's intentions were questionable for a number of reasons. Take the case of the water supply. While decentralizing its authority to the *panchayats,* the Kerala act on water authority simultaneously stipulated that issues relating to water had to be handed over to a state authority. Similarly, while village industry came under *panchayat* control, state-level boards were set up for dealing with *khadi* (woven cloth). And, while field channels for irrigation were once managed by *panchayats,* a law passed by the state on command area development took away their authority in this area. In Kerala, then, "while subjects were listed as powers and functions given over to local government institutions, in many cases the actual powers, funds and manpower were with the authority, boards, corporation, society or the state government" (Ramachandran 1995, 110).

In Madhya Pradesh, a new Panchayati Raj Act was introduced in 1990 whereby the state government could vest a local authority with any of its property, but it could also simultaneously assume any property vested in the *panchayat* (Singh and Misra 1991, 694). State bureaucrats were deemed competent to inspect the works of *panchayats,* and it was the duty of the officeholders, officers, and servants of these localities to provide access to all information and records demanded by the inspecting state authority. The state government or the prescribed authority could also suspend the execution of any resolution passed or order issued by the PRIs.

In Maharashtra, the Shiv Sena–led state government adopted three items of legislation in 1996 that vitally affected PRIs: the "provision for passing a no-confidence motion was changed to a simple majority from two-thirds majority . . . the provisions regarding holding of official position by a defected member [was deleted] . . . [and] on the eve of the zilla parishad elections, the government reduced the term of ZP office bearers from five years to one year" (*Indian Express,* 4 March 1997). The Shiv Sena–led government introduced these changes in a context in which most local governments in Maharashtra, prior to the elections, were controlled by the Congress Party. The actions of the Shiv Sena–BJP government belie the fact that local governments in India have some autonomous political authority, especially vis-à-vis state governments. In most states in India, then, state governments have not transferred enough authority to the PRIs.[27] This was largely due to the fact that state-level authorities were not prepared to part with their powers. A good example occurred in the late 1950s in the aftermath of the recommendations of the Balwantrai Mehta Committee on Panchayati Raj, which suggested that the relationship of state and local governments be reconsidered and that the state government retain only those powers that the *panchayat samiti* was not in a position to assume. This proposal was overruled by the National Development Council, which consisted of state chief ministers who were in the process of reorganizing district administration. An Administrative Reforms Commission report on state administration further reduced the autonomy of *panchayats* by recommending that only developmental functions be relegated to them, even as regulatory functions were retained by the state government; the "lack of regulatory powers with the PRIs has discouraged initiative at the grass roots level" (Singh 1994, 20). Consequently, there has been, in most cases, a half-hearted devolution of powers to local governments, and the states still retain tight control over many of the functions that ostensibly were the responsibility of the *panchayats.*[28]

What thwarts the development of these local bodies is that "wherever panchayats have not taken root or they have been uprooted after brief spells of success it has been observed that the MPs (Members of Parliament) and MLAs (Members of the Legislative Assembly) have been not too friendly to these institutions. Not only have these persons been indifferent to local governments, but at times they have also been hostile to these bodies" (Matthew 1995, 13). In Andhra Pradesh, the Vengala Rao Committee observed that "as of now, the legislators do not seem to appreciate the need for devolution of substantial powers to the local bodies. They feel their position and importance are threatened by the emergence of powerful local leaders" (Raghavulu and Narayana 1991, 46). State governments hence do not want to accede power to local governments, as "a large number of surveys and in depth studies have revealed that the State satraps, including MLCs (Members of the Legislative Council) and MLAs do not want to vest *panchayati raj* institutions with any substantial powers. Instead, they want to centralize all powers in their hands" (Verma 1990, 137). In Rajasthan, "Panchayati Raj Institutions came increasingly into disfavour with the Congress politicians who had created them . . . because these institutions were producing local politicians who competed with or threatened to compete with ministers and legislators in their constituencies" (Stern and Kamal 1974, 288). In all states, MPs and MLAs are members of the district government and have membership and voting rights in *panchayats;* the only exceptions are Maharashtra, where they are totally excluded from this body, and Gujarat, where the MLAs are permanent invitees but don't have the right to vote.

The repeal of the Karnataka local government act of 1983, which devolved real authority to local governments, and the adoption of the 73rd, but not the 64th, Amendment provide perfect examples of how the state governments still retain control over local governments and are loathe to give up their authority.

Local Government in Karnataka
In 1963, the state set up the Kondajji Bosappa Committee, which recommended setting up elected *zilla parishads* and excluding MPs and MLAs from local institutions. The governing Congress Party was not in favor of the recommendations of the committee, so a bill that was to implement the recommendations lapsed in the state house. In 1983, a new act was passed in which the *zilla parishad* was assigned responsibility for the planning and implementation of all development schemes. The state government, this time led by R. K. Hegde (who became chief minister in 1983), followed through with its commitment to decentralization, and in 1987–88, the first year of the functioning of the new institutions, 23.8 percent of states' own planned outlays (37.2 percent if centrally sponsored plans are included) were transferred to the district sector. Simultaneously, 30 percent of gov-

ernment employees, most of whom were primary school teachers, came under the administrative control of *zilla parishads.* Further, under the provisions of the new act no government official could suspend a *zilla parishad* or a *mandal panchayat;* there was no provision for any government official to exercise control over these local bodies, and any plans made by the *mandal panchayat* or the *zilla parishad* could not be altered by the state government. In providing this autonomy to local governments, the bill undermined the authority of MLAs in the PRIs.

In November 1990, however, the Congress Party introduced a bill in the assembly to amend the Karnataka Panchayati Raj Act of 1983. The basic idea was to vest more power in the state bureaucracy. Rajiv Gandhi, who had introduced the 64th Amendment to the Indian Constitution, which sought to establish the autonomous power and authority of local government, did not support the measure, and the move was shelved. In 1993, after Rajiv Gandhi's death, the government placed a similar bill before the legislature, where it passed within 30 minutes. The 1993 bill, which reconstituted the relationship of the state government to local institutions, was defeated in legislative council and sent back to the legislative assembly, where it passed again.

The real forces behind this change were the MLAs. While the Karnataka Panchayati Raj Act of 1993, in its preamble, says that *panchayats* were being established "for greater participation of the people and more effective implementation of rural development schemes [not local self-government] . . . it weakened the power of the chair of the *zilla parishad*" (Matthew 1994, 67–68). The act also detailed the power of state officials, who could now inquire into the affairs of local government at all levels. These officials also had power over civil courts under the code of civil procedure. Local governments could no longer post or recruit their own officials, and even the transfer of the lowest level government employee— the peon—in the *zilla parishad* now rested with a state official (68). Most important, the state could now "omit, amend, or add any activity, programme or scheme" introduced by the *panchayat* and suspend any order of the *zilla parishad* (70).

Thus, unlike in the case of the 1983 act, which delegated power to the local governments, the state government, by passing the 1993 act, reserved for itself considerable powers of supervision and control over the PRIs at all levels. The "Karnataka Panchayati Raj Act of 1993 which replaces the 1983 Act virtually restores the structures that existed prior to 1983 and has reduced the Panchayats 'autonomy' drastically" (Krishnaswamy 1993, 2185). The role of the MLA and the bureaucrat in local government has been restored. While Karnataka has reinstated the authority of the state government and the MLA, the 73rd Amendment, while introducing local government as a constitutional entity, has also placed significant constraints on its authority. Even in a well-funded city like Bangalore there was "an extravagant disregard in the State government for the needs of the city, and they have left the Municipal Corporation financially crippled" (Manor 1993, 41).

The 64th and 73rd Amendments

The unwillingness of state governments to cede authority and power to local governments is also apparent in the changes made in the 64th Amendment to the Constitution in order that it might be adopted as the 73rd amendment. The 64th Amendment to the Constitution was introduced as Bill No. 50 in Parliament in 1989. Its purpose was to reorganize local government in India by inserting Part IX into the Constitution. Article 243a would make it obligatory for all states to establish a three-tiered system of *panchayats* and provide for all seats in *panchayats* at all levels to be filled by direct election. The state legislatures, however, could allow state and national legislators to become members without voting rights; there would be a reservation for scheduled castes, scheduled tribes, and women. The act also sought to provide for devolution by the state legislature of powers and responsibilities upon the *panchayats;* to provide for sound financing of the *panchayats* by securing authorization from state legislatures for grants-in-aid from the Consolidated Fund of the State; to provide for the constitution of a Finance Commission to review local government finances every five years; and to empower the Comptroller and Auditor General of India to audit these accounts. The bill also sought to impose a uniform pattern of local government throughout the country instead of permitting individual states to legislate the details of local government. The bill got more than two-thirds of the votes in the Lok Sabha but failed in Rajya Sabha on 15 October 1989 by two votes.

In September 1991, the Congress Party introduced the 72rd and 73rd constitutional amendment bills. The bills were passed by the Lok Sabha on 22 December 1992 and by the Rajya Sabha on 23 December 1992 and were soon ratified by more than half the state assemblies and brought into force on 24 April 1993. The 73rd Amendment dealt with the same issues as the 64th—the power of local governments—but the new version incorporated some significant changes, which restored power to the state governments. It allowed the Gram Sabha to "exercise such powers and perform such functions at the village level *as the Legislature of the State may by law, provide*" (emphasis added). The state legislature was also permitted to provide for the appointment of members of the Rajya Sabha and members of the Legislative Council of the State as representatives in intermediate and district-level *panchayats*. The 64th Amendment, by contrast, had said that *only* those chosen by direct election could vote in local bodies. In 1992, that provision was changed and the word *only* was dropped, allowing non-elected members (MLAs for one) to vote in local bodies.

In addition to restoring the power of the state legislature, the 73rd Amendment also changed financial relations among states and localities. In the 64th Amendment bill, the state Finance Commissions' recommendations were to govern the "*determination* of taxes, duties, tolls and levies which could be assigned to, or appropriated by the Panchayats." This was deleted in the 73rd Amendment, thereby placing local finances in the hands of the state government instead of a commission. At the same time, references to audits of local government finance by the auditor and comptroller general of India were deleted and audits were now to be conducted by the state legislature.

Commentators observed that even after the adoption of the 73rd Amendment the *panchayat* would still remain an agent of the state government. Further, decentralized planning, as it is envisaged under the 73d amendment, has three problems. First, the "provisions are recommendatory rather than mandatory." Second, the list of items allotted to panchayats and municipalities is quite extensive, yet "not a single item has been allotted *exclusively* to Panchayats or Municipalities" (Prasad 1994, 532 [emphasis. added]). Finally, the financial position of the *panchayats* is still weak, as they do not have any independent basis for raising revenues and expenditures, which are still determined by the priorities assigned by state and central governments. State Finance Commissions have yet to complete their reports in many states; in some, such as Maharashtra, the Finance Commission was adjourned without having completed its work.

In India, then, the state has come to occupy a primary role in the economic and social transformation of the nation. While the central government has led these efforts, state governments, insofar as they enjoyed a measure of autonomy, have been key players in this process. Local governments, on the other hand, owe their existence to the state governments and possess little power, authority, or financial resources to undertake any autonomous action. The nature and structure of the state has influenced the development of the party system, which emerged as an executive-centered, state-based party in which the national party could influence the states and state parties controlled local politics.

Chapter 3

Electoral Laws, Associations, and the Organization of the Catchall Congress Party

Politicians in India, because of the federal structure of the Indian nation-state, seek to control the main instruments of power and authority, namely, the central and state governments. Most prominently, the Congress Party was organized coterminously with the center and the states in the two decades following independence. The federal structure, which allowed state governments to exercise independent power and authority, in conjunction with largely state-specific social and economic structures, led to the formation of the Congress Party as a collection of state-specific parties. The party, which was in power in all of the states as well as at center throughout the two decades following independence, built support for itself by controlling government resources. It was able to do so because there were few constraints on its using these resources to further its electoral considerations. The stage for this partisan use of state resources was set at independence when the party came to see itself as *the* agent of the state as far as economic development was concerned. Additionally, since the party continued to be electorally successful during most of the 1960s, there was no need for it to develop an organization. Not surprisingly, contrary to most perceptions, there is little evidence that the Congress Party had a well-developed organization, especially beyond the state level. The weakness of associational life allowed the party to develop links with social cleavages.

This understanding of the national Congress, as a collection of state-based parties, with the Congress Party in each state representing interests unique to its region and with a weak national organization, is different from many earlier characterizations. Most discussions of the Indian party system invoked a one-party-dominant model, which conceived Congress as a party that represented all salient social divisions. The initial formulation of the one-party-dominant model came from Morris-Jones (1964), who pointed to the Congress Party's capacity to absorb and retain various groups within its fold. Kothari (1964), who came up with the term *one-party-dominant model* independently of Morris-Jones, cited the party's ability to respond to and accommodate differing interests by means of politicians who occupied critical positions in the Congress's organization.[1] While political scientists who examined the Congress Party from a national perspective were addressing the catchall and accommodative nature of the party, case studies of party politics at the local level revealed that the Congress Party was tied to specific social groups (Brass 1965; Weiner 1967; Sisson 1972). These observations of the party's links to specific groups in each of the states called into question the catchall nature of the party. The one-party-dominant model, though formally accurate insofar as one party dominated the electoral scene in India, was seen as substantively misleading (Chhibber and Petrocik 1989).

This chapter discusses the impact of state structures, especially the role ascribed to the state, federalism, and electoral laws and the absence of associational life on the social basis of the Congress Party in the two decades following independence. The chapter also asks whether the Congress Party was in fact well organized in the period following independence and whether it drew its electoral strength from that organization. Congress Party documents and surveys of local elites suggest that it was not as organized as is commonly believed. A survey of party activists conducted in 1967, when the Congress was still well organized by most accounts, not only questions the notion that the Congress was as organized as is commonly believed, especially in relation to other parties, but also suggests that Congress activists were more geared toward gaining access to state office and building personal positions than were activists of other parties. This evidence forces us to reconsider whether Congress in the two decades following independence was truly an organized political party.[2]

This chapter will first provide evidence that the Congress Party is perhaps best understood as a coalition of state parties. Drawing on evidence from two postelection surveys, it will demonstrate that the party mobilized social groups at the state level far more effectively than it mobilized these groups at the national level. This state-level orientation of the party is a consequence of the state-specific nature of social cleavages in India, the single-member simple plurality electoral rule (which forced the building of coalitions across castes), and the federal division of power. The chapter will also discuss the nature of associational life in India. Most Indians do not belong to an association. In 1991, as noted in the first chapter (see table 3), fewer people belonged to associations in India than in any of the 25 countries for which comparable data on the extent of associational life are available. Further, even the associations that exist are often "demand groups," which are rarely, if ever, permanent fixtures of Indian political life (Rudolph and Rudolph 1987). Because associations were weak and the state has such an overwhelming presence, the party was the key link between state and society during this period. The Congress Party was, therefore, quickly made subservient to the needs of officeholders and soon transformed itself from an independence movement to an electoral machine. The final section of the chapter will describe this transformation and its impact on the party's organization.

The Social Basis of the Congress Party

The Congress Party's electoral dominance was built on the ability of the party to function as the major link between state and society, which was facilitated by its control over the state. As Manor (1991) notes, "when the British withdrew in 1947, Congress quickly and smoothly took control of the machinery of the state at all levels. Congress then became India's central political institution, more important than Parliament or the civil service or any other formal institution of the state . . . [and] the party's operatives soon came to dominate the civil service so that the formal machinery of the state was subordinated to the needs and demands of the party" (26).

    In India, the geographical nature of segmental cleavages generates interstate differences in the social basis of partisan support. For instance, caste, expressed as *jati,* is a local phenomenon, which has provided a consistent basis for political parties to mobilize support. As Brass (1990) notes, "at the local level, in the countryside, by far the most important factor in voting behavior remains caste solidarity . . . [and] large and important castes in a constituency tend to back either a respected member of their caste or a political party with whom their caste members identify" (85).[3] Because caste groups are geographically specific and power is dispersed across states but rarely devolves to localities, political mobilization along caste lines is territorially contained and rarely crosses state lines. When combined with the federal structure of the nation-state, the implication of this geographical nature of caste is that it is difficult for political parties to mobilize caste groups across states.

The Electoral System

The institutional framework of Indian politics, especially the single member simple plurality electoral system and federalism, reinforces the relationship of caste groups to the state government. SMSP requires politicians to build coalitions among castes at the local level in order to win elections. Consider two hypothetical cases. In the first scenario, a single caste is numerically dominant in an area. If only one party nominates a candidate from the dominant caste, that party would then win the election because the first past the post electoral system implicit in SMSP could ensure a plurality for the party. Competing parties are aware of the dominant caste in an area and tend to nominate candidates accordingly. In Chapproli, an assembly segment in Uttar Pradesh, *jats* were the dominant *jati.* For the 1969 state assembly elections, the three major parties all nominated *jat* candidates (Gokte 1995, 466–67). This selection annuls the advantage any one party may obtain by nominating a candidate from the dominant caste. Hence, for most parties competing in areas where there is one dominant caste, electoral success requires building alliances with other castes in the area so as to obtain a plurality of the votes cast.

In the second scenario, no caste is numerically dominant.[4] In such cases, parties have greater freedom to nominate candidates from any caste. For example, in the Secunderabad assembly segment of Uttar Pradesh, *gujars* and *thakurs* were the two numerically dominant *jatis,* comprising 24 and 21 percent, respectively, of the voting population. The Janata Dal (JD) and Bahujan Samaj Party put up *gujar* candidates, whereas Congress and the BJP nominated *thakurs* (*Amar Ujaala,* 5 November 1993). If a party wishes to win the elections, however, it still needs to build alliances across castes.[5] In other words, caste is important but only insofar as it places constraints on the alliances political parties have to build to be electorally successful.[6]

Political parties need to build alliances across caste lines for another reason. A well-established result in political science, Duverger's law, states that under an SMSP system electoral competition will be limited to two parties. Skeptics, especially students of Indian politics (because India is considered an anomaly in the electoral rules literature), question the validity of Duverger's law given the number of parties that contest elections in India. Data drawn from parliamentary constituencies for elections from 1957 to 1996, however, suggest that in most parliamentary constituencies in India electoral competition is limited to two parties. In most con-

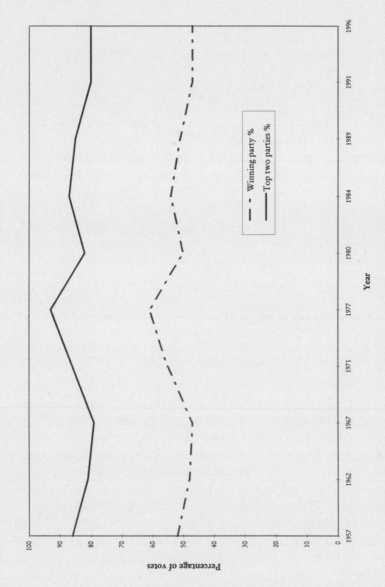

Fig. 8. Percentage of votes received in Lok Sabha elections by the winning party and top two parties combined, 1957–96

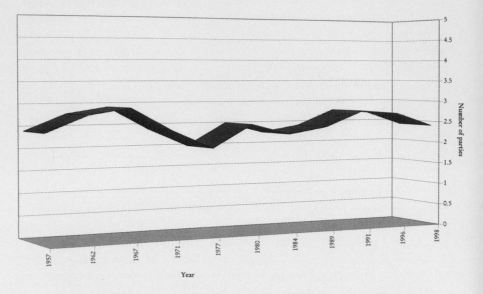

Fig. 9.   Effective number of parties in the Lok Sabha elections, 1957–98
(average across constituencies)

stituencies, the top two parties garnered well over 80 percent of the vote,
with the top party obtaining over 50 percent of the vote on many an occasion (see fig. 8).[7] Moreover, for most of the period since 1957 the effective
number of parties in India is close to two (see fig. 9).[8]

This finding is important because if only two parties are competitive in
a parliamentary constituency where, by any account, there are multiple
jatis, electoral success can only be guaranteed by building a coalition
across *jatis.* Hence, it was the interaction of electoral laws with the local
nature and small size of *jatis* that constrained the Congress to build
alliances across castes and appear as a catchall party—the only way it
could guarantee its electoral success in the SMSP system.

Federalism

The federal organization of government in India also had an impact on
the relationship of caste groups to political parties. The many hundreds
of principalities that constituted India at that time were combined into
larger units at independence. In 1956, the states were reconstituted, with

language being the organizing principle.[9] This reorganization of states gave linguistic and geographical boundaries to religious, ethnic, and caste divisions. Take the case of Andhra Pradesh, which is a Telugu-speaking state. Before the creation of Andhra Pradesh, the Telugu-speaking region was part of a larger state, Madras. A linguistic division of Madras created two states: Andhra Pradesh (Telugu speaking) and Madras (Tamil speaking). Prior to the separation, the major conflict in Madras state was over linguistic differences. As soon as Andhra Pradesh was created, conflict surfaced between the *kamma* and *reddi* castes (Horowitz 1984). Thus, ironically, while the creation of linguistic states removed language as a basis for political conflict, it institutionalized linguistic divisions that have become a prominent feature of the Indian political landscape.[10]

Indian federalism, especially the power vested in state rather than local governments, focused voter and candidate interests on gaining access to the state government. As it is the state government that makes most of the decisions on the allocation of resources, these decisions dominate voter preferences in local areas. Voters develop a set of preferences regarding the party composition of the state legislature and vote accordingly. Similarly, candidates affiliate themselves with political parties, which can make it easier for the candidate, upon election, to secure resources for local projects. Candidates, then, tend to form alliances that will allow them to come to power in a state.[11]

Given the significance of the power and authority vested in the state government, the importance of statewide caste coalitions for state politics is not surprising. It has been argued that the introduction of democratic politics has increased the power of the "numerically large castes" (Srinivas 1955, 571). The federal division of powers helped raise some kinds of caste conflict to the state level: *kammas* and *reddis* in Andhra Pradesh, the *vokkaligas* and *lingayats* in Karnataka, *rajputs* and *jats* in Rajasthan, and brahmans and nonbrahmans in Tamil Nadu (Kothari 1970).

Associational Life in India

The ability of the Congress to forge links with social cleavages at the state level was fostered because of the absence of associational life. As was discussed earlier, very few Indians belong to associations. A postelection survey conducted in 1991 makes this clear. Less than 2 percent of the respondents were members of caste and religious or neighborhood and peasant associations. About 4 percent were members of trade unions, and a similar number said they belonged to some other organization. How many Indians, then, belong to an association? Individual membership in associations was recoded, and 84 percent of those surveyed either said that they did not belong to an association or refused to respond to the question. Only 13 percent said that they belonged to at least one association (see table 3).

While associational life in India is limited, it does exist, and associations do exercise some influence over policy. The associations that have existed for a long time in India, particularly trade unions and student groups, are often linked directly to political parties. Others are typically more ephemeral, as they are mostly single-issue driven; they might organize to push for some policy change but dissolve once the particular issue has been resolved. Business associations, even when they have been in existence for some time, rarely operate as pressure groups to lobby the government.[12]

The major trade unions in India are all tied to political parties: for example, the Indian National Trade Union Congress (INTUC) is a Congress trade union, the Bharatiya Mazdoor Sangh (BMS) is affiliated with the Bharatiya Janata Party, and the Confederation of Indian Trade Unions (CITU) is a union of the Communist Party of India (Marxist). E. A. Ramaswamy (1988), in a study of trade unions in four Indian cities, noted that, except in Bombay, unions are affiliated with political parties. In Bombay, a survey of 119 enterprises revealed that in 29 of them leadership was homegrown and that party-affiliated unions, except the Bharatiya Mazdoor Sangh (tied to the BJP), were not doing very well. In the other major cities, however, it is a different matter. In Madras, the history of the labor movement is tied to party politics. For two decades after independence, the labor wing of Congress and the Indian National Trade Union Congress were at odds: "the fact of the union and the government being under the same leadership helped resolve disputes expeditiously and neutralize communist influence over the labour movement" (Ramaswamy 1988, 80). In 1967, when the Dravida Munnetra Kazhagam (DMK) came to power, Chief Minister Karunanidhi used coercion to "foist DMK leaders upon trade unions . . . and employers who had basked for so long under the benign rule of the Congress quickly changed their allegiance to the new party. Deeming it to be an advantage to be with whichever party is in power, they actually helped the new Chief Minister capture trade unions" (82). Similarly, in Bangalore employee unions such as those affiliated with the Motor Industries Company (MICO) switched union leadership away from the Congress once the party was defeated in the state assembly elections of 1983 (145–59). In the case of the Indian Tobacco Company (ITC) the union aligned itself with INTUC in order to get benefits from the Congress government (160–71, esp. 162). In other words, "the Indian labor movement is essentially an outcrop of politics" (102).

Students are indeed an interest group, but most of the prominent student organizations are led by political parties. The National Student's Union of India is affiliated with the Congress Party, the All-India Students Federation with the CPI, and the Student Federation of India with the CPI(M); the Akhil Bharatiya Vidyarthi Parishad is a wing of the BJP.

Rural organizations are few and far between, and where they do exist they arise in response to specific government policies. The Rudolphs note that the influence of self-employed cultivators was first felt in North India when, in Uttar Pradesh, Charan Singh brought down the Congress government of C. B. Gupta and formed a more agriculturally oriented government (in alliance with the Jana Sangh in 1967). With the new agrarianism of Sharad Joshi and Harekrishna Singh Surjeet and the agitational politics of 1980–81, "the issue of remunerative prices had moved out of party headquarters, secretariat corridors, and legislative chambers to the unmediated politics of *rasta rokos* (road-blocks), *gheraos* (sit-ins), and 'long marches'" (Rudolph and Rudolph 1987, 360). In the case of agricultural movements, "organized interest groups or social classes did not push the government toward a price and technology-oriented strategy. *Price-based interests appeared on the political scene much after the policy change*" (Varshney 1993, 49). Myron Weiner made a similar argument that "one could write the history of postwar agrarian policy in India, and of the political struggles which entered into making such policy, with little or no reference to farmer organization" (1962, 149). Varshney notes that "failed policy implementation was an aggregate effect of such discrete microstrategies, not of collective action or political organization" (1993, 78). Rural issues, he argues, became important in the 1980s at the national level (until then they were regional) because Charan Singh "made them into issues of central political concern" (111). Most of this mobilization by farmers during the 1980s was over prices. As political parties incorporated these ideas into their platforms, these groups lost their political relevance and often ceased to exist as independent political forces. As far as a large proportion of the rural population is concerned, especially the rural poor, there is no mention of their membership in associations. They are represented instead by political parties (Rudolph and Rudolph 1987, 379).

Business associations are quite prolific in India. They are not, however, an outgrowth of interest group activity; it is policy that exerts a great influence on the mobilization and behavior of business associations (Kochanek 1974). Robert Hunt, in a study of small business associations, found that most of them "generally are young, small, and lacking in financial resources" (1980, 256). While these associations grew rapidly in the mid 1950s, by the late 1970s they were reporting "little or at least diminished growth in membership" (256). They "appear[ed] to be seriously lacking in the capacity to receive, store, process, disseminate, or otherwise act upon pertinent information . . . consequently, they [were] doubtful allies of small manufacturers [and] none of these associations undertook systematic budgetary activities (257). Moreover, these associations seldom held regular elections, and those that did were often controlled by small cliques (258). Members did not identify with these associations (260). Studies of the functioning of and participation in Chambers of Commerce yield similar findings (Namjoshi and Sabade 1967).

Caste associations have been seen as playing an important role in Indian political life (Rudolph and Rudolph 1967). But are these caste associations so important? The survey data discussed earlier make it clear that most Indians do not belong to caste associations. Most caste associations that do exist are either tied to political parties or arise in response—like agricultural interests—to political considerations resulting from state policy. Eleanor Zelliot's work on the *mahars* a *dalit* caste, for instance, makes no reference to a *mahar* association and clearly shows that the caste realized the importance of forming an alliance with a political party. In 1956, "Ambedkar made an attempt to transform the Scheduled Castes Federation into a party" (58). Other scheduled caste groups also work through political parties (Suresh 1996, 380–81). Similarly, the *kshatriyas* in Gujarat, who began as a social movement but became organized for political reasons, joined the Congress Party, which they felt was the party that would best represent their interests (76—78). The Kshatriya Sabha, despite being an organization with strong leadership and a clear orientation, existed only until 1958. In Tamil Nadu, a *nadar* organization existed, but it was altered once a party representing the interests of the *nadars* came to power. This development undermined the community's political solidarity as well (125). In Andhra Pradesh, for the *reddi* and *kamma* castes "explicit caste organisation has little to do with the sustenance of [their] culture" (138); the *reddis* and *kammas* "found organising their caste on the lines of an association difficult" (150). Andre Beteille has suggested that castes influence politics through associations, yet he admits that the Vanniyakkula Kshatriya Sangam was politically inactive until 1967 (1970, 282). Beyond that, Beteille makes no mention of the caste association, its functions or its organization. Jalali (1993), also links the proliferation of scheduled caste associations in Karnataka to political considerations, particularly the role played by the Devaraj Urs government in the mid-1970s. Ironically, most of the growth in scheduled caste associations is in governmental or quasi-governmental organizations.[13]

This argument does not to seek to deny the significant role played by caste in Indian social life. All it seeks to assert is that there is no one-to-one correspondence between a political and a sociological meaning of caste. Scheduled caste, for instance, is a political, not necessarily a sociological, category. Within the scheduled castes in Uttar Pradesh, there are *jatis,* such as the *chamars* and *bhangis,* who have limited social interaction but are political allies. State policy can render this coalition unstable as, for instance, in Andhra Pradesh, where the government decided to classify the scheduled castes into four categories, A, B, C, and D (as a ranking) for purposes of allocating quotas in jobs and educational institutions. This led to an immediate fissure among the scheduled castes, especially between the *madigas* and the *malas,* as the former would have 7 percent of the seats in contrast to 6 percent for the latter (*Deccan Chronicle,* 10 November 1997).[14] The situation was similar with the so-called forward castes. Brahmans and *kshatriyas* may identify politically with each other, but neither would necessarily allow social relations to develop through intermarriage. When a postelection survey in 1991 asked voters whether they had relatives from other castes, only 2 percent responded in the affirmative. Caste, as a sociological phenomenon, works through well-developed networks. The claim made here is that caste is not an association like others, such as trade unions, which have officeholders and an organizational structure. Even the presence of an informal network of caste members is not sufficient grounds for treating caste like an association.[15]

There are a vast number of religious sects in India, some which could be treated as religious associations.[16] With a few exceptions, such as the Arya Samaj, which was involved in the independence movement, most of religious sects and associations (such as the Radhasoamis) have stayed out of electoral politics. There is one clear exception—the Rashtriya Swayam-

sevak Sangh (RSS).[17] This social association not only has provided organizational support but it has developed close ties with the BJP. Many of
the BJP's current leaders are from the RSS. Unlike other associations in
India, the RSS exists independently of any political party, even the BJP. If
anything, it is the BJP that is dependent upon the RSS, not vice versa.[18]

The women's movement, too, is fragmented and often tied to political
parties. Amrita Basu (1992) notes how women's issues were made subservient to the partisan interests of the CPI(M) in West Bengal. One reason for this is that the most prominent women's organization in West Bengal was affiliated with the CPI(M). The Anti–Price Rise Movement
(APRM) in Maharashtra, even though it was seen as a cross-party movement, was composed of women from different political parties (Gandhi
1996). Calman (1992) provides evidence for the development of women's
organizations, such as the National Federation of Indian Women and the
All-India Democratic Women's Association, out of major political parties. The absence of independent organizational life among women who
also noted in a report issued by a government appointed Committee on the
Status of Women in India. The report, commenting on the low levels of
participation by women in the electoral process, made a pointed reference
to the noticeable absence of women's organizations in India (Committee
on the Status of Women in India 1974).

Associational life in India, then, is weak. As the Rudolphs point out,
most of Indian political life is characterized by the existence of demand
groups, which rely on "ad hoc rather than bureaucratic organization," and
there is a tendency toward "excessive multiplication and fragmentation"
within these groups (1987, 247). As associations were weak, the Congress
Party's links to social cleavages were constructed through the state via the
distribution of state resources rather than by establishing links with associations of social groups. The weakness of associational life, insofar as the
Congress Party was not tied to any association, eased the ability of Congress to retain its catchall nature, as there was no one obvious group that
the party relied on for mobilizing the vote or an association for whose policy positions the Congress displayed an open preference.

The State-Specific Nature of the Congress Party

As social divisions are geographically contained and electoral success in
SMSP systems rests on building coalitions across *jatis,* coalitions in local
areas are formed around state government policy. State government pol-

icy is a basis for building coalitions because the federal division of power favors state over local governments. The SMSP electoral rules led to political parties mobilizing support locally, in contrast to nationally, as is typical in proportional representation systems such as those of Israel and the Netherlands. The federal division of power leads each of the state Congress parties to mobilize its own distinct bases of support, a move made easier by the fact that some important preexisting social divisions, such as those based on language, rarely cross state boundaries. Consequently, the ties of political parties to social groups should also be mediated by these social and political institutions

Given these constraints, one would expect that:

1. At the national level, where a voter lives—his or her state—should be a far stronger predictor of the vote than social factors such as caste, religion, or social class, which may be observed nationally.
2. However, because caste, class, and religion are major points of conflict, each will have a strong correlation with party support when examined at the level at which these factors are politically significant, namely, within each state.
3. The political significance of group conflicts varies by state, so the strength of the link between particular social cleavages and the party should vary across states.
4. The heterogeneity of the Congress Party reflects variation among the states in the commitments of the Congress Party to intergroup conflicts. Consequently, there will be considerable state by state variation in the social groups that are aligned with the Congress Party.

The data in table 6 confirm the first expectation: nationally, support for the Congress varies more by state than by caste, class, or religion.[19] In other words, the social variables turn out to be relatively poorer predictors of the vote compared to regional differences. This conclusion held for both of the elections, 1967 and 1971, that were analyzed; even though the explanatory power of the state variable fluctuates, geographic divisions are the most critical variable in explaining the Congress vote.

Tables 7 and 8 provide support for the second hypothesis: when examined nationally, the correlation of caste, religion, and class with the Congress vote is lower than it is by state. Again, this relationship holds for both the 1967 and 1971 elections. In both cases, the average correlation across states between caste, religion, and class is higher than it is when these variables are correlated with the Congress vote nationally. For 1967, the national figures for caste, class, and religion were 0.07, 0.09, and 0.03, respectively; the averages across the states, however, were 0.24, 0.27, and 0.13. A similar pattern holds for 1971.

TABLE 6.   Region, Social Cleavages, and the Vote, 1967, 1971 (zero-order correlations)

	Percentage Variance	
Social Cleavages	1967	1971
Caste	3.30	1.16
Religion	1.10	0.90
Class	0.02	0.30
Caste, religion, and class	3.50	2.00
State	7.10	26.10

Source: 1967 and 1971 postelection surveys

TABLE 7.   Within-State and Across-State Associations between the Congress Vote and Religion, Caste, and Class, 1967 (zero-order correlations)

State	Religion	Caste	Class	Percentage of Variance Explained
Andhra Pradesh	0.19	0.22	0.10	7
Bihar	0.11	0.32	0.16	16
Gujarat	0.24	0.28	0.12	7
Haryana	—	0.19	0.11	7
Kerala	0.53	0.27	0.15	31
Madhya Pradesh	0.10	0.25	0.24	16
Maharashtra	0.29	0.16	0.04	6
Karnataka	0.18	0.45	0.09	24
Orissa	0.23	0.25	0.20	16
Punjab	0.27	0.51	0.23	16
Rajasthan	0.35	0.49	0.23	38
Tamil Nadu	0.07	0.08	0.08	2
Uttar Pradesh	0.07	0.15	0.05	3
West Bengal	0.14	—	0.06	2
Average across states	0.24	0.27	0.13	14
National figures	0.07	0.09	0.03	0.7

Source: 1967 postelection survey

Note: The figures in the first three columns are correlation ratios; the figures in the fourth column are the coefficients of determination obtained through a dummy variable regression analysis.

TABLE 8. Within-State and Across-State Associations between the Congress Vote and Religion, Caste, and Class, 1971 (zero-order correlations)

State	Religion	Caste	Class	Percentage of Variance Explained
Andhra Pradesh	0.14	0.22	0.20	10
Assam	0.29	0.69	0.17	51
Bihar	0.08	0.30	0.05	7
Gujarat	0.30	0.29	0.22	18
Haryana	0.16	0.76	0.47	59
Himachal Pradesh	—	0.14	—	—
Jammu and Kashmir	0.17	—	0.38	15
Kerala	0.17	—	0.18	6
Madhya Pradesh	0.23	0.24	0.04	10
Maharashtra	0.22	0.28	0.08	14
Karnataka	0.09	0.29	0.13	10
Orissa	—	0.58	0.32	37
Punjab	0.28	0.30	0.28	15
Rajasthan	0.10	0.45	0.25	24
Tamil Nadu	0.12	0.37	0.10	14
Uttar Pradesh	0.21	0.11	0.08	8
West Bengal	0.10	0.24	0.09	10
Delhi	0.23	0.39	0.36	27
Average across states	0.19	0.30	0.20	20
National figures	0.10	0.11	0.06	2

Source: 1971 postelection survey
Note: The figures in the first three columns are correlation ratios; the figures in the fourth column are the coefficients of determination obtained through a dummy variable regression analysis.

Tables 7 and 8 also report on an analysis of the variation in Congress vote using religion, caste, and class. Together, these three variables account for only 0.7 and 2 percent of the variance in the party's national vote in the 1967 and 1971 elections, respectively. For the same elections, the average variance accounted for by these variables across the states was 14 and 20 percent, respectively. These tables highlight the stronger impact of social variables on the Congress Party's vote in the states as compared with the nation as a whole. The data provide further evidence for the observation that caste, class, and religion manifest themselves as political determinants more significantly at the state than at the national level.

The data presented in Tables 7 and 8 also support the third expectation: the political significance of social cleavages in India is state specific.

In a number of cases, the within-state correlation between the Congress vote and social cleavages is much larger than either the national or the across-state correlation. For instance, religion correlates highly with the Congress vote in Kerala (0.53), Rajasthan (0.35), Maharashtra (0.29), and Punjab (0.27) in 1967 and in Assam (0.29), Gujarat (0.30), and Punjab (0.28) in 1971. Caste ties to the Congress vote were high in Karnataka (0.45), Punjab (0.51), and Rajasthan (0.49) in 1967. In 1971, the ties were strongest in Assam (0.69), Haryana (0.79), Orissa (0.58), Rajasthan (0.45), Tamil Nadu (0.37), and Delhi (0.39). Similar sets of cases can be identified for class ties.

In the two decades following the first elections of 1952, the Congress Party retained its character as a collection of state-based parties, each of which mobilized interests unique to its region. Though social cleavages such as caste manifested themselves at the state level and not nationally, Congress managed to draw support from most groups within a state and present itself as a catchall party. Each of the groups supported the party because Congress controlled the instruments of the state, appeared electorally invincible, and was therefore best positioned to represent its interests.

Executive Office and the Congress Party

That the Congress Party mobilized support through its ability to deliver state resources to its supporters and its general willingness to engage in patronage politics (or constituency service) has been noted by a number of scholars (e.g., Brass 1965, Weiner 1967, Frankel 1978, Manor 1981, Kohli 1990, and Mitra 1992).[20] Congress Party activists understood the significance of using the state's resources to mobilize and maintain support. In a 1967 survey of party elites conducted by the Center for the Study of Developing Societies, party activists were asked a series of questions about what motivated party workers (see table 9). Congress Party activists were more likely than those of other parties to say that their main motivation for joining the party was to enhance their personal positions, to be close to important people, and to enhance their status in the community. Other activists had more frequently joined their parties in order to influence policy.

Party elites were also asked about the prerequisites for getting a ticket to contest elections on a party label (see table 10). The Congress could be distinguished from other parties, even in 1967, in that the backing of special groups and connections with leaders were more important for Congress Party elites than they were for those belonging to the other parties. A candidate's own ability, work done in the area, and status in the party organization were far more important for obtaining a ticket in parties other than the Congress.

In other words, the Congress Party maintained its electoral dominance insofar as those who joined the party did so to gain access to the state. For at least two decades following independence, since the Congress was seen as electorally invincible it was the vehicle for providing access to the state. Gaining this access enabled Congress politicians to exercise a significant influence over the allocation of resources and regulation of eco-

TABLE 9.   Why Workers Affiliate with a Political Party, 1967 (mean scores)

Reason	Other Parties	Congress	F
Build personal position	2.17	2.38	7.75**
Access to important people	2.28	2.41	2.95*
Build status in the community	2.36	2.52	2.95**
Influence government policies	2.56	2.38	6.68**

Source: 1967 elite survey
Note: Responses were scaled from 1 to 3, with 1 indicating that a particular issue was not important and 3 that it was very important.
   *Significant at 0.05   **Significant at 0.1
$N = 550$

TABLE 10.   Basis for Nomination as a Party Candidate, 1967 (mean scores)

Basis	Other Parties	Congress	F
Candidate's own ability	1.25	1.43	10.386**
Recognition of work done in the area	1.27	1.41	5.96**
Status in party organization	1.59	1.71	2.78*
Connection with leaders	2.00	1.70	15.00**
Backing of special groups	1.95	1.84	3.16*

Source: 1967 elite survey
Note: Responses were scaled from 1 to 3, with 1 indicating that a particular issue was important and 3 that it was not of great importance.
   *Significant at 0.05   **Significant at 0.1
$N = 550$

nomic activity. The executive, or office-seeking, orientation of the party was also visible in intraparty struggles over which branch, the executive or the organizational wing, would control the party.

As there quickly emerged an emphasis on holding executive office within the party, its organization became subservient to the executive wing very early in independent India. Even under Nehru's leadership, when the national party was supposed to emphasize its socially constructive role and was ostensibly focusing on its organization, the composition of the Congress Working Committee, the party's top body, underwent significant institutional modification. At the Indore session of the All-India Congress Committee (AICC), the Congress Party president was given complete freedom to select a Working Committee. The one-third rule, which permitted only one-third of the members of the Working Committee to be government ministers, was dropped, giving the committee a strong executive bias. "As a result the organizational element, . . . was replaced by a strong ministerial element drawing not only upon central Cabinet Ministers but also upon important Chief Ministers . . . [and] most long term members of the Congress Working Committee came from parliamentary wing Chief Ministers or Cabinet members while short term members of the committee were from the organizational wing" (Kochanek, 1968,124–25). In other words, the national organization of the party began to be dominated by the parliamentary wing.[21] In essence, the process of transforming the Congress from a movement for national independence to a ruling party began with the elimination from its ranks of organized groups not amenable to control by the leadership and ended as early as 1951 with the final subordination of the organization to the executive, so that the party became subservient to the government.

A similar trend was witnessed in the various states in which the party organization was used by rival factions to gain control over the government. Factions within the Congress Party employed the power and patronage associated with executive office to control party organization and minimize dissidence within it. State chief ministers who wished to ensure control over the state governments felt it essential to maintain a grip on their party organizations. Importance was attached to the office of the Pradesh Congress Committee president and membership in the Executive Committee of the Pradesh Congress Committee and the Election Committee. Organizational elections in the Congress were keenly contested largely because of the "realization that office bearers who were to be elected would play a decisive role in the party's machinery for selecting candidates" (Kochanek 1968, 27–28). Even in elections for the Congress Party's Central Election Committee, it was alleged that "the bribes of office and other advantages were freely used by some of those in possession of the organization and the government" (35–36). Election to this committee was important, since it had the final say in selecting Congress candidates for any forthcoming election.

The party's organization was tied to executive office at the local level as well. Weiner reports an interview with a member of the Congress Party in Guntur who said: "*My belief is that there is no Congress party organization in India.* Congress has identified itself completely with the government machinery. When the government is lost, then Congress will disappear. . . . I have yet to see a meeting of the Congress workers. They only meet when some minister comes. Otherwise they do not meet to pass resolutions or carry on any party business" (Weiner 1967, 176; emphasis added). Nehru, as early as 1955, realized that the party organization at the local level was controlled by officeholders. Addressing a conference of the presidents of the Pradesh Congress Committees and the leaders of the Congress legislative parties, Nehru observed that in Congress the party boss had become the organization's leader (Indian National Congress 1955). This problem was evident especially at the local level. A meeting of the Subcommittee on Organizational Affairs in the Congress noted that the Pradesh and even the District Congress Committees (DCC) were controlled by executive officeholders; either members of Parliament or members of the legislative assembly (Indian National Congress 1956).

The national Congress organization attempted throughout the 1950s to convert the party into an organization, emphasizing the need for constructive activity. Congress Party activists were aware of their party's largely electoral focus. U. N. Dhebar, who became the Congress Party's president in 1995, noted that "for the last five or six years, all our energies have been concentrated upon elections, whether they are Parliamentary elections, state legislature elections, or the local board elections or the Congress elections in general. I think they are sapping the vitality of the organisation." He asked that the party be revitalized as a field organization, for the "result[s] of the last elections . . . point to one fact, that we are going fast in the direction of being a cent per cent Parliamentary party" (All-India Congress Committee 1958, 4). According to Dhebar, "the function of the Congress now is virtually that of a vote-getting body and experience of the last ten years, after the Congress Party came to power, shows that, although efforts are honestly made by Congressmen to take interest in constructive and other activities the real enthusiasm is generated just a few months before the general election takes place" (20). In the Nehru era, then, the Congress organization was a "highly fractionalized, internally competitive party, ruled by personal opportunism rather than ideology" (Brass 1990, 66).

Further evidence for the state-specific and executive nature of the party during this period comes from the basis of electoral competition with the Congress. During the period of electoral dominance, the most significant opposition to Congress came from within the party itself, especially from disaffected politicians who had lost in the Congress "sweepstakes," that is, who had not been nominated by the party as a Congress candidate in the next election (in most constituencies, being nominated was a sure ticket to success both in the election and in access to government patronage, as the Congress generally won most of the seats in the Lok Sabha). A Congress Party report in 1953–54 noted that "narrow party reasons and internal factions have in many cases been the cause of the Congress defeats. From almost all the constituencies where the Congress suffered defeats, representations have been received from local Congressmen to the effect that reverses have been due to the bad selection of candidates and lack of united support from the Congress workers" (Indian National Congress 1954, 110).[22] In Gujarat, a *khadiata* (*jati*) candidate was denied the Congress ticket in 1957. He then worked against the Congress Party in the elections. The candidate was later given a ticket to contest elections from another constituency in the same district and was elected as a member of the legislative assembly. The candidate and those associated with him then returned to the Congress fold and worked for the party (Kothari and Shah 1965).[23]

That the principal threat to the ascendancy of the Congress came from its own internal factional disputes was also demonstrated in the midterm elections in Kerala held in March 1965. Competition between the Congress Party and its breakaway faction, the Kerala Congress, was responsible for the party losing 10 percent of its seats in the Kerala legislature. Factional disruption also led to the defeat of a number of Congress candidates in Madhya Pradesh in 1962. By 1962, dissidents in Karnataka (then Mysore) had already formed a party of their own, while in Uttar Pradesh and Punjab the situation was precarious and dissension had just been patched up in Rajasthan. For Congress Party politicians, then, the sense of party loyalty was minimal, as a substantial number of them, upon failing to receive party nominations, contested elections against the official candidates of the party. In 1962, for instance, 884 Congress Party members were suspended or expelled for contesting elections against official nominees.

Until 1967, however, factional defection was limited and has been characterized as partial factional defection (Chhibber and Sisson 1990). A sense of the Congress Party's invincibility left individuals with little incentive to shift allegiance to another party, for there were no competitors that could guarantee access to the state. Clearly other parties in India were seen as the "opposition"—as if Congress was the natural holder of power, which was not far from the truth given that other parties, such as the Jana Sangh and the Communists, did not seek to replace the Congress but merely to check its power.

Organization of the Congress Party

The largely electoral nature of the party and its executive does not necessarily preclude the development of an effective organization. As has been argued, however, Congress was a party that activists joined because it provided them access to the state and helped them build a coalition that could ensure electoral success. Since aspirations to executive office were the most important reason why many joined the party, within the party those who held executive office at the national, state, and local levels came to dominate it. This phenomenon stymied the growth of the party's organization. Congress, however, did not develop as effective an organization as has been argued.

Whatever organization the party did develop paralleled the administrative divisions of the state, not electoral demarcations. Congress had, apart from national and state offices, district offices.[24] Considerable research on the Congress Party's organization has been devoted to the functioning of the party in these district offices (Weiner 1967; Kohli 1990). A district, however, is an administrative demarcation, not an electorally drawn geographical unit. The party did not organize itself in electoral constituencies for either the Lok or Vidhan Sabhas. Even when party leaders acknowledged the need to improve the party's organization, they emphasized either the district or the mandal (a level lower than the district), neither of which were electoral units. In other words, the party saw and organized itself as an adjunct to the state. Given the predominant role assigned to the state and Congress's vision of itself as its agent, the party's organization mirrored the state, not electoral, constituencies. This is quite unlike the case in other democracies, such as the United States and England, in which parties have organizations in electoral districts.

Elite Attitudes

Even at the district level, Congress was not well organized. Evidence for the weak organization of the party comes from the party activists themselves. In the 1967 elite survey, respondents were asked to delineate the causes for the weakness of their party.[25] Almost a third (32 percent) pointed to a lack of material resources and organizational deficiencies. Fifteen percent did not see any weakness in their party, while the remaining (21 percent) gave a myriad of other reasons.

The cited reasons for weakness varied by party. A large majority of Congress Party activists attributed weakness in their party to its organization (42 percent), while activists from other parties were more likely to point to a lack of material resources (51 percent) such as money. Obviously, Congress activists, given the party's control over the state, had little reason to feel similarly. The weakness of the Congress Party's organization is also apparent from the party elites' responses when they were asked whether they discussed party matters with elites at higher and lower levels of the party's organization. A party is considered well organized when there is effective communication concerning party matters across different levels of the organization (Eldersveld 1982). Compared to other parties, Congress elites in 1967 were less likely to engage in a discussion with elites from other levels of the organization.[26] The organizational weakness of the party, acknowledged by party activists themselves, as well as the lack of communication between various levels of the organization, suggest that claims of the strength of the Congress's organization should be reexamined.

Further evidence for the poor organization of Congress in 1967 comes from a comparison with elite attitudes in 1993. By all accounts, Congress's organization had atrophied by 1993. If the attitudes of Congress Party activists in 1967 are similar to those in 1993, it could be said that the nature of the party organization at the local level had not undergone much change during this period. Further, if this is indeed the case and Congress Party activists' attitudes in 1967 and 1993 are similar, then, if in 1993 there was no organization to speak of, doubts could also be raised about the extent of the party's organization in 1967. It could be argued that even if the Congress Party was poorly organized in 1967 its organization was still better than its organization in the 1990s. There is little doubt that at the national and state levels Congress in the 1990s is mostly the preserve of a few individuals. An elite survey conducted in 1993, however, displays remarkable similarities between the attitudes of Congress elites in 1967 and 1993. In 1993, as we would expect, Congress Party elites were less likely to identify with their party, were less committed to party ideology, and did not see their organization as effective. As in 1967, the motivations of workers associated with the Congress Party were focused more on building personal contacts and being close to important people (see table 11). Similarly, to get a ticket to contest elections as a Congress candidate, contacts with leaders and the backing of caste groups (as in 1967) were more important than experience in politics. In 1993, wealth was also cited as an important criterion for getting a Congress ticket. Party elites were also asked a series of questions on what they thought was important for success within the party. Once again, Congress Party elites were more likely than those of other parties to stress the role of the leader, wealth, and association with castes (see table 12).

Organization of the Party—Preindependence

The lack of organization is also supported by the fact that the Congress Party, prior to independence, did not extend to all of the provinces. There was no party organization in the princely Indian States, which were incorporated into the union only at independence. Even in British India, historians have questioned whether the party was in fact organized. D. A. Low, for example, notes that "the Mass Contacts Committee was under considerable pressure to submit its report at an early date. On May 6, 1936, it accordingly issued to each District Congress Committee a small four-page printed questionnaire and asked responses to it be sent to the local Provincial Congress Committee so that these committees could send their consolidated replies to Doulatram by the end of June. This, however, was more than many local committees could manage, and by the end of the year Doulatram had received a miscellany of replies from ten Pradesh Congress Committees, from a *dozen or so* District Congress Committees direct, and from *six to eight* other bodies in addition" (1988, 140; emphasis added).

The reach of the Congress at the local level was also limited by the self-interest of those joining the party. Numerous studies have shown how local notables who had captured the party at the local level used it to further their interests (Gallagher, Johnson, and Seal 1973). C. A. Bayly noted that the Congress was essentially a secondary organization that facilitated the persistence of "circumscribed local and sectional aims which derived from lower levels of politics" (1975, 4). Discussing Madras, David Washbrook argued that "the Congress parties which won in the dry and wet regions were of different characters, indicating the . . . different nature of district politics in the two areas [and] . . . even as the Congress stood proclaiming victory for a national ideal, the ambiguities of trying to construct provincial politics on a base of district-level institutions stood out clearly" (1973, 209). This was also the case in Bengal. The Bengal Pradesh Congress Committee observed of its primary committees that they "cannot all be said to be actually functioning today." Moreover, "the effective influence of its [Bengal Congress] workers was small. Even by their own estimates, the popular appeal of the District Congress Committees did not spread far" (Gallagher 1973, 316).

TABLE 11.   Why Workers Affiliate with a Political Party, 1993 (mean scores)

Reason	Other Parties	Congress	F
Building personal contacts	2.08	1.96	9.362*
Access to important people	2.08	1.86	9.185*

Source: 1993 elite survey
Note: Responses were scaled from 1 to 3, with reponses closer to one reflecting greater importance placed on an issue.
*Significant at 0.05
$N = 472$

TABLE 12.   Basis for Nomination as a Party Candidate, 1993 (mean scores)

Basis	Other Parties	Congress	F
Experience	1.66	1.44	4.134**
Connections with leaders	1.55	2.02	9.674**
Wealth of candidate	2.04	2.37	6.321**
Backing of caste groups	2.12	2.27	3.062*

Source: 1993 elite survey
Note: Responses were scaled from 1 to 3, with 1 indicating importance placed on an issue and 3 suggesting that the issue was not important.
*Significant at 0.1   **Significant at 0.05
$N = 472$

Organization of the Party—Postindependence

The fragmented and amorphous nature of Congress organization did not change after independence.[27] The report of the general secretaries of the Congress Party for the period January 1953 to January 1954 noted that the Congress Working Committee had passed a resolution on 11 September 1953 stating that "in certain areas, especially those which used to be in the Indian States before, even District Congress Committees have not been formed" (Indian National Congress 1954, 54). An All-India Congress Committee representative, Mahesh Saran, toured the former princely states in September 1953. In Orissa, he observed that "there are some energetic Congressmen in each of the ex-States but the Congress organization is not very strong" (55).

While there was no Congress structure at all in the former princely states, even in the rest of India the party was not well organized. Nehru, discussing the 1952 election, observed that it was "true to say that the Congress organization has not usually played a satisfactory part in many States. . . . where we have won, this was not always due to the Congress organization. Indeed, the Congress organization, as a whole rather failed in this test" (Indian National Congress 1954, 56). By 1955, Congress Party politicians were openly complaining about the lack of organization. Bhojubhai Shah, a senior Congress leader, noted that "we must be clear about the ideals and objectives. Some feel that Congress is a Parliamentary party and beyond its parliamentary activities, nothing is needed to be done. We must bear in mind that the Congress is a full fledged political party. It must have three sections—Parliamentary, organizational and constructive. The parliamentary work was creditable but it needed better toning up. *What about the other 2 sections?*" (Indian National Congress 1955, 68; emphasis added). G. B. Pant, another Congress leader, acknowledged that "the Congress organization is not as effective and powerful as it should be. There would be places where no Mandal organisations of the Congress exist. *It would not be wrong to say that there may be districts without a Congress organisation. Even where we have got the district organisation, they are not active and functioning.* Congressmen today have a tendency to jump into activity only on two occasions—one, on the occasion of the elections or by-elections to the State Assembly or the Parliament or local bodies, and, secondly, on the occasion of the elections to the Congress organisation" (All-India Congress Committee Economic Review 1955, 4; emphasis added). In 1953, the party resolved that the attention of the Pradesh Congress Committees (PCC) was invited on Articles 2, 12, and 14 of the Congress Constitution, which required them to organize and function through District Congress Committees (DCCs) and other subordinate bodies. There would have been little reason for the national party to exhort the PCCs to organize DCCs if the latter had existed and were functioning as organizational units.

Sadiq Ali, a Congress general secretary, observed that at the lower levels the "organisation . . . was weak, loose and riven by group politics. . . . The Congress has of course always been a mass party but hitherto its mass character has been rather more on the emotional side. The organizational framework was there but it was far from adequate to the needs of the people and the pressures of democracy. The Congress has now to turn its attention to its organizational weakness at the foundation level" (1959, 6). This weakness was most apparent in the responses to the All-India Congress Committee circulars that were sent out in this period. The response was seen as "meagre and no regular information and reports about the activities of the Congress organisation were supplied by the PCCs. The District Congress Committees practically showed no interest and it seemed that only 20 to 25 District Congress Committees were active" (reported in Zaidi 1986, 330). They went on to note that in many places Congress Committees had practically ceased to exist, and it served no useful purpose in trying to counteract the party's organizational weakness (334).

Organizational weakness and disarray were most evident when intraparty organizational elections were held. As was the case during the preindependence period, there were complaints regarding irregularities and malpractices in Congress elections. The All-India Congress Committee had to send representatives to at least nine provinces to look into complaints about intraparty election irregularities: Dev Kanta Barooah went to Delhi, Patiala and East Punjab States Union (PEPSU), and Kanpur; G. K. Vijayavargiya and B. S. Mehta to Vindhya Pradesh; G. H. Deshpande to Agra; Radheylal Vyas to Himachal Pradesh; Mahesh Saran to Chattisgarh States and Orissa; and G. S. Gupta to Bihar. In the United Provinces, "the organization was from the start, riven by cliques and individual ambitions" (Gopal 1976, 91). Nehru acknowledged this in a letter to Tandon, saying that "the Congress is in a bad way . . . it seems to have lost much inner strength that it possessed and we are concerned chiefly with faction fights and maneuvering for position and place" (93).

It could be argued that these observations, which suggest a nonexistent or weak organization that was faction ridden, are not really accurate insofar as the party had a large membership.[28] While the fact of membership cannot be denied, those figures are not real indicators of party strength for three reasons. First, despite its membership of 8.5 million in 1954, the party had only 71,000 active members in 1954. This was only a few thousand more than the Communist Party, which was much smaller in terms of its membership rolls and electoral strength. By 1958, despite a growing electorate, Congress Party membership had been reduced in half and its active workers reduced to 54,000.

Second, Congress membership figures were not reliable because the party was dominated by office-seeking individuals who, when they came to power, subordinated themselves to those above them so that they could gain access to positions of greater power. Because of this emphasis on the benefits that could accrue through the state, party functionaries tended to inflate membership figures in their districts, and this falsification enabled competing factions to assert control over the party. In Uttar Pradesh, for instance, during elections in 1959 to the state bodies, a million member names were found to be bogus.[29]

Third, party membership figures also appear to be tied to elections. The 1961 report of the general secretaries of the Pradesh Congress Parties observed that in an election year there was generally a big drive for membership (Indian National Congress 1961). For instance, in 1960 the total number of primary members in the Congress Party was 4.7 million. In 1961 (the next general elections were to be held in early 1962), the number of Congress members almost doubled, to 9.5 million, only to drop to 2.4 million in 1962 and 2.7 million in 1963. Party membership figures also varied by state, with approximately 4 percent of the electorate as party members in Punjab and less than 0.5 percent in Himachal Pradesh, Tamil Nadu, and Orissa.

Attempts by the Congress to build up a party organization at the district level and below did not begin until the presidency of U. N. Dhebar. There is no evidence, however, to suggest that Dhebar's attempts to set up an organization succeeded. "He knew that the Pradesh Congress Committees were functioning but he did not know how many of the District Congress Committees functioned. Some DCCs had no offices even" (Zaidi 1981, 70). Dhebar, since he found that the soundness of the organization varied across states, questioned whether the party was truly organized at the state level as well. The party's organization, he noted, was reasonably sound in some states; in others, it was outwardly strong but inwardly it rested upon the influence and hard work of one or a few men. In a few states, the organization either simply limped along because of the absence of an effective opposition or worked only under strains of internal discord, while in the rest it was simply nonexistent.[30] At a meeting of presidents and secretaries of the Pradesh Congress Committees at Avadi, Dhebar reaffirmed this situation when he said that "the trend of power politics evidenced in the attempt to capture Legislatures and offices, has produced its own reactions, thereby adversely affecting the Organisation itself. Organisational and parliamentary complaints are received from most of the Pradeshes. All these indicate the growth of a disease. . . ." He added that the party should be more than "an organisation which works only for elections or as go-between the people and the administration" (Zaidi 1986, 281).

Data drawn from the surveys of party elites in 1967 and 1993 suggest that the Congress Party was not a well-organized party in the two decades following independence. Party activists had limited communication across different levels of the organization and tended to join the party to gain access to the state. Since the Congress was deemed to be the party that would inevitably be returned to power and control the resources that the state commanded, the party developed an executive bias. The federal structure of the Indian state allocated resources and independent authority to state governments, and thus the party developed as a collection of distinct state parties, each representing interests particular to its region. During this period, when the primary purpose of the national Congress was the formation of the national government, it was able to gain the cooperation (sometimes half-hearted) of state leaders. These leaders were secure and influential only by virtue of their command over executive office. Since maintaining political power depended largely upon retaining control over the instruments of the state, there was little need to develop an organization. The Congress Party continued to win elections as long as state political leaders continued to mobilize support for the party; the national Congress, in turn, met their political needs. Because no other political party was competitive during this period, the major political tension was that within the Congress Party—factional conflict within the state parties and between the state and central parties. Factional conflict within the state parties was over who would control the state government; that between the center and the states was over the autonomy of the state Congress parties from the central party.

Chapter 4

Electoral Competition and the Growth of Central Intervention in the States

It has been argued thus far that the Congress Party was a coalition of state-based parties. This territorial orientation of the party is influenced by social divisions, particularly caste and language, which are more politically salient at the state level than they are at the national level. These demarcations were reinforced by institutional structures—the federal devolution of power and the SMSP electoral law. These factors forced the Congress Party to mobilize support locally and aggregate this support on a state by state basis, giving it the appearance of a catchall party at the state level. The Congress during the period of one-party dominance was "a collection of state based factions linked not by a common constituency, but by elites who cooperate in the pursuit of office" (Chhibber and Petrocik 1989, 191).

Given the state-based nature of the Congress Party and the absence of other electorally competitive parties during this period, the major political conflict was between the national and the various state parties. This conflict openly manifested itself during the 1960s. Following the death of two Congress prime ministers in office, state leaders came to control the national party. The electoral debacle that followed the 1967 elections was in large part due to this intraparty conflict, though the consequences of factionalism within the Congress Party were exacerbated by an economic crisis that preceded the elections.

In the 1967 general elections, the party lost control, for the first time, of eight state governments and came to Parliament with a much reduced majority. Since then, even though the Congress then was "restored" periodically, as in 1972, a single party has not retained exclusive power in Delhi.[1] The Congress won pluralities in the elections of 1980, 1984, and 1991 and sat in the opposition after the elections of 1977, 1989, 1996, and 1998. Similarly, in the states Congress has not been able to retain its electoral dominance of the pre-1967 era, losing every state government at least once in the elections that have taken place over the past three decades.

The 1967 elections had important consequences for the party system. In the aftermath of the elections, it became clear that the Congress Party could be beaten. The party could no longer rest its electoral success on its historic legacy as the party of independence. Most importantly, for the Congress Party to win national elections it had to ensure that either it or a party favorable to it won elections to the state assemblies. Seeking to secure its electoral position, the national Congress Party responded by reestablishing the authority and power of the center (made easier by some of the unitary features of the Constitution) and politicizing the distribution of state resources. Once again, these responses were made possible because of the role ascribed to the state at independence and the fact that the Congress Party occupied a controlling position and saw itself as the agent of India's economic development. The federal structure of the state and the electoral laws, however, still forced the Congress Party to mobilize support on a state by state basis, and opposition to the Congress Party has been largely state specific.

The first part of this chapter lays out the reasons for the relatively poor performance of the Congress Party in the 1967 election. The Congress Party, it will be argued, was unable to hold together its coalition in the states because state politicians became more autonomous of the central Congress Party in the mid-1960s. As power devolved to the state leaders, the national party lost its ability to intervene in state politics. This intervention had been key in maintaining a semblance of unity within the state-level Congress parties. The waning of Congress's appeal as the party that had ushered in independence, combined with the effects of an economic crisis marked by a drop in food production and inflation, exacerbated the political tensions within the party. These factors led to the poor performance of the party in the 1967 elections. For the national Congress Party, the lessons of 1967 were clear: in order to continue its electoral success in national elections, control over the state parties, which could be achieved through increased and selective intervention in the states by the central government, was critical. The second section of this chapter discusses how the national party, under Indira Gandhi's tutelage, adopted measures to ensure its electoral success. The implications of these developments for state politics and electoral competition are discussed in the concluding section.

The Rise of Political Competition: 1967

The first serious threat to the electoral dominance of the Congress Party came with the general election of 1967, in which the party lost electoral majorities in eight states and was returned to national power with a reduced majority in Parliament.[2] The Congress Party suffered electoral setbacks in almost all of the states compared to the 1962 election: not only did it have a lower overall vote share, but it also lost seats in the state assemblies and to the Lok Sabha in almost all states. The party's vote share for the Lok Sabha, compared with the 1962 election, dropped by 22 percent in Orissa and between 5 and 10 percent in Bihar, Gujarat, Uttar Pradesh, and West Bengal. Its vote shares for the state assemblies also registered a decline in every state but Kerala, Madhya Pradesh, and Rajasthan. This trend was repeated in the number of seats the party held in the Vidhan Sabhas. The Congress Party lost 89 seats in Tamil Nadu, and over 50 seats in each of the Bihar, Orissa, and Uttar Pradesh assemblies. For the Lok Sabha, the party did better in 1967 only in Andhra Pradesh and Assam, where it managed to gain just one seat more than it did in 1962. Competition emerged in the mid-1960s, with the unraveling of the coalition that the Congress Party had built up over the years. The Congress Party had won almost every election since 1952, state or national, by mobilizing votes on a state-specific basis. What accounts for the party's inability to hold its coalitions together in the states in 1967?

The answer to this question has two parts. The first has to do with whether the source of this competition was national or state specific. In other words, did opposition to the Congress Party come from a national movement or was it directed more against the state-level units of the party? Second, what was the nature of this competition? Did the successful opposition parties mobilize hitherto unmobilized segments of the electorate (or bring new groups into the electoral process) or was it largely a result of the defection of existing supporters of one party to another?

The major source of electoral competition to the Congress Party, in the years leading up to and including the 1967 election, was at the state level. In Punjab and Tamil Nadu, regional parties—the Akali Dal and Dravida Munnetra Kazhagzam, respectively—provided opposition to the Congress and emerged as political forces in their own right. Opposition parties also emerged in Gujarat, in the form of the Congress(O) and the Swatantra Party, and in Maharashtra as the Republican parties, the Shiv Sena, and the Congress Party breakaways. Madhya Pradesh has been the scene of ongoing political battles between the erstwhile Jana Sangh, now the Bharatiya Janata Party, and the Congress. Kerala politics has long been characterized by multiparty electoral battles, with the CPI(M), the Muslim League, the Congress Party, and the Kerala Congress as the major contestants. Orissa was initially the home of the Ganatantra Parishad; later it became a stronghold of the Swatantra Party, and subsequently it saw the ascendance of a regional party, the Utkal Congress and now the Biju Janata Dal. Bihar and eastern Uttar Pradesh have been influenced by a variant of the socialist parties, while western Uttar Pradesh and Haryana have been home to the Bharatiya Kranti Dal and its successor, the Lok Dal. Rajasthan at independence was home to an informal *rajput* coalition that subsequently merged with the Congress. Over the years, however, the state provided the Jana Sangh and Swatantra parties with substantial support. West Bengal saw the ascendance of the CPI(M), along with a host of smaller leftist parties such as the Forward Bloc, all of them specific to the state.[3]

Second, why is it that this state-specific opposition to the Congress Party provided an electoral challenge in the mid-1960s? The Congress Party did relatively poorly in the 1967 election (and after that as well) largely because groups whose interests it no longer accommodated exited the party. Exit from the Congress Party in 1967 took place for one primary reason: the party could no longer ensure the accommodation of different interests in the various states. Most of this difficulty arose over access to state largesse. The intense intraparty conflict over the nomination process to contest elections as a Congress candidate was often settled through the active intervention of the national party (Kochanek 1968). The weakness of the national party was most apparent when it was unable to successfully to contain intraparty conflict over nomination proceedings within the states.

Organizational Changes in the Congress Party

A major factor mitigating against a reconciliation of the various factions that characterized state-level Congress parties was the central party's loss of control over the state units. Until then, factional conflict within the state-level parties had been resolved by intervention from the center (Kochanek 1968). As central authority weakened, mediation of factional conflict within the state-level parties became problematic for the Congress Party. The trend toward diminished central authority was evident as early as the third general elections in 1962 (Weiner 1965). By that time, there had been a transformation of internal competition within the Congress Party, and one could witness open dissidence, defiance, and electoral sabotage within the party in many states (Kothari 1961d).

This dissatisfaction came to a head over the issue of nomination for the fourth general elections in 1967.[4] By the time of the election, the national Congress Party was a divided house. The party had seen two succession battles following the deaths of two sitting prime ministers, Nehru and Shastri, in 1964 and 1966, respectively. The central party had been weakened relative to the state units following the assumption of control of the national party organization by state leaders. This change in control was reflected in the composition of the working committee. Until the early 1960s, the Congress Working Committee was essentially an extension of the office of the prime minister, as the entire Committee was nominated by the president of the party, who, in turn, was handpicked by the prime minister. By 1964, however, state-level Congress leaders had managed to break the stranglehold of the prime minister on the Working Committee by electing almost half of the Working Committee members. These elections gave state leaders the opportunity to influence national Congress politics directly. The death of Nehru and then Shastri provoked intraparty conflict over who would be the next prime minister. The "Syndicate" (a euphemism for a collection of state leaders who controlled the national party) did not want a strong prime minister who could usurp its authority within the party. On both occasions, it bypassed the claims of Morarji Desai, who had the potential to be a strong prime minister, and picked a weaker candidate—Shastri to succeed Nehru and then Indira Gandhi after the death of Shastri (Brecher 1966; Kochanek 1968).[5]

These organizational changes in the party had a major impact on factional accommodation within the party for two reasons. First, since the national party was already divided, factional conflict was more likely to occur within the states. National leaders, especially those who had risen through the ranks from the states, had an interest in state politics since they were always tied to one faction or another . For instance, the appointment of N. Sanjiva Reddy as Congress president did not keep him from intervening in Andhra politics. In fact, his encouragement of dissidents led to a cabinet crisis in Andhra Pradesh in the late 1950s. The same was true of Morarji Desai, who maintained an influential presence in Gujarat politics after his election to the national Council of Ministers, as did Y. B. Chavan in Maharashtra. Further, as the national party was divided over the issue of succession, there was a pronounced incentive for the various holders of national office in the party to reestablish political control at the state level in order to ensure their political survival. This intervention in state politics by central leaders did not go unopposed. More often than not, central leaders, because of their factional ties, ran into opposition from state leaders, who saw central intervention as a usurpation of their authority.[6]

Second, since the Congress Party in the center was divided and weak, it could not mediate conflict within a state. With the weakening of the central party and the emergence of powerful state chief ministers, the national party lost its ability to arbitrate factional conflict in the states. This left state parties in the control of the chief minister. In this period, the central party had lost its control and states were run by largely autonomous chief ministers. Signs of this trend were observable even when Nehru was prime minister. In the early 1960s, the central party had begun to lose its grip over the party. Much of this trend was due to power in the states having congealed around the office of the chief minister.

The influence of the chief ministers was visible most prominently in nominations to contest the 1967 elections on the Congress ticket. For the first time since the 1952 elections, chief ministers were able to exercise power over the selection of candidates, with the end result being that their requests were favored over those of dissidents in the states. The larger role played by chief ministers in nomination politics made compromise among the different factions difficult (Kochanek 1968). In Rajasthan, the chief minister, Mohanlal Sukhadia, had a difficult time dealing with the demands of factions within the party. If he did not "accommodate the dissidents [that] might drive them out of the party, and if, on the other hand, they had already decided to leave the party, the attempt to accommodate them was to play their game. This dilemma was very much present in the calculations of Mohanlal Sukhadia" (Kumar 1968, 124).

Data drawn from the postelection survey of political activists in 1967 provides supportive evidence for the observation that an individual's ties with powerful state leaders and social groups was paramount in determining nomination as a Congress candidate. Congress activists were divided into two groups: those who came from states with a great deal of factional conflict and those from states in which the party was more cohesive. Party activists had been asked a battery of questions regarding candidate selection. Sixty-three percent of those from more cohesive states were likely to think that factors such as the candidate's ability were more influential in candidate selection, whereas only 37 percent of party activists from factionally divided states felt similarly.

One reason for groups deserting the Congress was the party's catchall image—the result of its attempts to accommodate a very broad range of interests in order to maintain its electoral dominance. Most groups supporting the Congress did so because of the party's control over the state; this association was facilitated by the perception that the Congress could not lose an election. As a result, diverse groups whose interests were often at odds were brought into the party's fold. This strategy had its drawbacks. Sooner or later, the large number of groups with competing demands would compromise the ability of the party to satisfy those demands, and dissatisfied groups would be convenient targets of mobilization by other parties. Also, the strategy of appealing to a wide constituency generally works well only during times of economic expansion, when it is easy to build large coalitions that encompass competing interests.[7] In the mid-1960s, however, the Indian economy was facing its first postindependence crisis.

Economic Crisis, the Independence Mandate, and the 1967 Elections

The years prior to the elections of 1967 were marked by sharp price increases for a multitude of reasons, including a drought that had plagued the country for two years prior to the elections, the war with Pakistan in 1965, and the devaluation of the rupee in 1966. A standard economic voting model—"people vote their pocketbook"—would suggest that, given the poor economic conditions in India at the time, the Congress, as the incumbent party, would lose support. Further, since the Congress faced budgetary restraints, it was difficult for it to adopt policies that would ensure the support of each member of its heterogeneous coalition.

By 1967, the Congress Party's independence mandate was waning, particularly with the entry into the political process of those who had attained political awareness after independence. Up until then, the party had been able to maintain its electoral success because it was the party that had brought independence. The momentum of that movement lasted until at least 1962, when for the first time since the first elections in 1952 the Congress made only a passing reference in its election manifesto to its role as the party responsible for India's independence. In the 1967 election, the party once again talked about its role in the independence movement, but this was more in the context of discussing the great leaders that the party had produced.

The impact of the growing number of new entrants into the political process was reflected in the monotonic increase in turnout for every general election through 1967. Turnout rose from 48 percent in 1957 to 55 percent in 1962 and to 62 percent in 1967. Moreover, those who entered the political process in the postindependence period—that is, who voted for the first time in the 1952 election or after—were less likely to vote for the Congress.[8] One-fourth of the postindependence generation said they voted for Congress in 1967. This contrasts with the preindependence generation, two out of five of whom voted for the Congress. Further, the postindependence generation was more likely to switch allegiances: 53 percent of those who were politically socialized in the preindependence period voted for the same party in the 1962 and 1967 elections, whereas only 38 percent of the postindependence era respondents retained similar political preferences between the two elections.

Table 13 assesses the relative impact of these variables on voting for the Congress Party in 1967.[9] In the 1967 postelection survey, respondents were asked to assess whether the party had failed to keep prices down and maintain law and order. Those who felt that the party could not be blamed for the price rises and the deteriorating law and order situation could be expected to vote for the Congress. At the same time, respondents who had attained their political awareness in the postindependence era (to reiterate, those who were first eligible to vote in the 1952 general elections or after) should be less affected by the Congress's role in the independence movement than those who became politically aware during the independence struggle. The logistic regression detailed in table 13 relates the decision of whether to vote for the Congress Party with the respondent's partisanship (i.e., whether the respondents felt close to Congress or not), party performance issues, the respondent's age cohort, and a dummy variable that takes on the value 0 if the respondent resided in a state that was factionally divided and 1 otherwise (i.e., states where Congress was more cohesive).[10] The results quite clearly indicate that the decision to vote for the Congress was affected by the factional nature of the state party, with respondents more likely to vote for the Congress in states where the party presented a relatively cohesive front. Factionalism, as the table suggests, had an impact on the vote for the party, controlling for partisanship, positive perceptions of party performance, and age cohorts. In other words, one important reason why Congress did poorly in the elections of 1967 was that various state-level Congress parties could no longer successfully mediate factional conflict within their states. The impact of factions is confirmed by the fact that after the election five of the eight chief ministers in states in which Congress lost the elections were defectors from the Congress Party and led parties that borrowed the Congress's name but added the name of their state as a prefix.[11]

TABLE 13.   Government Performance, Factionalism, the
Independence Mandate, and the Congress Vote, 1967 (logistic
regression)

	Coefficient	Standard Error
Government performance		
Prices	0.28**	0.16
Law and order	0.09	0.11
Factionalism in Congress	0.46*	0.15
Congress identifiers	2.71*	0.16
Postindependence generation	−0.26**	0.15
Constant	−1.368*	0.24

Source: 1967 postelection survey
*Significant at 0.05   **Significant at 0.1
N = 1,176
−2 log likelihood = 1,143.8
77.83 percent predicted

   The coefficients for partisanship and party performance were positive,
whereas the coefficient for the age cohort was negative. That coefficient
indicates that those who were socialized into politics after independence
were less likely to vote for the Congress Party, even if party performance,
partisanship, and the extent of factional conflict in the party are taken into
account. Thus, the entry into politics of a new generation for whom the
independence mandate of the Congress had little resonance and the presence of factional conflict within state-level Congress parties, together with
the effects of the economic crisis of the mid-1960s, led to the electoral
debacle of 1967.

   The increased factionalism that preceded the 1967 election and the
entry of a less committed electorate led in the 1967 elections to "economic,
personal and regional considerations . . . [having] an edge over the traditional, ideological, nationally cohesive forces" (Narain and Lal 1968, x).
Several representative cases elucidate the large role played by local and
regional considerations in the 1967 elections. In Uttar Pradesh, a study of
the Azamgarh parliamentary constituency revealed that caste was the
most important factor in elections, even more decisive than considerations
of the candidates' local affiliations with the area. Thus, the parliamentary
candidate of the Congress, Chandrajit Yadav, in an attempt to build a
multicaste coalition,

when he saw that the election wind was not in favour of the Congress, . . . started approaching voters of different castes through their caste leaders. For each of the Vidhan Sabha constituencies, he enrolled a team of about 100 workers from different castes to work among their own castes and communities. He distributed leaflets with a personal appeal to vote and support his candidates, ignoring the Assembly candidates of his party, so as to avoid confrontation among his castemen. Yadav managed to have an electoral pact with the candidates of his caste [rather than with candidates of his own party], contesting Assembly seats for reciprocal support *irrespective* of their party affiliation. (Singh 1969, 1602; emphasis added)

The lack of partisan loyalty that characterized Azamgarh was not an isolated instance. B. Maheshwari, in a study of Jaipur (1968), noted that the Congress Party suffered from a lack of dedicated workers and that its activists in fact had conflicting loyalties. In Jaipur, the city Congress office was nominally responsible for elections in all four of the assembly constituencies in the city. In practice, however, the city office neglected three of these constituencies, concentrating on just one of them, Johari Bazaar, and a rural constituency nearby. This action was motivated by personal interests on the part of the officeholders, who wanted to strengthen their own positions in Johari Bazaar and gain favors from the dominant groups in the Pradesh Congress Committee by supporting the PCC chief in a neighboring constituency rather than concerning themselves with the success of the party across the entire city.

Garald C. Papachristou (1968) observes that the lack of partisan loyalty was equally apparent in the local elections of 1967. The *sarpanchs* (heads of the *panchayats*) had party affiliations, but they did not blindly support their parties' candidates. Of those who claimed party membership, 46 percent supported the candidate of the party they professed to belong to whereas 38 percent supported independent candidates largely because they were dissatisfied with the candidate representing their party (154). For most of the local political elites, affiliation with the Congress was more a matter of expediency than anything else. Seventy percent of *sarpanchs* interviewed said that most Congress *sarpanchs* would change their support to a new ruling party if there were a change in government at the state level. A *sarpanch* who was willing to change his political loyalties explained it this way: "I want development of my area and this is only possible if I join the ruling party" (154). These observations underscore the fact that at all levels support for Congress was undergirded by the fact that the party controlled the state. State elites supported the Congress party because it held the reins of the central government, whereas local support for the party was contingent upon its control of the state governments.[12]

Given these developments, it is no surprise that the attachment of voters to political parties also registered a decline. The proportion of those identifying with the Congress Party dropped from 39 percent in 1967 to 22 percent in 1971 and 12 percent in 1980. Furthermore, the proportion of the electorate that identified with any party also decreased, from 67 percent in 1967 to 35 percent in 1971 and 23 percent in 1980.[13]

To summarize, this analysis of the 1967 elections suggests that the Congress did not perform well because of factional conflict within the party, the economic situation at the time, and the waning of the importance of the legacy of independence. Since factions within Congress were often linked to interests (either economic or political), increased factionalism meant that group politics would become more prevalent in the aftermath of the 1967 elections. Even though the Congress retained its electoral majorities in some of the elections that followed, most notably in 1972, the nature of how the party built its coalition had changed forever. The Congress was no longer able to assume automatic electoral success. It could not mobilize support as the party that had brought independence, especially with the introduction of a new generation to politics. Factional accommodation, as it became clear after the 1967 elections, was only possible through access to the state. As long as the Congress was guaranteed electoral success, the various factions had little leverage over what they could expect from the party. Once the Congress appeared vulnerable, the need to build, maintain, and keep coalitions together became ever more urgent. As involvement with Congress (and other parties) became the means for gaining access to the state, loyalty to political parties declined rapidly—parties came increasingly to be seen as vehicles for accessing the resources of the state. The 1967 election also made it clear to Indian politicians, especially those from the Congress Party, that there was a need to ensure favorable economic conditions at election time.

There were two other significant outcomes associated with the 1967 general elections. First, for Congress to be returned to power nationally, it had to retain the support of its state-level parties. How did the national Congress Party respond to the emergence of this competition in the states? Furthermore, how did the various state parties attempt to hold together the multiple groups that were not loyal to any party but formed the basis of a party's electoral coalition? The next section discusses the political and economic measures taken by the national party, especially during Indira Gandhi's regime, to ensure the electoral success of the national Congress Party. Second, the politics of exit came to dominate electoral politics.[14] Now that politicians and voters realized that no political party was electorally invincible (especially not the Congress), they began to switch allegiances if they felt that the party no longer represented their interests. Since the Indian party system is characterized by a state-specific party system, exit is a state-level phenomenon. Chapter 5 examines in detail the politics of exit in the states in more detail. It also addresses attempts by the state-level parties to hold together viable coalitions.

The National Congress Party and State Politics, 1967–84

Between 1967 and the next national elections in 1971, which saw the emergence of Indira Gandhi as the unchallenged leader of the Congress, the party suffered the first of a succession of splits. The initial split, in 1969, was between Prime Minister Indira Gandhi and a coalition of powerful state leaders—known as the Syndicate—which controlled the party organization but had become disturbed at its inability to control the prime minister it had placed in power. The 1969 split, ostensibly over who was to be the official Congress candidate for the presidency of the country, resulted in two national Congress parties, the Congress (O), for "organization," was the party of the Syndicate and maintained titular and in most cases actual control over state and local party organizations as well as national party institutions. The Congress (R), for "ruling," enjoyed the support of a majority of incumbent Congress MPs during the interval between the split and the 1971 elections. The Congress (R) was left with a decimated party organization in 1969.[15]

Prime Minister Indira Gandhi called the 1971 national election separately from the state elections. The immediate impact of this decision was to separate local issues, which were an important basis of voter mobilization, from national ones and to buffer national politics from state-level factional conflict. A demobilization of the electorate followed. In contrast to 1967, when 62 percent of eligible voters turned out in the national election, in 1971 only 55 percent of the voting population exercised the franchise. In these elections, the Congress (R) was returned with a two-thirds parliamentary majority, having garnered 44 percent of the vote. It benefited from the "multiplier effect" associated with SMSP systems in which large parties get a greater proportion of seats than their vote share. The Congress (O), sending 238 candidates to the hustings, saw but 16 return victoriously, with the party attracting only 10 percent of the vote.

The election results of 1971, especially the Congress (R)'s win with such overwhelming support, demonstrated two things: first, that elections could be won without the benefit of an elaborate party organization to serve as an instrument of electoral mobilization and a mechanism for screening candidates; and second, that the existence and operation of a party organization does not guarantee electoral success. As elections could apparently be won without an organization, there was little need to build one. Consequently, after 1972 no organizational elections were held within the Congress Party. This led to a centralization of decision making within the party (Manor 1991).

Another clear lesson of the 1967 elections was that a state-focused mobilization strategy by the national Congress Party had its drawbacks. If the Congress lost control over a state government to another party, it was then more likely to do poorly in that state in the national elections. As most state governments were controlled by Congress until 1967, the party also managed to retain its electoral majority. Competition to Congress in 1967 came from state-specific parties whose objective was control over the instruments of the state government.

Facing competition from these state-based parties, the national Congress Party attempted to ensure that states were governed by its allies. The first preference of the national party was that a state be governed by a unit of the Congress Party. If that were not feasible, the national party was willing to form a coalition with regional parties that supported Congress, either in national elections or in Parliament. The latter was the case with the Dravida Munnetra Kazhgam (DMK) in Tamil Nadu in the early 1970s. After the 1967 state assembly elections, the DMK came to power in Tamil Nadu where the Congress had won three seats and the DMK 25 for the Lok Sabha.[16] By 1971, however, the DMK had formed an electoral alliance with Indira Gandhi's Congress Party, whereby Congress won all nine of the seats it contested from Tamil Nadu (the DMK, its ally in the Lok Sabha, won another 23). Since then, the success of the Congress Party in Tamil Nadu is largely attributable to the fact that it cedes control over the state government to its regional ally, either the DMK or the All-India Anna Dravida Munnetra Kazhagam (AI-ADMK).[17] Andhra Pradesh provides another example. The Congress Party lost control of Andhra Pradesh to the Telugu Desam, a regional party, in 1983. In the next election to the Lok Sabha, held in 1984, even though the Congress was returned to power by the largest margin ever, it still did not win a majority of seats to the Lok Sabha from Andhra Pradesh. Instead most of these seats went to the Telugu Desam. Andhra politics, in the 1990s has been characterized by electoral competition between the Congress and the Telugu Desam.

Additionally, the Congress Party in the Indira Gandhi years allocated resources to states it governed to influence electoral outcomes. The political concerns of the center increased the amount of loans granted to the states by the center. Central loans to states increased by more than Rs 28 million in the years in which the center had political considerations to address, such as supporting a Congress government in power in the state. This contrasts with an average increase of only Rs 13 million in other years.[18] Electoral motives account for these differences in the amount loaned to the states. The assumption behind this disbursement was that, with these extra resources, the state party would be able to continue to mobilize support. A similar set of reasons explains why Congress began to increase its intervention in state politics as elections became more competitive. If a state was controlled by a state unit of the Congress Party, the party was likely to do better in that state in the national elections.

The emergence of electoral competition to the Congress around the time of 1967 election, from political parties interested in gaining control over the state, led the national party to adopt a two-pronged strategy to enhance its electoral prospects in the states. First, it increased the role of the state, which made defecting from the party that controlled political power difficult. Second, the center increased its political and economic intervention in the states and redirected resources such as industrial licenses, loans, and food to states in which its electoral prospects were in jeopardy.[19] Within the states, however, the onset of competition made the executive office the locus of contention. An expansion of executive offices followed.

A Larger Role for the Center

Since the Congress Party used state resources to build continued support for itself, and opposition to the party has come from those who could not obtain access to the state from within the state-level Congress parties, the national party responded to the emergent competition after 1967 by increasing the role of the central government in matters formerly handled by the states. Economic centralization began with the elections of 1971, when Indira Gandhi initiated a policy of consolidating power and resources in the hands of the central government. In addition to centralizing power (Rudolph and Rudolph 1987; Kohli 1990), the central government increased its spending (nondefense) vis-à-vis the states. Central government spending (nondefense) as a proportion of GNP increased most noticeably after 1971 (see fig. 10). As figure 11 suggests quite clearly, the proportion of total central government expenditures on the current account as a proportion of total government expenditures (by both the central and state governments) on the current account also shows a remarkable increase beginning with the Gandhi regime.

A number of developments have further increased the imbalance between the center and the states over the years. First, the center redefined the income tax to exclude corporate tax from the tax receipts it had to share with the states. This change is significant because the corporate tax became a larger proportion of the direct taxes collected by the central government than personal income tax. Whereas in 1950–51 personal income tax composed 77 percent of direct taxes, in 1960–61 it was 60.5 percent, in 1970–71 it was 56 percent, in 1980–81 it was 53 percent, and in 1988–89 it was 49 percent (Chandok 1991). Second, the center began to raise revenues by resorting to administered price increases rather than raising excise taxes. The latter, unlike the former, had to be shared with the state governments. Third, the central government expanded its control over the economy by appropriating revenues from broadcasting. During the emergency period from 1975 to 1977, when fundamental rights were suspended in India, the central government introduced the 42nd Amendment to the Indian Constitution. This amendment was a source of much controversy because of the limits it placed on individual liberties. The last item in the long, mostly political amendment gave the center the right to appropriate resources gathered from commercial advertising on government-owned radio and television stations. Within the framework of the unamended Constitution, these monies would have been appropriated by the states. When the political features of the 42nd Amendment were repealed in 1977, the Janata government—which ostensibly had a larger commitment to federalism in its election manifesto than did the Congress—did not repeal this particular amendment.[20] The states were thereby deprived of an important source of revenue. Fourth, there is an increasing tendency on the part of the center to impose schemes of expenditures for the states devised at the center (these are known as the

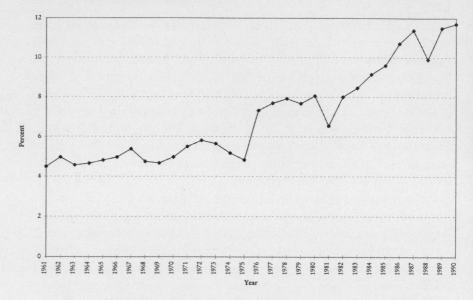

Fig. 10.   Central government expenditures as a proportion of GNP, excluding defense spending. (Data from Chandhok 1990; Ministry of Finance, *Indian Economic Statistics,* 1996.)

centrally sponsored schemes). This encroaches on the powers and functions of the states, as these schemes also call for matching grants from the state governments. The latter requirement forces state governments to alter their spending priorities.

There has also been a tendency on the part of the center to circumscribe the independence of the Finance Commission by laying down strict guidelines for the commission. The Finance Commission is a constitutionally mandated body whose express task it is to preserve the fiscal balance between the center and the states. Its terms of reference, however, are controlled by the center. Since the time of the fifth Finance Commission (which was set up in 1967), the terms of reference laid out for the body by the central government have not given it any leeway, as the government quite explicitly insists that the commission shall follow its directives. Further, these terms of reference are unilaterally imposed by the Union Finance Ministry without any prior consultation with the states. The fourth and fifth Finance Commissions also accepted the position that they should restrict themselves to assessing nonplan revenue gaps (nonplan rev-

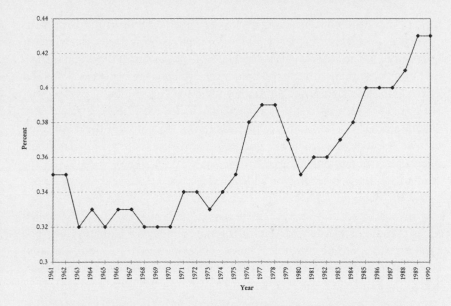

Fig. 11.   Central government expenditures as a proportion of total government expenditures, excluding defense spending. (Data from Chandhok 1990; Ministry of Finance, *Indian Economic Statistics,* 1996.)

enue gaps are shortfalls in the revenue accounts of the state governments only on spending that is not incurred as part of the five-year plans) and not concern themselves with the totality of the financial position of the states. Since 1972, following the recommendations of the Administrative Reforms Committee, a member of the Planning Commission, a central body with little consideration for the interests of the states, has been nominated to the Finance Commission.[21]

The central government has also extended its role in social policy, an area that traditionally was in the realm of the states. The central government introduced its National Policy on Education in 1986 and established *navodaya vidyalayas* (composite schools) in each district. Eight hundred *kendriya vidyalayas* (schools meant for central government employees who might be transferred) are now operational in the country; the improvement of science education has been pursued under a centrally sponsored scheme, which began in 1987–88; and a Computer Literacy and Studies in Schools program was initiated by the departments of Education and Electronics of the central government. Central policies have also been established for scheduled castes and scheduled tribes. The central government provides special assistance to states for the economic advancement of these groups, and it also releases special funds to states, Union Territories, and even private institutions to coach scheduled castes and tribes for the competitive examinations that qualify them for government jobs. In 1992, the central government set up a National Backward Classes Finance and Development Corporation to provide economic aid to the backward classes. Further, the center has initiated a national program for the mobilization of rural women through the Mahila Samakhya (education for women's empowerment). For children, there is a central Balwadi Nutritional Program, which is run by the Central Social Welfare Board.

In addition, there has been increased central incursion into policy areas that are explicitly reserved for the states under the Constitution. The center has, according to Mitra, "made massive inroad[s] . . . into jurisdictions reserved for the States" (1988, xi). One such area is agriculture, where the center has enlarged its influence. Until 1967, the central role in agriculture was limited. Provisions for agriculture in central government and centrally sponsored programs fell below 10 percent of total government expenditures on agriculture (by both central and state governments). In the Fourth Five-Year Plan, initiated in 1970, the proportion of central expenditures on agriculture increased to more than two-fifths of total government agricultural expenditures by both the center and the states (National Commission on Agriculture 1976, 104). This increased resource allocation by the center is significant given that under the Indian Constitution agriculture is itemized as a state subject; it is an issue area over which states are supposed to have complete jurisdiction.

In the area of rural employment and development, the role of the central government has also increased over time. The Jawahar Rozgar Yojana (Jawahar Employment Plan), a centrally sponsored scheme that addresses rural unemployment, is implemented by the state, but 80 percent of the funds come from the central government. Similarly, the Integrated Rural Development Programme, which is designed to help small and marginal farmers, agricultural laborers, and rural artisans with low incomes, is a centrally sponsored scheme with half the resources coming from the central government.

Thus, since 1971, when Indira Gandhi came to power, the central government has increased its intervention in the fiscal elements of federalism through economic centralization of finance and greater involvement in the economic affairs of states, exemplified by the increase in central programs for social development. While the overall level of central government intervention has increased, political considerations have played a role in the transfer of resources from the center to the states.

Political and Economic Intervention by the Center in
the States

Political Intervention

To ensure its electoral success in the states, the national Congress increased its intervention in state politics and economics after the mid-1960s. Political intervention by the center in the affairs of states was facilitated by constitutional provisions, detailed in chapter 2, that favor the center. The most egregious intervention was justified through Article 356 of the Constitution. From 1951 to 1966, "president's rule" was imposed on states 10 times. Political problems caused by the reorganization of states and the inability of parties to form a ruling coalition on two occasions rendered president's rule inevitable. In seven instances, the center used its power under the Constitution to influence state politics, even intraparty politics. For example, in 1951 the (national) Congress Parliamentary Board decided that the Punjab chief minister, Dr. Bhargava, should resign because of intraparty factional conflict. Yet, despite an absolute majority in the state legislature, the state Congress could not agree on an alternate leader. President's rule was imposed on the Punjab following the chief minister's resignation to resolve factional differences within the party (Kochanek 1968). The most famous example of Congress intervention in state politics during this period was in Kerala in 1959. There the national Congress managed to have the duly elected Communist government dismissed and imposed president's rule on the state. Having gained control over the state government, Congress, not surprisingly, did much better in the next round of elections in Kerala.

From 1967 through 1984, in sharp contrast to the earlier phase, president's rule was imposed 72 times.[22] On 20 occasions, as no coalition government could be formed, central intervention was perhaps justified. In the 52 other cases, central intervention in the states was made for partisan reasons. These were of two types: one, as in the case of Punjab in 1951, when there was intraparty factional conflict; and the other when a state government was formed by a party other than the party in power at the center. From 1967 to 1987, intraparty factionalism was the impetus for invoking president's rule on seven occasions. In these cases, severe intraparty factional conflict prevented the emergence of a relatively stable ruling coalition in a state. As the national party could not bring about a compromise among the different factions in the state party, it introduced central rule until factional differences within the state party could be resolved. On the 45 other occasions, the power of the central government was invoked by the ruling national party to undermine a state government that was in the hands of an opposition party or coalition. More often than not, this intervention was successful. The national party performed much better in almost three-fourths of the state assembly elections subsequent to the period of central rule. Political intervention in state politics, therefore, was one reliable way for the national party to ensure its electoral success.

Economic Intervention

A 1988 report of the Commission on Centre-State Relations reveals that state governments feel that the national government plays too large a role in their economies, especially in the areas of industrial development and agricultural policy.[23] Karnataka, a state that was not governed by the Congress Party when the commission was making its inquiries, cited instances of industries not located in Karnataka for political reasons. The most egregious example was the relocating of the Indian Telephone Industries, a public sector factory that manufactured electronic telephone exchanges to Gonda in Uttar Pradesh. Relocation was pursued by the central government despite the fact that perhaps the best infrastructural facilities for producing the exchanges were available in Karnataka.

Not only was the location of public sector facilities influenced by political considerations but the Karnataka government also noted that private sector corporations such as Glaxos, the Tata Electric Locomotive Company, and Tractors India wanted to build plants in Karnataka but were asked by the Congress-controlled central government to locate them elsewhere. The Kerala government summed up the position of the states generally when it observed that no objective criteria had been followed in deciding where investment by the center in the public sector would occur and that locational decisions were largely made arbitrarily, that is to say, politically.

Political Considerations and Central Allocations to the States

The complaints by Karnataka and Kerala provide some anecdotal evidence of the national government's recourse to politics in permitting industrial investment. A more systematic political bias can be seen in the allocation of loans and food to the states by the national government during the Indira Gandhi years.

Allocation of Loans from the Center to the States
As the national party has traditionally mobilized electoral support on a state by state basis, we would expect to find a political element at work in the disbursement of resources by the center to the states.[24] Two issue areas were examined to determine whether politics figured in any measurable way in center-state economic relations, the first concerning loans granted and the second concerning the allocation of food by the center to the states.

The administration of loans is important, for states rely on the central government's apportionment of the nation's financial resources. Most of the allocation of funds to states is determined the Finance Commission, but the center can disburse loans to the states outside the parameters set by the commission. Thus, the center has some discretion in dispensing loans to the states. This dispensation of loans by the center might be expected to vary from one year to the next based, in part, on electoral considerations.[25] The center cannot alter the assignment of loans on a completely random basis and has to take into account loans given to a state during the previous year. Consequently, it is crucial to focus on changes in the loans allocated to a state from one year to the next. In modeling this relationship, therefore, the dependent variable measures second-order differences, that is, the change between the difference in loans granted to a state say between 1970 and 1969 and the difference in loans granted to the same state between 1969 and 1968. We would also expect, in an entirely apolitical world, that the central disbursement of loans would cover any shortfalls in the economic performance of a state. If a state faces an economic downturn, the center would provide it with additional resources to make up for the poor performance of the state's economy. The measure used for assessing the economic performance of a state was change in the per capita income of the state. The expectation was that loans received by a state would be negatively associated with movements in per capita income. If the per capita income of a state went up, that would signal better economic performance in that state; the state would then need less financial assistance from the center, and the loans allocated to it would be lower in that year. The opposite would be true if per capita income declined. The amount of loans disbursed is also constrained by the resource position of the center. The center can distribute more loans to the states when its own revenues have increased. Most students of center-state financial relations in India have noted an increased role of the center in financial matters. Thus, the final control introduced in the model was a time trend to account for the increasingly larger role the center might play in dispensing loans to the states.

The political variable was a dummy variable constructed by determining the political situation of the central party in a state. Three criteria were used to determine the values of this variable: first, whether a state faced either a national or state election; second, whether the state and national governments were controlled by the same party prior to the election; and, third, whether there was serious intraparty factional conflict. The central party could be expected to provide extra support to states in which an intraparty factional fight had just been resolved so that the new chief minister could put together a more stable coalition (app. C lists the years in which it is hypothesized that political considerations might have influenced changes in loans granted by the center to the 15 states analyzed). The final model estimated was:

$$L_t = \beta_0 + \beta_1 I_t + \beta_2 R_t + \beta_3 T + \beta_4 P + e$$

where

L_t is the second-order difference in loans disbursed to a state;
I_t is the change in the income of a state;
R_t is the change in the revenue position of the center;
T is the time trend; and
P is the political situation in a state in the year under consideration.

Since the allocation of loans from the center to an individual state is not independent of the loans allocated to other states and since the process was noticed to be time dependent, a GLS-ARMA AR(1) estimation with cross-sectional dummies was used to estimate the impact of political considerations on resource disbursement.[26] Table 14 reports the results. As expected, changes in revenue accruing to the center had a positive and significant influence on loan allocations to the states. Changes in the economic situation of a state also had the expected effect, with the center disbursing more resources to a state whose economy showed a downturn. While the sign is correct, the coefficient is not significant. The same is true for the coefficient on the time trend variable—it, too, has the expected sign—but it is not significant. The coefficient for the political variable was positive and significant, suggesting that the central government used political considerations to disburse resources to the states.

Disbursement of Food by the Center

The assignment of loans to states is one way that a ruling party at the center can help its state unit build and/or maintain a winning coalition. For a ruling party to be successful in elections, it is also important that inflation-

TABLE 14.   Loan Disbursement by the Center to the States, 1967–84 (GLS-ARMA specification with state dummies)

Variable	Coefficient	Standard Error	t-ratio
Constant	−1,146.45**	624.78	−1.83
R_t	0.01*	0.05	2.16
I_t	−2.99	2.57	−1.16
T	125.53	74.72	1.67
P	1,081.80*	531.07	2.03
Andra Pradesh	−119.08*	1,011.02	−0.11
Assam	296.06	654.61	0.45
Bihar	353.16	1,450.86	0.24
Haryana	−65.40	870.99	−0.07
Karnataka	756.82	943.35	0.80
Madhya Pradesh	264.25	718.94	0.36
Maharashtra	2,968.43*	1,087.23	2.73
Orissa	−418.16	936.93	−0.44
Punjab	2,522.01	1,536.85	1.64
Rajasthan	142.67	1,041.70	0.13
Tamil Nadu	342.11	1,049.67	0.32
Uttar Pradesh	2,155.49	2,488.85	0.86
West Bengal	1,368.90	1,339.12	1.02
Gujarat	762.63	1,051.36	0.072

Source: Reserve Bank of India, Bulletin various issues
*Significant to 0.05   **Significant to 0.1
$R^2 = 0.14$
$N = 270$
Rho = −0.108

ary tendencies, especially food prices, be kept in check. In addition, it is important that food be readily available. The central government can influence the availability of food, insofar as it plays a large role in the procurement and distribution of food.[27]

In 1977, for example, just before the elections—when Congress controlled most state governments—the central party asked states to increase the sale of rations by 50 percent, to sell wheat and milo to certain areas without ration cards, and to draw additional grains from the Food Corporation of India. The national government also lowered the price of wheat and milo (*Hindustan Times,* 1 January 1977). There have also been cases in which the state administration did not oblige the national government and allow more food into a state. In 1980, the Delhi administration, under the control of the Bharatiya Janata Party, did not use the extra sugar allocated to it by the central government despite a sugar shortage in Delhi just before the 1980 parliamentary elections (*Hindustan Times,* 29 November 1979). The rationale behind the party's decision was to let the voters vent their anger on the then ruling national party—a splinter group of the Janata Party—to which the BJP was opposed.

To assess whether the central disbursement of food to the states was based on political considerations, as in the case of loans, the dependent variable in the model measured the second-order difference in the amount of food distributed by the center to a state in a given year. Focus on the change in the amount of food allocated to a state is important. We expect that the center cannot alter the assignment of food completely at random and has to take into account the food distributed to a state in the previous year. Modifications in the parceling of food from the central pool to a given state could also be affected by variations in the amount of food produced in a state. And the ability of the central government to provide food to states facing shortages could be affected by the total quantity of food procured by the center. Larger procurements by the center are more likely when more food is produced; consequently, there will be less need for the center to allocate food to the states when that is the case. In other words, greater production of food enables more disbursement but simultaneously suggests greater production, which alleviates the demand for food support. The political variable for the distribution of food is a dummy variable that takes the same values as those used for discerning political patterns in the assignment of loans by the center to the states.

There is some prima facie evidence that the central government's political considerations did influence changes in the amount of food allocated to the states. Central disbursements to states increased, relative to the previous years, by almost 75,000 tons in years in which the center had a political interest in the states. In other years, central assignments, from the previous years, decreased on average by about 26,000 tons.[28] To make sure that this increase was not influenced by nonpolitical factors, however, the final model estimated was:

$$F_t = \beta_0 + \beta_1 PS_t + \beta_2 PC_t + \beta_3 P + e$$

where

F_t is the second-order difference in the food allocated to a state by the center;
PS_t is the change in the amount of food produced in a state;
PC_t is the change in the amount of food procured by the center; and
P is the political situation in a state during the year under consideration.

The results, reported in table 15, support the hypothesis that political factors have a positive and significant influence on the distribution of food by the center. The coefficient on the changes in the amount of food procured by the center also has the expected sign. Moreover, the significant coefficient suggests that the center's procurement of food does in fact influence the distribution of food to the states.

This analysis of the disbursements of loans and food by the center provides evidence for the proposition that electoral considerations led the party governing at the center to direct economic resources to its supporters, the state parties. In addition, the national party also tried to influence economic conditions at election time in the period after 1967, when it became clear to the party's leaders that economic conditions could affect election outcomes. In particular, the Congress earmarked subsidy allocations along electoral cycles in the belief that economic conditions influence election outcomes and voter attitudes. This move was buttressed by the fact that Congress also began to face challenges to its electoral dominance at the national level at that time.

The Bifurcated Party System
It could be argued that, since the success of the national party depended on its state units, the national party need not influence perceptions of its performance in the electorate.

Since 1971, when national elections were delinked from state elections for the first time, national elections have followed a cycle independent of state elections. Whereas elections to the national Parliament took place in 1971, most state assembly elections were held in 1972. This institutional change, the separation of state and national elections, led to a bifurcation of the party system in 1971 (Rudolph and Rudolph 1987). Now that national elections were held separately from state elections, the national party had to mobilize support somewhat independently of the state parties. In 1977, for instance, the national party for the first time decided to play a direct role in the elections in each constituency instead of leaving the campaigning to its candidate (*Times of India,* 8 February 1977). Data drawn from a 1989 postelection survey provide further evidence for the separation of the national and state Congresses. In 1989, 86 percent of those who voted for the Congress Party in the national elections said that they also voted for Congress in the state elections. On the other hand, only

TABLE 15.   Food Disbursement by the Center to the States, 1967–84 (GLS-ARMA specification with state dummies)

Variable	Coefficient	Standard Error	t-Ratio
Constant	7.53	48.57	0.15
PS_t	0.04*	0.01	4.00
PC_t	−0.01	0.00	−0.97
P	70.58*	29.47	2.39
Andhra Pradesh	26.72	64.21	0.41
Assam	−9.30	54.16	−0.17
Bihar	−56.24	124.14	−0.45
Gujarat	−58.63	70.69	−0.82
Karnataka	−22.68	59.07	−0.38
Madhya Pradesh	−44.71	71.84	−0.62
Maharashtra	−96.15	116.07	−0.82
Orissa	−17.56	57.94	−0.30
Rajasthan	−57.61	64.78	−0.88
Tamil Nadu	11.53	70.20	0.16
Uttar Pradesh	−74.15	103.66	−0.71
West Bengal	−6.25	107.73	−0.05

Source: Bulletin on Food Statistics various issues
*Significant to 0.05   **Significant to 0.1
$R^2 = 0.13$
$N = 234$
Rho = 0.083

56 percent of those said that they voted for the Congress in the state elections also voted for the Congress in the national elections. A likely explanation for this phenomenon is that the Congress's coalition for state and national elections is not the same. Hence, it would be equally important for the national Congress also to ensure favorable perceptions of its performance along national election cycles.[29]

This separation of national and state elections had an unintended consequence. As most the political opposition to the Congress came from parties rooted in the states, the separation of national and state elections made it easier for other parties to form coalitions to oppose the Congress. With the delinking, it was easier for the other state parties to form a national coalition without necessarily impairing their social bases within their states. Under the Janata coalition in 1977, for instance, it was far easier to nominate candidates for the national elections. Parties were more willing to compromise and form preelectoral coalitions for the national elections. State assembly elections were held shortly after the victory of the Janata Party. Whatever cooperation among the various constituents of that party that had marked the selection of candidates for the Lok Sabha broke down when it came time to select candidates for the state assembly elections. Maintaining the coalition became much harder. The experience of the Janata Party suggests that, at the state level, political parties were less willing to compromise and form preelectoral coalitions with their national partners. Quite simply, since the fundamental interests of these parties were not compromised at the state level, these parties could enter into pre- or postelectoral coalitions with other parties for national elections.

Not surprisingly, beginning with the 1971 election, in which the Congress was returned to power, political parties have essentially alternated in winning elections to the Lok Sabha. In 1977, the Janata Party was elected, while 1980 saw a return to power by the Congress. In 1984, the Congress won on a sympathy vote following the assassination of Indira Gandhi, only to be turned out of office five years later, again by a coalition of state-based parties. In 1989, the Janata Dal, a party based in North India (Bihar, Haryana, and Uttar Pradesh) was supported by the CPI(M) from West Bengal; the BJP, which was then strongest in Madhya Pradesh and Rajasthan; and the Telugu Desam and DMK, which are strong regional parties from Andhra Pradesh and Tamil Nadu, respectively. These parties formed a coalition government at the center. In 1991, Congress retook control of the national government, but after the next round of elections in 1996 a coalition of small parties, the United Front, came to power. In 1998 it was the turn of a BJP-led coalition of regional parties to govern from Delhi.

National governments, therefore, from 1967 onward allocated subsidies along electoral cycles to ensure favorable perceptions of their performance among the electorate. Allocations of subsidies by the central government increased dramatically in the period after 1967. Until then, the average change in subsidies from one year to the next, in real terms, was Rs 130 million. From 1967 through 1985, however, the average increase in subsidy allocations has been over Rs 850 million. This jump in the level of subsidies disbursed by the central government was most noticeable in election years, when subsidy allocations increased by an average of Rs 1,070 million.

Electoral Cycles and Subsidy Allocations

The national party could be expected to seek to ensure positive perceptions of its performance among the electorate for two reasons. As noted earlier, the national party operated somewhat independently of its state units after 1967. In addition, holding national elections separately from state elections made the national party a central focus of these elections. To this end, the party would attempt to keep inflation low, and, since most Indians spend much of their income on food, food prices were also kept low. Since most food distributed by the government is sold through fair price shops, keeping a plentiful supply of food grains in those stores helps ensure positive perceptions of the party in power. For instance, just before the 1977 elections the central government decided to provide its employees with interest-free loans to buy food and urged state governments to do the same (*Hindustan Times,* 1 January 1977). Just a couple of weeks before the election the government also decided to sell eggs, onions, and potatoes at ration shops to ensure that these items were available to the consumer (*Hindustan Times,* 3 March 1977). Food prices could be kept in check through higher food subsidies. Consequently, we might expect that subsidies allocated by the government would increase in times of electoral competition. Electoral cycles will have an independent and positive impact on the extent of subsidies provided by the government.[30]

To determine whether the subsidy provided by the central government was influenced by political considerations, a time series model was estimated. The political variable used in the model was the number of elections held in a year. Since the allocation of food to the states by the central government was assumed to be influenced by political considerations, and since food subsidies constitute a large proportion of government subsidies, the political variable incorporated both national and state elections. If there were only national elections in a year, it was assumed that the electoral pressures on the center were equivalent to those when elections were held in all states simultaneously, and the political variable was accorded a value of 16 (the number of states plus one under consideration). If state and national elections were held together, there was no need to give the state elections a separate value. For the year 1957, for example, the value of the political variable was 16. Only one state election was held in 1961, so that year took a value of 1.

$$S_t = \beta_0 + \beta_1 T + \beta_2 EP + e$$

where

S_t is the change in subsidies provided by the center;
T is the time trend; and
EP is the number of elections during the year in question.

As table 16 indicates, increases in government subsidies were affected by election cycles but only from 1967 onward; from 1952 to 1967, by contrast, subsidy disbursements were not influenced by electoral considerations. The significance and positive sign of the other independent variable, a time trend, suggests that increases in subsidy allocations may indeed be due to other political factors. These factors could include the role of state

TABLE 16.   Electoral Cycles and Subsidy Allocations by the Center, 1952–85[a]

Years	Constant	Time-Trend (T)	Politics (EP)	R^2
1952–66	−10.45	0.78*	1.84	0.06
	(−0.30)	(−0.25)	(−0.87)	
1967–85	−175.9	8.26*	6.17	0.36
		(−2.34)	(−2.14)	

Source: Economic data were collected from the *Economic and Functional Classification of the Budget* various issues

Note: Figures in parentheses are *t*-ratios

[a]Regression estimates include a time trend and electoral cycles; estimates at 1970–71 prices.

*Significant at 0.01

actors and dominant classes in appropriating larger amounts of state subsidies for themselves (Bardhan 1984). The results clearly suggest that the role of electoral politics cannot be overlooked insofar as electoral pressures have an impact on subsidy allocation independent of the other variables.

The evidence provided in this section suggests that the ruling party in India during the Indira Gandhi period directed the allocation of subsidies along electoral cycles. Increased allocation of subsidies because of electoral pressures, the granting of loans to the states, and the disbursement of food based in part on political considerations support the claim that electoral politics plays an important role in the central government's relationship with the states. One way to ensure electoral success has been to increase central intervention in the states, which Indira Gandhi practiced almost to perfection. State chief ministers, on the other hand, facing electoral competition within their states, need to maintain a coalition of multiple factions. In most states, the response of the chief ministers has been to expand the number of offices that could be held by the state legislators and, following the lead of the central government, to increase the role of the state government within the state to ensure continued support for the governing party.

Chapter 5

Building Coalitions in the Indian States

The Congress Party, even after 1967, remained a party that mobilized support on a state by state basis and one whose social basis was state specific. Within the states, however, the Congress faced increased electoral competition. Most of this competition came from state-specific parties. The increased competition was not due to the entry of new groups into the electoral arena but was a result of voters shifting support between political parties. After providing evidence for the increased competitive nature of electoral politics in the states, this chapter will, using aggregate and survey data, demonstrate that the emergence of opposition to the Congress after 1967 was not attributable to the entry of new groups but instead to the exit of elements of its coalition. These changes were caused by a drop in the partisan commitment of voters. The lower levels of allegiance to political parties and the decline in votes received by Congress was aided by the emergence of a generation in politics whose members had not been socialized during the independence movement. Therefore, the Congress Party's reputation as the party that had brought about independence did not resonate as much with this segment of the electorate as it had with previous generations. The factionalism that characterized the Congress, the various splits within the party, and the fact that the party did not attempt to rebuild whatever organization it once had, further loosened the ties of voters to parties.

Since 1967, political parties keen on retaining electoral majorities have relied on an expansion of the state to hold together the various factions present within each party. A group or faction would support a party only as long as access to the state was possible. One way of signaling this access was through the allocation of state offices. The second section of this chapter, then, provides evidence that in the era of electoral competition in the states larger cabinet sizes and cabinet instability have become endemic features of state politics.

Despite the many changes in the political landscape, the Congress Party managed to retain a measure of electoral success until the 1989 election, after which its decline was clear. The last section of the chapter discusses the reasons for the party's electoral debacle in 1989, focusing on the role of Rajiv Gandhi. It concludes with the observation that since 1989 the decline of the Congress has been most noticeable in the northern Indian states of Bihar and Uttar Pradesh.

Electoral Competition after 1967

The competitive situation, as far as the Congress Party is concerned, has not improved since the 1967 elections. The party has not done as well in terms of either the party's vote share or the number of seats it has held in state assemblies. The party's average vote share in state elections has declined slightly, from 42 percent in the elections between 1957 and 1967, to 36 percent in the elections between 1967 and 1985, and 31 percent thereafter.[1] At the same time as the opposition parties were doing better, the Congress's vote share was fluctuating, reflecting more fluid electoral support for the party and making for greater uncertainty as far its electoral fortunes were concerned. Through 1967, the Congress's vote share varied by roughly 6 percent around the mean. Over the succeeding 18 years, the variance of the Congress vote more than doubled—to approximately 13 percent in the national and state elections between 1967 and 1985. The variance has since dropped to 8 percent.[2]

Furthermore, the Congress Party did not have the same kind of success in state elections after 1967 as it did during the period of one-party dominance. The average number of seats Congress held in state assemblies fell to 68 after 1985, having already slipped from an average of 119 in the elections before 1967 to 106 in the elections between 1967 and 1985. During the earlier period, the party controlled almost all of the state governments most of the time. The major exceptions were Kerala, where the party lost elections to the Communists, and Orissa and Andhra Pradesh, where the party had to deal with strong opposition. Since 1967, the party has lost control over every state at least once. Indeed, during the period 1967 through 1985 the party lost control of over half of the governments it could have formed in the states. A total of 78 elections were held in the 15 states under consideration: non-Congress parties formed the government 42 times, leaving the Congress in control of only 36 of the possible 78 governments. Between 1985 and 1996, 34 elections were held in these states and the Congress managed to win a majority in only nine of them. At the same time as it faced competition in the states, Congress faced successful challenges to its electoral dominance at the national level in 1977, 1989, 1996, and in 1998, when it lost to the Janata Party, a Janata Dal-led coalition, and came in second to the BJP in terms of seats in the Lok Sabha, respectively.

What explains Congress's decline in the 1967 elections and thereafter? The argument developed so far has suggested that the party's electoral fortunes were linked to its maintaining coalitions comprised of different interests. As a consequence, the party had an image as a catchall party that did not represent sectional interests but rather stood for all Indians. In a situation in which only one party could win an election, as was the case with the Congress until 1967, exit was not a real option for disaffected groups. With the emergence of a viable opposition that could best the Congress in an election, however, the threats of exit have become real. A party can be forced to toe a line closer to the needs of the coalition it represents. Social groups have, in turn, become more aware of the utility of electoral strength as a political resource. A group's combined vote can go a long way in satisfying its interests. Take, for instance, the farmers' movement in western India. This group held talks with various political parties to draw appropriate policy concessions before announcing which political party it would support. Similarly, the farmer's group in Uttar Pradesh, supported Congress, Janata Dal, and the BJP in different elections (*Amar Ujaala,* 3 November 1993).[3]

This argument, which links electoral outcomes to exit, is different from observations of Indian politics that argue that opposition to the Congress since the mid-1960s emerged because of the entry of hitherto unmobilized groups into the political arena (Brass 1990).[4] In this line of reasoning, the emergence as political actors of groups that had not previously participated in the political process, such as the backward castes, explains the growing opposition to Congress after 1967. This argument, if correct, questions whether Congress's electoral failures can be better explained by the politics of exit. The debate about whether it was the entry of new groups or the exit of its supporters that affected Congress's electoral fortunes is important, as the nature of party competition could potentially influence whether the catchall party system will be replaced by a cleavage-based party system, the extent of the Congress's electoral decline, and even the electoral success of the BJP.

The Mobilization of New Groups or the Politics of Exit?

The 1967 elections saw the highest turnout for a national election since independence.[5] An examination of voter turnout in both national elections since then suggests that turnout in national elections since 1967 has increased in only two states, Bihar and Orissa. In Punjab, Rajasthan, and Tamil Nadu, turnout never attained the level of 1967. In Uttar Pradesh it increased by 2 percent over the 1967 level but only for the 1977 national election.

As opposition success in the 1967 national election was a result of exit from the Congress, it is safe to say that any change in the electoral balance between the opposition and the Congress Party after 1967 cannot be attributed to the entry of hitherto unmobilized groups into either the Congress or the opposition. The data suggest that the fluctuation in the Congress's vote (or the vote for any other party for that matter) is the return to the party of those who abandoned it at other times. There have been no large increases in the Indian electorate for much of the period under discussion.[6] In other words, the party system is extremely fluid, with groups not necessarily supporting the same parties continuously.

For state elections, however, the picture is different. Turnout in many states has gone up since the 1967 elections. It could be asserted that since the Congress Party's success in the national elections is dependent upon its state units, and since turnout has increased in the states, the argument attributing the Congress's electoral decline to the entry of new voters cannot be ruled out. An investigation of the relationship between the votes mobilized by Congress and its competitors, however, yields results that support the exit thesis. Since 1967, the votes mobilized by other parties have been acquired at the expense of the Congress. Tables 17 and 18 report on the relationship between the vote mobilized by the Congress and its competitor parties in national and state elections.[7]

Let us examine the national elections first. Following the approach that has been adopted before, the elections were divided into three groups: those held through 1967, those held between 1971 and 1984, and those of 1989 and 1991. The positive coefficient for the vote mobilized by the Congress until 1967 suggests that during this period Congress and the other parties were bringing new voters into the electoral process. That is, the mobilization efforts of the Congress did not hamper the efforts of other parties to mobilize voters. From 1971 onward, however, the relationship between the mobilization efforts of the Congress and other parties changed. The negative coefficient suggests that as the opposition mobilized more support it was acquired at the expense of the Congress and vice versa. In other words, in national elections after 1971 new voters were not brought into the electorate but voters were switching allegiances between the Congress and other parties. The trend began to change in 1989. The lower coefficient (compared to the period between 1971 and 1984) and the smaller coefficient of determination (R^2) imply that the inverse relationship between the mobilization efforts of the Congress and those of the other parties is still significant but not as powerful as before.

A similar result obtains for state elections. Table 18 reports the relationship between mobilization by the Congress and its competitors in state elections held between 1962 and 1967, state elections from 1967 to 1989, and those held thereafter. For the first and third periods—that is, prior to 1968 and after 1988—the mobilization efforts of the Congress and the other parties are not statistically related. For the period between 1967 and 1989, there is a clear and negative relationship between mobilization by other parties and by the Congress: the votes mobilized by other parties go up as the Congress captures a smaller vote share. These results provide further evidence that electoral competition during this period was characterized by the politics of exit and not the entry of hitherto unmobilized groups.

TABLE 17. Opposition Party Mobilization in National Elections, 1957–91 (OLS estimates)

	1957–67	1971–84	1989–91
Mobilization by Congress	0.105*	–0.685*	–0.335*
Constant	45.84*	22.56*	40.38*
R^2	0.006	0.31	0.099
F	7.503	909.86	108.0
N	1152	1988	992

Source: Singh and Bose 1985, 1994
*Significant at 0.01

TABLE 18. Opposition Party Mobilization in State Elections, 1957–91 (OLS estimates)

	1957–67	1971–84	1989–91
Mobilization by Congress	0.133	–0.769*	0.174
Constant	24.36	49.470	33.930
R^2	0.007	0.249	0.019
F	0.17	18.65*	0.436
N	25	57	23

Source: Butler, Roy, and Lahiri 1996
*Significant at 0.01

A State by State Look at the Politics of Exit

Further evidence for the dominance of exit in state elections comes from observing shifts in voting patterns among the states. Since exit is a major reason for the Congress's electoral successes and failures, we can expect that its vote share would fluctuate from one election to another. For exit to be the dominant variable in explaining a political party's electoral successes and failures, a party's electoral successes and/or failures in the states should be influenced by the changing nature of group support.

Consider the case of Andhra Pradesh. The Congress was ousted from power by a regional party, the Telugu Desam. The rise of this a regional party in Andhra was ostensibly due to members of the *kamma* caste reaffirming their rivalry with the *reddis,* who controlled the Congress. The *kammas* had supported Congress until the 1983 election. In this election, compared to the 1978 election, which Congress won, the vote mobilized by the party dropped by close to 6 percent. Prior to 1983, the vote mobilized by Congress in state elections in Andhra Pradesh had varied between 29 and 32 percent. In 1983 it dropped to 23 percent, suggesting that some part of the party's coalition had defected. During the early 1980s, the Telugu Desam, was supported by, in addition to the *kammas,* another caste—the *kapus.* In 1989, however, the *kapus,* dissatisfied with the Telugu Desam government, shifted their backing to the Congress, which managed to mobilize a third of the electorate in the state elections.

In Assam, the Congress lost the state elections for the first time in 1978. The vote mobilized by the Congress dropped from 33 percent in 1972 to 6 percent in 1978; mobilization rebounded in 1983, when Congress won the elections. Bihar, meanwhile, has a matrix of caste relations that are, as far as their range and intensity are concerned, specific to that state. To begin with, there are conflicts among the upper castes and between the upper and the backward castes. Scheduled castes are at loggerheads with both groups. The tribal belt in the Jharkand region of Bihar has its own subregional party (the Jharkand Mukti Morcha [JMM]). Bihar politics has been marked by shifting coalitions, which are reflected in the aggregate election data. The Congress did poorly in the 1967 elections, when the share of voters it managed to bring to the polls dropped by about 2 percent from 1962 levels. The party's loss in the state elections of 1977 was accompanied by an even smaller proportion of the electorate turning out for the Congress (12 percent). In 1980, the Congress came back to power in Bihar, bringing in an additional 8 percent of the electorate. By 1990, however,

Congress's decline in the state was apparent: it managed to mobilize only 10 percent of the electorate for the 1990 assembly elections. The Congress suffered its first electoral loss in Gujarat in 1975. In that election, the vote mobilized by the party, which had been consistently about 29 percent in previous elections, dropped to less than 25 percent.

Support for the Congress in Haryana politics has been subject to unpredictable fluctuations, which can be accounted for by changes in the support it receives from particular sections of the electorate (Ranbir Singh 1990). Changes in the vote mobilized by the Congress support this observation. In 1972, the Congress won the state elections, mobilizing 8 percent more voters than it had in 1968. The party's failure in 1977 can be attributed to its inability to hold onto its coalition—especially as the proportion of voters supporting it dropped from 33 percent in 1972 to 11 percent in 1977. When the party won again in 1982, its success can be ascribed to the additional 15 percent of the electorate that came out in its favor. In 1987, the Lok Dal came back to power in Haryana largely because of the inability of Congress to hold onto 6 percent of the electorate that had supported it in the previous elections.

In Karnataka, too, the Congress's loss of control over the state assembly in 1983 was accompanied by a 5 percent drop in the vote mobilized by the party. Similar patterns are observed with regard to the Congress's electoral defeats in Madhya Pradesh, Orissa, Rajasthan, and West Bengal in 1977. Congress's successes in Madhya Pradesh in 1972 and 1980, in Orissa in 1974 and 1980, in Rajasthan in 1972 and 1980, and in West Bengal in 1972 could be attributed to the Congress being able to mobilize a larger share of the electorate than it managed to do in the preceding election.

A similar pattern is evident in Maharashtra. The Marathas, the dominant group in the Maharashtra Congress, exited the party in 1978 as a consequence of Indira Gandhi's efforts, through S. B. Chavan, chief minister of the state, to break the Marathas' monopoly. In 1978, not surprisingly, the vote mobilized by Congress dropped to 12 percent, compared to 34 percent in 1972. Once the Congress lost the state elections in 1978, Indira Gandhi, on her return to power in 1980, gave up the attempt to break the Maratha lobby's monopoly. The Marathas return to the Congress was reflected in a doubling of the electorate who turned out in support of the Congress in 1980. In Uttar Pradesh, too, as the scheduled castes and Muslims defected from the Congress in 1977 to the Congress for Democracy, the vote mobilized by the Congress Party dropped by 4 percent. In the 1980 elections, these groups returned to the fold of the Congress, and the party managed to mobilize an additional 2 percent of the electorate.

Survey data from election surveys of 1971 and 1980 provide further support for the exit model. Table 19 shows the absolute deviation of the Congress vote within state-specific social groups between the 1971 and 1980 elections, controlling for state-level results. Since Congress is a collection of state-specific parties, examining the simple difference between the vote of the groups from one election to another would hide state- and time-specific political circumstances. Table 19 was constructed by computing the absolute deviation between the deviation of the groups from the state mean. Take, for instance, Andhra Pradesh. The upper castes were more supportive of the Congress in the 1971 election, voting 6 percent over the state mean for the Congress. In 1980, they were far less supportive of the party, voting 23 percent below the state mean. That gives us an absolute deviation of 29 percent. In this case, the simple mean difference, without controlling for state and time effect, would have been only 11 percent. While here the difference is exaggerated, in many other cases the absolute deviation suppresses the mean difference. Thus, while the numbers do not have an immediate intuitive meaning, they are substantively more accurate.

Each state provides differential support for the Congress. So, in the election of 1971 in Andhra Pradesh, when the upper castes were more likely than other groups to support the Congress, we could say that the party's success was based more on the upper castes in Andhra. On the other hand, if in the 1980 election the upper castes were voting below the state mean for the Congress, we can assume that the upper castes were not the foundation of the party's coalition in that election. Table 19, using this algorithm, reveals that group support for the Congress varies across time within states. For instance, while the upper caste vote in 1980 swung by 29 points in Andhra Pradesh, it moved by only two percentage points in Uttar Pradesh. In sum, the upper castes formed the basis of Congress support in 1971 and moved away from Congress in 1980 in Andhra Pradesh. The Congress, it can thus be said, based its electoral success in 1980 on a coalition in which the upper castes did not play a major role. In Uttar Pradesh, however, upper castes have consistently been an essential element of the Congress's coalition. At the same time, for the lower castes the swing was the largest in West Bengal, while it was modest in Andhra Pradesh, Karnataka, and Uttar Pradesh. Examining the data by state we find that the pattern of group exit varied. In Andhra, it was the upper castes and the harijans who switched their votes for the Congress Party most often, while in Maharashtra it was the middle castes and the scheduled tribes. In Uttar Pradesh, it was the merchant and upwardly mobile castes who were most likely to exit the Congress.

Executive Office and Political Parties

Exit has been responsible for the Congress's electoral failures and successes in state elections. The reasons for exit lay in whether or not the interests of a group were accommodated by the ruling party. More often than not, the interests of a social group revolved around the benefits that accrued from its control over executive office. For instance, the emergence of backward castes as a political force in Bihar and Uttar Pradesh was accompanied by a greater number of their ranks receiving state government cabinet positions (Frankel 1989b; Hasan 1989a). As group politics has become more prevalent during the post-1967 era, there has been a sharp increase in the number of executive offices held by legislators. As the allocation of executive office has become the locus of coalition building, those groups or factions that could not attain office became dissenters, initially within the party and ultimately outside it. To keep dissenters in check, with the increased emphasis on executive office, we would expect greater instability in state cabinets.

TABLE 19.   Change in Group Support for Congress between 1971 and 1980 (absolute differences in percentage of caste vote for congress)

State	High	Upper	Merchant	Middle	Lower	Harijan	Scheduled Tribe
Andhra Pradesh		29		6	6	22	
Bihar	19				16	12	
Gujarat					10		
Karnataka		4		3	6		
Madhya Pradesh	22		21		9	11	29
Maharashtra				37			32
Orissa				18			
Rajasthan							30
Uttar Pradesh	2		20		7	7	
West Bengal	12				25	8	33

Note: See text for details on the algorithm used to calculate table entries. Data are drawn from the 1971 and 1980 election surveys.

Cabinet Size

Cabinet size, in the period following 1967, increased. Other executive offices, such as the chairmanship of public undertakings and membership in land tribunals, were also extended to legislators. The implicit idea behind this expansion of executive offices was to minimize dissent by incorporating as many groups as possible. For instance, when V. D. Patil became the chief minister of Maharashtra, all but three districts were represented in his cabinet, resulting in the largest cabinet in Maharashtra's history. In Punjab, 41 of the 87 Congress legislators occupied some ministerial position in January 1996. A senior minister, Kewal Kishan, commenting on the size of the body, reportedly said that the expansion was due to electoral concerns: "we have to fight the Lok Sabha polls. There was a need to empower these [legislators] to canvas for the party" (*Hindustan Times,* 8 January 1996). The most egregious example comes from Uttar Pradesh. In 1997, to maintain a minority government, the BJP chief minister, Kalyan Singh, offered cabinet positions to Congress and BSP defectors who supported the BJP. The resulting cabinet had 92 members.

Since 1967, cabinet size has increased in all states.[8] We find that the largest cabinets in from 1967 to 1994 averaged over 20 more members than the largest cabinets in the period up to 1967 (table 20). Cabinets, then, have increased in size in all states, even disproportionately, with regard to increases in the size of the state assemblies.

Filling cabinets, however, is not the only way to dole out executive positions in an effort to keep factions together. Making other executive appointments, such as the chairmanship of state-level public sector undertakings, provides a way of placating those who were not given cabinet positions. The increase in the number of public sector undertakings during the period from 1970 onward is indicative of this phenomenon. Before 1970, there were only 200 state-level public sector undertakings (SLPEs). During the 1970s, 300 new units were added, and in the period from 1980 to 1987 another 350 were added. In most of these undertakings, positions on the board of directors and the chairmanship are politically determined. Other executive positions can be awarded to loyal party supporters, and even to potential foes in the party, such as control over district cooperative banks. Maharashtra provides the best example of cooperatives serving as the foci for local party activity, especially the sugar cooperatives and district banks. In Karnataka, with similar effect, members of the legislative assembly are appointed as members of the land tribunals, which gives them control over such vital issues as land redistribution.

A pair of analyses of the caste composition of the Bihar and Uttar Pradesh cabinets since independence conducted by Frankel (1989b) and Hasan (1989b) suggest that the increases in cabinet size are attempts to incorporate all castes in order to minimize dissent. Even though castes other than the traditionally dominant ones are being incorporated into the state cabinets, their inclusion has not been at the expense of the existing groups, which still have a similar number of seats. In Uttar Pradesh, for example, the number of backward caste ministers did increase between 1974 and 1985, but so did the number of forward caste cabinet members (Hasan 1989a, 198).

Cabinet Instability

The increased use of state government offices to build coalitions had another immediate consequence: the use of executive positions to cement coalitions led not only to larger cabinet sizes but also to higher degrees of cabinet instability. Cabinets were now the focus of factional conflict; those who were not incorporated within the power structure in a state were also

TABLE 20. Cabinet Sizes, 1957–94

	Pre–1967		Post–1967	
State	Cabinet	Legislature	Cabinet	Legislature
Andhra Pradesh	16	300	61	294
Assam	16	108	38	126
Bihar	22	318	70	324
Gujarat	16	154	31	182
Haryana	—	—	33	90
Kerala	11	133	41	140
Karnataka	25	208	40	224
Madhya Pradesh	24	288	45	320
Maharashtra	31	264	42	288
Orissa	15	140	37	147
Punjab	—	—	41	117
Rajasthan	24	176	33	200
Tamil Nadu	9	206	25	234
Uttar Pradesh	33	430	49	425
West Bengal	37	252	43	294

Note: Data were collected by the author from various issues of the *Asian Recorder* from 1957 to 1994.

more likely to oppose the ruling coalition. In fact, according to Forrester, "large ministries . . . are more liable to instability than small ministries. Indeed, they are large because they are coalitions of parties or factions within one party and it is fairly clear that many ministers continue to act primarily as factional leaders" (1970, 474). In other words, increased factionalism can lead to larger and less stable cabinets. The ruling coalition can seek to resolve this conflict in one of four ways: it can add ministers to the cabinet after its initial formation; it can drop ministers who provided opposition from within the ruling coalition; it can reshuffle the cabinet, effectively demoting some and promoting others; or it can replace the chief minister (and hence the cabinet).

In the period up to 1967, 21 chief ministers resigned or saw their ministries fall, 50 ministers resigned from cabinets, 23 cabinets were reshuffled, and 101 ministers were added after the announcement of the initial cabinet. In the period of increased instability (post-1967), 195 chief ministers resigned or saw their ministries fall, there were 627 resignations by ministers from state cabinets, 135 cabinets were reshuffled, and 2,406 ministers were added after the announcement of initial cabinets.[9]

An index of cabinet instability shows a sharp increase after 1967. The index was constructed using a probability model. The notion underlying the calculation was that events that are less likely to occur should be given the most weight when computing an index. For instance, the most common form of cabinet instability was the addition of ministers, while the fall of a ministry was the least likely event to happen; thus, the latter event is more significant. This empirical observation is also substantively valid insofar as adding ministers is not a politically difficult move for a ruling coalition. Dropping ministers is more problematic, followed by reshuffles. Losing power is the least preferred outcome for a ruling coalition, and hence it is something ruling coalitions generally avoid. The probability of each event occurring was constructed by subtracting from unity the proportion that event (such as a cabinet reshuffle) occupied out of the total number of events (i.e., additions, dropping of ministers, reshuffles, and the fall of ministries). These probabilities were then used as weights for the actual number of the event.[10] The final index was a weighted sum (by the probabilities) of these events.

Average annual cabinet instability at the state level jumped from slightly under one, for the years 1957 through 1967, to just over three for the years 1967 through 1994. Figure 12 shows average cabinet instability across the states since 1967.

Fig. 12. Average cabinet instability, by year, 1967–91, across the 15 major states. (Data from *Asian Recorder*, various issues.)

The index of instability was, however, higher in some states, such as Andhra Pradesh, than in others, like West Bengal. Haryana, which came into existence in 1967, has had a high level of cabinet instability throughout this period (fig. 13). Some states have had far more unstable cabinets than others.

Why is factional accommodation more difficult in some states? The higher index of cabinet instability suggests that it was becoming increasingly more difficult for the party to form stable coalitions. As was observed earlier, in the two decades following independence factional conflict within the Congress was kept in check, so the party could form a stable coalition. After the mid-1960s, however, there has been an increase in intraparty factional conflict. One explanation for the greater intraparty factionalism is the central government's interference in state politics. Observers note that Indira Gandhi, in order to secure her own position, imposed weak chief ministers on states—with Andhra Pradesh providing the most egregious example. In a five-year period leading to the state elections in Andhra Pradesh in 1983, four Congress chief ministers were changed, with each new one appointed by Indira Gandhi. An argument that places full blame for these changes on the prime minister, however, exaggerates the control that the center can exercise over state politics. Often overlooked is the fact that most state politicians wanted central intervention in order to settle factional conflicts within in the state party.[11] Moreover, not only Indira Gandhi but also Morarji Desai and Rajiv Gandhi followed similar strategies. Thus, a personality-based argument cannot really account for increased central intervention; other reasons may be a more appropriate place to look for an explanation.

Increased cabinet instability can be attributed to two developments. First, as electoral politics became more competitive, political parties began to mobilize groups to gain support. Much of this mobilization was done around promises of access to state offices. In order to ward of this competition, the Congress—or most other parties for that matter—found it in their interests to increase cabinet sizes. Greater competition within the state assemblies also led to more cabinet instability. Consider the following interpretation. Regardless of which cabinet posts were assigned to whom, another party (or a faction with the governing party) could find some assignment of cabinet posts that would be preferable to a large enough number of members of the existing cabinet and some who are outside the current cabinet. The repetition of this process generates greater cabinet instability. Rapid changes in the cabinet in Bihar between March

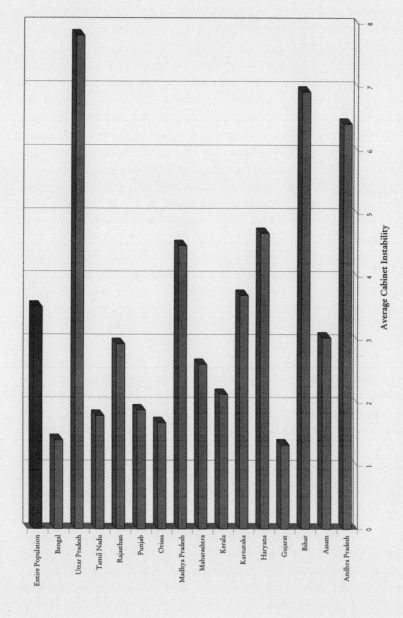

Fig. 13. Average cabinet instability in the states, 1967–91. (Data from *Asian Recorder*, various issues.)

1972 and April 1975, when a reassignment of cabinet posts led to three separate Congress Party–led cabinets headed by Kedar Pande, Abdul Gafoor, and Jaganath Misra respectively, was an instance in which various factions within the Congress Party offered more attractive reallocations of cabinet positions.

An institutional change, the absence of organizational elections to party offices at the state level spurred on factional conflict within the party. Organizational elections for positions within the state and national Congress were no longer held beginning in 1972. The unintended effect of this institutional change was that, unlike during the period of one-party dominance, when factional conflict within the party could be expressed as ministerialists versus dissidents (drawn from the organizational wing), nowadays there are a multiplicity of factions.[12] In other words, party organization provided a focus for dissidents in the period up to 1971; when there was dissension, the party usually divided into two factions. Organizational elections forced factional leaders to form coalitions so as to be able to muster the necessary majority to unseat the chief minister.

As no organizational elections are held anymore, the political environment today is much more fluid. Factional leaders who oppose a chief minister do not necessarily coalesce into a single group of dissidents. Instead, groups now retain their independence and provide conditional support only after determining which faction can muster the most support. These factions often revolve around caste, region, religion, economic pressure groups limited to a state, or some combination thereof. Hence, what was formerly the role of organizational elections has now been left to the central party—that is, to determine which challenger for the chief ministership in a state office has the requisite following among legislators.

Thus, the inadvertent impact of this institutional change was an increase in the power of factions as political actors within parties. This change in the political environment also affected the ability of state chief ministers to build cohesive factional alliances. Traditionally, they had attempted to build this coalition by dispensing executive office; those left out of positions of power gravitated to the organization and waited their turn. As the organization withered away, allocating executive position was the only avenue through which Congress politicians' interests could be accommodated. This institutional change exacerbated divisions within the party and made coalition building more difficult.

Second, cabinet instability is linked to the nature of electoral competition. Table 21 reports the results of a regression in which the dependent variable is the extent of cabinet instability in a state. The key independent variable is the kind of party competition in a state. Party competition after 1967 was coded into four categories: where the electoral competition was between two parties and was ideological (e.g., as in West Bengal), multiparty competition, competition between two centrist parties; and where one party dominated electorally. As these were dummy variables (which took on a value of 1 if the kind of competition specified existed and 0 otherwise), the existence of a dominant party was used as the control variable. Four control variables were also included in the model: per capita loans received by a state from the center (as a measure of the soft budget constraint), the per capita revenue of the state (to test whether wealthier states would have an easier time keeping a coalition together), per capita expenditures on education by a state (which reflect the social commitment of a state government) and the law and order situation in a state (the number of riots and murders per capita). The results, reported in table 21, indicate that cabinet instability is higher when there is either multiparty competition or electoral competition between two centrist parties in a state. States in which party competition is ideological do not exhibit higher cabinet instability.

TABLE 21.   Party Competition and Cabinet Instability

Variable	Coefficient	Robust Standard Error
Law and order	3.043	2.917
Per capita revenue of the state government	0.164	0.441
Per capita loans received from the center	0.046	0.624
Per capita expenditures on education	−1.446	1.936
Ideological competition	0.186	0.654
Multiparty competition	2.871*	1.507
Competition between centrist parties	2.648*	0.897
Constant	1.997	0.764

*Significant to 0.05
$N = 264$
$F = 2.42$
$R^2 = 0.06$

The 1989 Elections: Rajiv Gandhi and the Congress Party's
Electoral Losses

Rajiv Gandhi came to power in 1984 with the largest majority the Congress had ever received in any election. The party managed to garner close to 50 percent of the vote and won more than three-fourths of all seats in the Lok Sabha. In the 1989 elections, however, the Congress was not able to obtain a majority, and even though it was still the single largest party a Janata Dal–led coalition with V. P. Singh at its head came to power in New Delhi. Why is it that Congress could not retain a majority?

Over the years, power within the Congress Party had been centralized. As power was centralized, the prime minister became the manager of all intraparty conflict. Accompanying this dependence on the prime minister was, as noted earlier, greater factional conflict within the states.[13] While Indira Gandhi was fairly skilled at managing coalitions, Rajiv Gandhi found it far more difficult to manage the various state Congress parties and hold them together. There are various reasons for this. First, Rajiv Gandhi was not reared in Indian politics. Even as general secretary of the Congress (I), he associated with businessmen, intellectuals, and journalists, not with Congress Party members or the party's state chief ministers. Rajiv's lack of association with the Congress rank and file was exhibited most clearly when, upon becoming prime minister, he launched an attack on midlevel party leaders, claiming that these power brokers rode on the backs of the masses to "dispense patronage [and] . . . convert a mass movement into a feudal oligarchy. They are self-perpetuating cliques who thrive by invoking the slogans of caste and religion." (quoted in Jaisingh 1989, 127). While this criticism received much favorable press, it isolated Rajiv Gandhi from those who could mobilize support for Congress—the midlevel elites.[14] Further, Rajiv found managing intraparty conflict within Congress more difficult that Indira Gandhi had because he was not equally respected among those associated with the Congress Party; Rajiv was not the vote getter that Indira was, and, consequently, Congress activists in the states were more independent of him.

The Role of Leadership in Indian Electoral Politics

Much commentary on the Congress Party's dominance since 1967 by pundits and professors alike has focused upon phenomena such as the "Indira wave," the "anti-Indira wave," and the "Indira factor" in accounting for the success or defeat, as in 1977, of the Congress Party. Commentators have argued that personality dominates electoral politics in India and that the electoral success of the party was built around the charismatic appeal associated with the Nehru family.[15] In each of the national election surveys since 1961, except for 1967, respondents were asked questions to appraise the performance of public figures. There has indeed been a "progressive increase in the proclivity of voters who register a favorable evaluation of the preeminent leaders, Nehru and Indira Gandhi, and vote for the Congress in national elections" (Chhibber and Sisson 1990). Leadership is a key variable in explaining the vote for the Congress Party in all areas of India, in the cities and in the villages, and across all social groups, whether of high or low status (ibid.).[16]

Leadership has an impact on the vote even when controlling for a number of other variables that influence support for the Congress. An analysis of the postelection survey of the 1971 elections supports this hypothesis. To ensure comparability with data from the 1989 election study, respondents who lived in the six states that formed the basis of the 1989 study—Andhra Pradesh, Bihar, Madhya Pradesh, Maharashtra, Uttar Pradesh, and West Bengal—were selected from the 1971 study for the analysis. The dependent variable was whether a respondent voted for the Congress or some other party. A number of dummy variables (which take the values 0 and 1, 0 if absent and 1 if present) were introduced as controls. Since the Congress is a collection of state-based parties, and the performance of the party varies across states, the various states were introduced as dummies. Additionally, the caste of a respondent, either forward or scheduled caste, the class of a respondent (i.e., economic status, a combination of respondent education and income) were included since Indira Gandhi's electoral success has been attributed to the mobilization of the poor through the electoral slogan of "Garibi Hatao" (remove poverty). Two other controls were added: perceptions of the Congress's performance (on the assumption that those who felt that Congress's performance had been poor would vote against it) and an interaction between performance and leadership evaluations. The interaction was introduced because evaluations of leadership are tied to perceptions of the government's performance.[17] As the results in table 22 make clear, in 1971, even after controlling for other factors that could influence the vote for the Congress, evaluations of the leader had a significant influence on the vote. The impact of class, however, is negative, suggesting that there was a class basis to the Congress vote in 1971 but that it was not those of low economic status who were overwhelming supporters of the Congress Party. As expected, the dummies for each of the states had a significant influence on the vote, providing further support for the hypothesis that the Congress mobilized support independently in each state. Forward and scheduled caste respondents, meanwhile, were more likely to express their support for Congress. None of the performance variables had any influence on the vote. Attitudes toward Indira Gandhi, however, had a significant impact on whether a respondent voted for the Congress or not.

Rajiv Gandhi, on the other hand, did not have the charisma of Indira and was not able to mobilize votes as well as she could. In Maharashtra, for instance, it was reported that Rajiv Gandhi's potential as a vote getter was barely discussed in the Congress camps (*Hindu,* 20 November 1989). Similarly, in Saurashtra, Rajiv Gandhi was not a factor in the party's ability to mobilize support (*Indian Express,* 13 November 1989).

An analysis of a postelection survey of the 1989 national elections shows that favorable evaluations of Rajiv Gandhi did not have a significant influence on whether a respondent voted for Congress or not. The 1989 postelection study was conducted in six states—Andhra Pradesh, Bihar, Maharashtra, Madhya Pradesh, Uttar Pradesh, and West Bengal. As with the analysis of the 1971 elections, a number of controls

TABLE 22.   Perceptions of Indira Gandhi and the Vote for the Congress Party, 1971

Variable	Coefficient	Standard Error
Financial position	0.1256	0.1104
Class	−0.2017*	0.0448
Andhra Pradesh	0.5477*	0.2434
Bihar	1.0103*	0.2647
Madhya Pradesh	0.9469*	0.2660
Uttar Pradesh	0.5473*	0.2325
Forward Castes	0.5048*	0.1604
Harijans	0.4431*	0.1882
Perception of the leader	−0.5325*	0.8064
Leader's performance	−0.0048	0.0452
Constant	0.4914	0.3295

Source: 1971 postelection survey
*Significant at 0.05
$N = 1,782$
−2 log likelihood = 1,454.1304
65.85 percent predicted

were introduced, such as whether the Congress Party had done all it could to solve the problems facing the nation with the assumption that negative perceptions of Congress performance would lead to a vote against the party. Demographic variables, including the respondent's class, caste, and state of residence were also incorporated in the model. Two variables particular to the 1989 elections were added. The first was whether a respondent had heard of the Bofors scandal; the second had to do with exposure to radio and television, which in 1989 were still state run.[18] Evaluations of Rajiv Gandhi and an interaction term of leadership evaluation and Congress performance completed the set of independent variables.

The results, listed in table 23, point to the continuing influence of class, perceptions of the Congress's performance, and the state a respon-

TABLE 23. Perceptions of Rajiv Gandhi and the Vote for the Congress Party, 1991

Variable	Coefficient	Standard Error
Performance of Congress	−1.1994*	0.2574
Improvement of financial situation	−0.1279	0.0876
Evaluation of Rajiv Gandhi	0.8371	0.5292
Age	0.0125*	0.0043
Education	0.1311*	0.0483
Income	0.0300	0.0422
Forward Caste	−0.3226	0.2361
Backward caste	−0.3232	0.2367
Scheduled caste	−0.5241**	0.2940
Muslim	−0.3765	0.3020
Madhya Pradesh	−0.4592*	0.2135
Uttar Pradesh	−1.2293*	0.1992
Andhra Pradesh	1.0182*	0.2432
Bihar	−0.7667*	0.2432
Maharashtra	−0.2385	0.2025
Knowledge of Bofors scandal	0.2449*	0.1376
Watched TV	0.4183*	0.1414
Listened to radio	0.2206	0.1355
Interaction of performance, evaluation	0.2811	0.2937
Constant	0.0267	0.6659

Source: 1991 postelection survey
*Significant at 0.05   **Significant to 0.1
$N = 1,685$
−2 log likelihood = 1,805.487
70.87 percent predicted

dent lives in as determinants of the vote for the Congress Party. In 1989, the scheduled castes defected from the Congress, while none of the other castes seem to have had an independent impact on whether a respondent voted for the party. Those who had heard of Bofors were less likely to vote for the party, while those with more exposure to the state-run media were more likely to vote for the Congress. After controlling for these variables, as well as the interaction between performance and leadership, attitudes toward Rajiv Gandhi did not influence whether a respondent voted for the Congress.

The third reason that Rajiv Gandhi was unable to forge a winning coalition was his inability to intervene as effectively in state Congress politics as Indira Gandhi had. An indicator of this is that Rajiv was unable to exercise similar control over the Congress Party.[19] He did intervene in state politics during his tenure as prime minister, but these interventions were seldom as decisive as those of Indira Gandhi. As a result, cabinet formation in Congress-run states was more difficult. Average cabinet instability in the states during Rajiv Gandhi's tenure as prime minister was greater (4.2) than it was during other periods of postindependence Indian politics (3.4).

Diverse scholars have also pointed to the ineffectiveness of Rajiv Gandhi as a party leader. Kohli (1990) states that Rajiv Gandhi could not rebuild the Congress as a result of being stuck in an impossible position. Reinvigorating the party would have required that the existing party structure be replaced, which was not possible. Rudolph (1989) takes a similar position on the inadequacies of the Rajiv Gandhi regime in dealing with the Congress Party. Likewise, Manor (1988) notes the hesitant and inconsistent handling of the party by Rajiv Gandhi. The increased factional conflict that manifested itself within the state Congress parties during this period, then, can be accounted for by the relative inability of Rajiv Gandhi to deal with these problems (Weiner 1987).

The changes wrought by the emergence of electoral competition in 1967, then, had two major consequences. First, the central government increased its intervention in the affairs of the state governments, especially during the Indira Gandhi regime. Second, there was an expansion of the role of the state during this period. As the state began to play a larger role, and the central government introduced social programs that were to be implemented by the state governments, control over the state governments became ever more important. This was consistent with fluctuations in electoral outcomes. In many Indian states, the parties in power alternated quite frequently. The larger variance in the vote shares of the major parties also supports the exit model, support for a party depending upon its performance. Thus, control over state governments and the prevalence of the exit model characterize contemporary electoral politics in India.

The Formation of a State-Specific Party System

The argument outlined earlier in this chapter and in previous chapters accounts for the emergence of a state-specific party system in India in the 1990s (see table 1). The Congress Party, as we observed in chapter 3, was a collection of state-based parties. These parties came together under a national umbrella, less united by a social or economic interest and ideology, but more through the common pursuit of office. The party was held together by the cooperation of activists in the independence movement and the active role played by national leaders such as Nehru. With the death of Nehru, and then Shastri, the party returned to its state-specific roots. The centralization of political authority under Indira Gandhi, accompanied by a nationally controlled disbursement of economic resources brought the Congress Party together again. This time, however, the party was held together explicitly by a central allocation of resources and the center's willingness to use its political authority to keep the state Congress Parties in line and prevent defection from the party.

In the states, party politics revolved around the allocation of executive offices, such as cabinet posts and positions of authority in state public sector undertakings and cooperatives. With the weakening of central authority that accompanied the ascent of Rajiv Gandhi, the Congress Party returned to its constituent self—a collection of state-specific parties. As the Congress Party in most states represented varying sets of interests different parties came to oppose the Congress Party in those states. With the solidification of the electoral presence of these parties in the state assemblies (made easier by the weakening of the Congress Party at the national level) electoral competition in each state began to look different from the other states. The emergence of the current state-specific party system can then be attributed to the large role played by the state and its federal structure which allocated some autonomy and authority to state governments (and none to localities); the state-specific nature of social conflict and economic considerations; a central party that relied on state parties to mobilize support for it; and the absence of national associations that could have forced political parties to respond to national, not state-specific, considerations.

In 1998, as we saw in table 1, the nature of interparty competition was different in each of the states. With the exception of Rajasthan and Madhya Pradesh, where the BJP and the Congress are the major parties, in no two states do we see the same profile of interparty competition. The party system in India retains one of its basic characteristics—that the Congress, still barely the largest party in terms of its vote share in the 1998 Lok Sabha elections, mobilizes support on a state by state basis. There are, however, significant differences in the Congress's mobilization of votes across different sets of states.

For the set of national elections held between 1971 and 1984, the Congress Party mobilized 26 percent of the electorate in states other than Uttar Pradesh and Bihar and 20 percent of the electorate in those two states. These proportions are not very different for the Lok Sabha elections from 1957 to 1967. In the national elections of 1989 and 1991, however, the Congress's mobilization yielded similar dividends in states other than Uttar Pradesh and Bihar—where it still managed to mobilize 24 percent of the electorate. In those two states, the Congress fared poorly, as only 13 percent of the electorate turned out in its favor; similar patterns obtain for the state elections: Congress managed to mobilize 17 percent of the vote until 1985 but only 11 percent thereafter. In all other states, Congress lost ground during the period between 1967 and 1985 but has since managed to sustain itself at 1985 levels. In other words, there are two distinct phases to the electoral fortunes of the Congress. Between 1967 and 1985, it did poorly in all states but Uttar Pradesh and Bihar. After that, however, its electoral debacle is most pronounced in these two states, and, given the electoral significance of these states (they control 16 percent of the seats to the Lok Sabha), it has suffered a greater loss nationally.

In addition to the increased factionalism that characterized the Congress Party and accounts for many of its electoral losses during this period, are there any other reasons for the poor showing of the party in many states prior to 1985. For one, the centralization of power by the Congress Party and greater intervention in the state governments provided an opportunity for state politicians to exploit regional sentiments against the Congress. Andhra Pradesh is the archetypal case: a state leader, N. T. Rama Rao, managed in 1983 to exploit regional sentiments and bring electoral success to his party—the Telugu Desam (TDP). The Congress, however, has been able to respond to these challenges and rebuild its coalition in Andhra Pradesh. Even in West Bengal, where a Left Front led by the

CPI(M) has been in power since 1977, the Congress retains a significant presence as the second largest party in the state.

The party system in most states has, not surprisingly, remained remarkably constant. The effective number of parties for the Lok Sabha elections from 1967 to 1996 has mostly remained unchanged for many states.[20] If one compares the effective number of parties in the period of electoral competition and when Congress still retained its dominance— from 1967 to 1989—to the effective number of parties after 1989 the dominant feature is similarity. In most states, the party system has remained unchanged. Andhra Pradesh, Gujarat, Kerala, Tamil Nadu, and West Bengal have retained close to a two-party system throughout this period. Madhya Pradesh, Maharashtra, Karnataka, Orissa, Punjab, and Rajasthan have retained their close to two and a half party systems throughout this period. Bihar has persisted with its three party-system, and Uttar Pradesh has shown the largest change in its party system—gaining almost one effective party and averaging close to four parties in the Lok Sabha elections.

Chapter 6

From a Catchall to a Cleavage-Based Party System in an Indian State: Uttar Pradesh

In Uttar Pradesh, the Congress Party has virtually no electoral presence in 1998. The chief reason for the Congress's decline in UP is that the catchall politics associated with the Congress and Janata parties has been replaced with a party system rooted in social cleavages. In 1998, in Uttar Pradesh—the state that had provided all of Congress's prime ministers except Narasimha Rao, the Congress Party is a shadow of its former self. The Congress won five of the 85 seats to the Lok Sabha in the elections of 1991, two in 1996, and none in 1998. For the 1996 state assembly elections, the Congress was a junior partner in an alliance with the Bahujan Samaj Party. Why is it that the Congress Party has fared so poorly in the state?[1]

Congress's poor electoral performance is directly attributable to the dilemma the party faced when a coalition government led by V. P. Singh in Delhi decided to adopt, based on electoral considerations, the report of the Mandal Commission, which advocated quotas in government jobs and admissions to educational institutions for the backward classes.[2] As a result of the fallout associated with the acceptance of the report, the forward, backward, and scheduled castes in Uttar Pradesh began to support the Bharatiya Janata Party, the Samajawadi Party, and the Bahujan Samaj Party, respectively. The Congress Party was left with almost no support in the state. As this chapter notes, issues raised by the Mandal Commission influenced party politics as much as they did because they provided an alternative to the catchall politics of the Congress Party. The acceptance of the Mandal report by the government forced the Congress's hand: it then had to take a stand either in favor of the report or against it. Depending on the position it adopted, the Congress would have lost the support of either the backward or the forward castes. The active position taken on the issue by the SP and the BJP allowed them to garner the support of the backward and forward castes, while Congress's attempt to placate both sides left it with no support at all. Why is that these social cleavages emerged as salient when they did?

The Congress had been able to garner support from most sections of society through the 1980s.[3] Until the 1989 state assembly elections, the party system in Uttar Pradesh was characterized by the dominance of a centrist catchall party, either the Congress or the Janata. The relationship of social cleavages to political parties for much of the period since independence was localized. As Paul Brass (1993a, 1993b) notes, caste had a significant influence on the vote in localities and was far less important at the state level, where factions dominated the political landscape. Caste influenced party politics mostly as *jati*.

The social basis of the party system changed after the elections of 1989, when Mulayam Singh Yadav of the Janata Dal became chief minister of Uttar Pradesh and V. P. Singh led a non-Congress coalition and became the prime minister of India. In 1991, when the next state assembly elections were held in UP, the party system was showing signs of its transformation from a one-party-dominant system, which maintained its success through catchall politics, to a multiparty system, to one in which the major parties—the BJP, SP, and the BSP—represented specific cleavages, the forward, backward, and scheduled castes, respectively. Why does caste structure the party system at the state level now, when in earlier times it was significant only at the local level? In other words, why is it that *jatis,* which are local, come to form statewide political coalitions of forward and backward castes? Is it because they occupy different class positions, as Frankel (1989) and Hasan (1989) have argued?[4] Or is it related to intra- and interparty competition?

This chapter begins by delineating the changes in the electoral fortunes of the Congress and the other parties in UP assembly elections since independence. An analysis of surveys conducted after the 1971 and 1989 national elections demonstrates that the Congress's dominance was built on obtaining support from the forward, backward, and scheduled castes. By 1996, each of these social groups supported a different party. This transformation in the social basis of the party system, from catchall to cleavage based, is attributed to electoral considerations: the adoption of the Mandal Commission report, which advocated quotas for the backward castes in government jobs and educational institutions, by the V. P. Singh government in 1990; the response of political parties to the adoption of the report; and the structure of the state in Uttar Pradesh, where local government has little authority. The final section of the chapter provides evidence based on postelection surveys of the 1993 and 1996 state assembly elections that the caste basis of the party system is linked to voter preferences about state policy and to the positions of the various parties.

The Catchall Party System in Uttar Pradesh

The Congress Party has been the electorally dominant party in Uttar Pradesh, in terms of votes received and seats gained, for much of the period since independence. As figure 14 shows, it was only in the aftermath of the 1989 election that the party's electoral fortunes took an ominous turn. By 1996, the Congress Party was not even among the three largest parties in the state, and for the 1996 assembly elections the Congress Party was the junior partner in an electoral alliance with the BSP. Before 1991, the Congress Party had maintained its electoral dominance through a mixture of catchall and vote bank politics. The former was particularly evident insofar as the policies it adopted were geared toward meeting the interests of most groups. When opposition to the Congress Party arose in the state, it usually sought to incorporate those interests within its fold.[5] It was supported by all segments of society, including the forward, backward, and scheduled castes as well as Muslims. Though all these groups were accommodated within the party, their competing interests were sometimes reflected in factional politics (Brass 1983).

While the Congress Party appeared as catchall at the state level, at the local level the party relied upon mobilizing support from particular *jatis*. An analysis of polling booth data for the 1971 elections reveals that a high proportion of all *jatis* in each polling booth in Uttar Pradesh voted for the same party (Chhibber and Petrocik 1989, 203–4). Paul Brass, who has studied Uttar Pradesh politics for a generation, also notes that *jati* influenced the vote in localities (1983). Any caste alliances that existed in Uttar Pradesh, especially beyond the assembly segment, were based on "mutual convenience" (23).[6] The Congress Party, because of the nature of the electoral system (SMSP) and the inability of any one *jati* to determine electoral outcomes, relied on cross-*jati* coalitions to win elections, and it therefore continued to maintain its status as a catchall party.

The catchall nature of the party shows up clearly in an analysis of data from the 1971 postelection survey. In 1971, the Congress Party, in contrast to the Jana Sangh, and the socialist and Bharatiya Kranti Dal (BKD) alliance was supported by a majority of the forward and scheduled castes

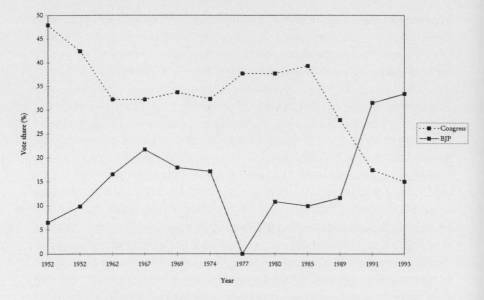

Fig. 14.   Congress and BJP Vote Shares, 1952–93. (Data from Butler, Roy, and Lahiri 1996.)

(59 and 75 percent, respectively). A plurality of the "other backward castes" also favored the Congress Party (45 percent), though a substantial proportion (a third) voted for the socialists or the BKD.[7] This pattern held for the 1989 elections, when, even though the Congress lost, it was still the second largest party (with 28 percent of the votes polled), with a Janata coalition just edging it out as the largest vote getter (30 percent of the vote). For the 1989 assembly elections, the Congress Party and the Janata Dal drew support almost equally from all of the backward, forward, and scheduled castes.[8] A plurality of the forward castes, 48 percent, voted for the Janata Dal, which also received the support of 37 percent of the back-ward castes and 40 percent of the scheduled castes. The Congress's support profile looked similar: Thirty-eight percent of the forward castes, 48 percent of the scheduled castes, and 40 percent of the backward castes voted for the party. The BJP, which garnered only 12 percent of the vote, was supported by 14 percent of the forward castes.

The catchall nature of the party system in Uttar Pradesh changed after the events of 1989 and 1990. In 1989, Mulayam Singh Yadav became chief minister of Uttar Pradesh and V. P. Singh became prime minister of India. While Yadav was from the backward castes and represented backward caste interests, Singh headed a coalition government in which his party was the weakest member. To bolster the standing of his party, Singh announced that the government would accept the recommendations of the Backward Classes Commission (the Mandal Commission) and that quotas for the backward classes would be introduced in government jobs and educational institutions. As noted earlier, this decision was taken without any societal pressure for quotas in 1990. There was no backward caste association agitating for quotas. The student unrest and self-immolations that followed in 1990 played a key role in the fall of the V. P. Singh and Mulayam Singh Yadav's governments in Delhi and Lucknow, respectively.[9]

State assembly elections to the Uttar Pradesh legislature were held in 1991. The aftermath of those elections made it clear that the nature of the party system in UP had changed. There was no catchall party that dominated the electoral scene. The Congress Party's vote share dropped by 10 percentage points (from 29.7 percent in 1989 to 17.4 percent in 1991) while the BJP garnered 31.5 percent of the vote, up from 11.6 percent in 1989. Collectively, the Janata Dal, SP, and the BSP managed to get close to 40 percent of the vote.[10] An analysis of the 1991 postelection survey reveals that 58 percent of the backward castes voted for the Janata alliance, whereas 61 percent of the forward castes voted for the BJP. In other words, by the time of the state assembly elections of 1991 the party system was rooted in social cleavages and not dominated by catchall parties.

Figure 15 presents a graphical representation of the transformation of the party system in Uttar Pradesh. The figure reports the ratio of the share of forward and backward caste voters who supported each of the two major parties in Uttar Pradesh in the national elections of 1971 and the state assembly elections of 1989 and 1991. A value close to one would suggest that an equivalent share of forward and backward caste voters supported the party in question. For the elections of 1971 and 1989, both major parties (Congress and the BKD in 1971 and Congress and the Janata Dal in 1989) got nearly equal amounts of support from both groups. In 1991, however, the two major parties, the BJP and the Janata Dal/SP alliance, drew support from very different groups. A greater proportion of the forward castes (almost two and a half to one) voted for the BJP, whereas a far smaller share of them, relative to the backward castes, exercised their franchise in favor of the Janata Dal/SP alliance.[11] Why did the acceptance of the recommendations of the Mandal Commission lead to the emergence of a party system in UP that was based on divisions between the forward and backward castes?

The Emergence of a Cleavage-Based Party System in Uttar Pradesh

A number of explanations have been suggested to account for the emergence of a cleavage-based party system in Uttar Pradesh. The first has to do with the observation that backward and forward castes occupied different positions in the economic hierarchy. Forward castes are generally large landowners, industrialists, and traders, and in addition they occupied more senior positions in the state bureaucracy (Frankel 1989; Hasan 1989).[12] Second, the proportion of the population that belongs to the forward castes in Uttar Pradesh is much larger than it is in many other states, especially in the south. Thus, it was more feasible for them to support a single party and be an effective political force as a consequence (Hasan 1989). Third, the economic situation of the backward castes had improved with the coming of the green revolution first to western and then to eastern Uttar Pradesh. As the backward castes became wealthier, some members could garner the resources needed to enter politics and mobilize other members across the state. In other words, with the agricultural revolution, they had the resources to form a successful backward caste party (Brass 1993).[13]

Undoubtedly, these factors are important insofar as they provide some preconditions for the emergence of a party system based on social cleavages. They do not, however, explain why a cleavage-based party system emerged when it did. First, by itself the position occupied by the forward and backward castes cannot explain why the Congress Party, which had managed to accommodate a broad range of interests for much of the period since independence, failed to do so in the 1990s. Further, while improved economic well-being allowed the backward classes to mobilize as a caste, it is not clear why this mobilization was undertaken on a statewide basis and led to the emergence of a party system based on statewide social cleavages given that the electoral system, SMSP, encourages local mobilization. Moreover, *jati,* the unit of social organization, is geographically contained, and there is no obvious reason as to why the various *jatis* should have come together on a statewide basis as forward and backward castes.

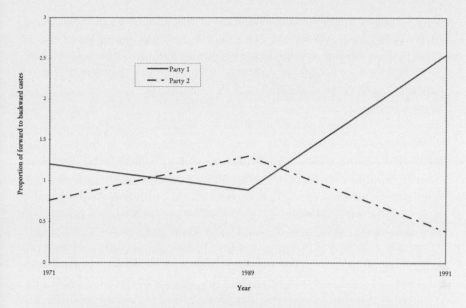

Fig. 15.   Proportion of forward to backward castes voting for the two major parties. Numbers close to one represent equal proportions of forward and backward castes voting for a party. See text for details of the calculation and parties included in the analysis.

The argument developed in this chapter is that the role played by electoral factors cannot be downplayed when discussing the reasons for the formation of backward and forward castes as viable coalitions of *jatis* and for their emergence as the basis of the party system. Three political factors, in particular, stand out. First, local government in Uttar Pradesh is virtually nonexistent. Voters are concerned about state policy more than they are about the actions of the local government and hence develop preferences about the policies adopted by the state government. Since it is the state government that makes most of the decisions affecting a locality, such as those concerning the allocation of resources, these issues dominate voter preferences in local areas. Voters then develop a set of preferences about the party composition of the state legislature. It is in this context that the Mandal Commission report had the impact it did. Once the report was accepted, voters developed preferences around it. Second, the SMSP electoral system makes building coalitions at the local level necessary to win elections. As discussed earlier, these are often cross-*jati* coalitions, and since local government has little authority they are constructed by focusing on the policies of the state government and the access to that government that a candidate can provide. Third, the dilemma faced by the Congress Party as a catchall party played a key role in the emergence of a cleavage-based party system in Uttar Pradesh.

Local Government in Uttar Pradesh

As in many other states in India, the state government in UP exercises significant control over local government. One measure of the relative neglect of local government by the state in Uttar Pradesh is the percentage of the state's development expenditures that is provided as loans to the local government: Between 1971 and 1989, the state government dispensed 3 percent of its total development expenditures as loans to local governments.[14] As local government does not have much autonomous power and authority in Uttar Pradesh, much like in other parts of India, voter and candidate preferences center around the policies of the state government. The report of the Mandal Commission, insofar as it sought to restructure who has access to the state government by providing quotas for the backward castes, had a large influence on the development of the party system in Uttar Pradesh.

Backward Classes Commissions

Why did the Mandal Commission report have the impact it did? The Mandal Commission was actually the second commission appointed by the national government to investigate what, if anything, it could do to help the backward classes in India. The first, known as the Kaka Kalelkar Commission, was appointed in 1953 by the Congress government.[15] The idea that the state was responsible for uplifting the backward classes came from the socialist orientation of the Congress Party. The notion that there were distinct backward classes in Indian society and that the government should adopt policies to look after these classes was written into the Constitution.[16] Who composed these backward classes and what specific measures the state should undertake, however, remained unclear. A commission was therefore appointed to identify these classes and propose measures for ensuring their welfare.

The Kaka Kalelkar Commission, which submitted its final report in 1955, was divided in its recommendations. Each member of the commission apart from the chairman, Kaka Kalelkar, gave dissenting opinions. Much of the dissent centered on whether caste was an appropriate basis for categorizing who belonged to the backward classes. One reason that the dissent took this form is that the report accepted and propagated the modernization paradigm. For some members of the commission, it was difficult to reconcile a policy based on a modernization perspective, with its emphasis on the individual, with the desire to make caste a basis for setting policy.[17] The report of the commission made it clear, however, that backward classes in the "present context [can] mean nothing but castes, and no other interpretation is feasible" (Backward Classes Commission 1955, xiii).[18] The commission went on to root backwardness in social, not economic, characteristics. Indian society was seen as being built on the medieval ideas of caste and social hierarchy, not economic structures alone (39). But, while social structure was key to explaining backwardness, it was not posited as its sole cause. Backwardness was also attributed to physical and economic circumstances such as the lack of a communications system in rural areas, the dearth of educational opportunities, and the limited availability of fewer government jobs.

Social backwardness, however, was a major cause of a lack of educational achievement, which was a key definition of backwardness. Differences in educational levels among individuals, too, were drawn mostly along caste lines, and the commission suggested that "those enjoying a higher social status with influence and power over other social groups and enjoying wealth or means to educate themselves; those occupying positions of power and authority on Government service or in trade, commerce and industry; should all be classified as advanced" (45).

The commission enumerated four criteria for defining who belongs to the backward classes: first, those who held a low social position in the traditional caste hierarchy of Hindu society; second, groups that lacked general educational advancement among the major sections of the caste or community; third, those who had inadequate or no representation in government service; and, fourth, those who were inadequately represented in the fields of trade, commerce, and industry.

The solutions offered by the commission also followed the modernization paradigm. Neither additional nor special political representation for the other backward classes was seen as necessary, since the right to vote was considered to provide all individuals with equal opportunity to express political preferences. The commission focused instead on introducing economic changes such as increased production, land ceilings (the amount of land an individual or family could own), the distribution of surplus land, the consolidation of small landholdings, the regulation of tenancy rights, improving conditions for the poor through government programs, price supports, the removal of rural indebtedness, and better irrigation to increase production. Improved communications would also help people in remote areas, as would better public health, rural water supplies, and housing. These large-scale economic changes, the commission suggested, would ensure better conditions for the backward classes and help lift them out of poverty.

As far as social backwardness was concerned, the commission saw it as central to the problem of backwardness in general and felt it could be alleviated through laws and government messages designed to educate the people. The commission also advocated reserving a proportion of all government jobs for the backward classes, but it simultaneously emphasized the need to reduce the power and prestige of government service.[19] It concluded, however, that as long as government service was attractive quotas would be necessary. The commission suggested for the backward castes quotas of 40 percent in class 3 and 4 jobs, 33 percent in class 2, and 25 percent in class 1 (these quotas were to be separate from those already in place for the scheduled castes and tribes).[20]

The Kaka Kalelkar report was submitted in 1955. The Congress government at the time was not interested in referring to the issue of backwardness in caste terms. Its reluctance to do so could have been either because the government was composed mostly of members of the forward castes or because the socialist orientation of the Congress's leaders made them more concerned with class than caste. Either way, the Congress sought to discover criteria other than caste that could be used to determine who was backward. The government of India then sought to conduct a "pilot survey to see if backwardness could be linked to occupational communities instead of caste." Subsequently, the Congress government decided that it would be better to apply economic tests than to use caste as a measure of socioeconomic development (Backward Classes Commission 1991, 7). As the government could not come up with a satisfactory criterion, in the end it took no action on the Kaka Kalelkar Commission's report. Further, even though the report was tabled in the Lok Sabha, it was never brought up for discussion (Chatterji 1996, 297).

When the Janata Party government came to power in 1977, it appointed a new commission to examine the question of backwardness in India. Unlike the Kaka Kalelkar Commission, the Mandal Commission was composed only of members of the backward castes. The commission submitted its report in 1980. By then, however, a Congress government was in power in the center, and the report was shelved for a decade. The Mandal Commission had one dissenter, who wanted a more nuanced categorization of the backward classes than was offered in the report and suggested that there should be intermediate and depressed backward classes, not just one category of backwardness. The commission's recommendations, to provide a quota for the backward classes in government jobs, were later accepted by V. P. Singh's Janata Dal government in August 1990.

The Mandal Commission had a different perspective than the Kaka Kalelkar Commission on the causes of backwardness. It noted that the caste system in India was similar to the political alliance between the aristocracy and the priests in medieval England (Backward Classes Commission 1991, 19). Equating the caste system with an alliance between the aristocracy and the priests (analogous to the *kshatriya* and brahman in the Varna scheme) pointed to a definition of caste that was more explicitly related to the state than the one adopted by the Kalelkar Commission, which had sought to ground its definitions in religious texts. The political definitions were made even more explicit later when the Mandal Commission report noted that discussions of caste based on *shastras* (texts) did not necessarily correspond to reality and that "caste restrictions have loosened considerably as a result of the rule of law introduced by the British, urbanisation, industrialisation, spread of mass education and, above all, the attainment of Independence and the introduction of adult franchise." Caste, however, "has endured over the ages owing to its great resilience; like the proverbial cat, it has nine lives" (23). The endurance of caste was attributed to democratic politics, in which "the institution of caste . . . played a useful role by providing ready-made traditional channels of mobilisation and articulation. Yet the hard fact remains that the excessive and unrestrained use of these channels has only helped deepen and broaden them." The resilience of caste, the Mandal Commission report went on to argue, was a direct result of the formation of caste associations, most of which were comprised of leading and important regional castes (24). Hence, "what caste has lost on the ritual front, it has more than gained on the political front" (25).[21]

The Mandal Commission's proposed solutions, in contrast to those of the Kaka Kalelkar Commission, also focused on state policies. The Mandal Commission noted that, as "the state is by far the largest employer and the greatest dispenser of all sorts of patronage . . . employment under the state and admission to various technical and professional institutions represent to an Indian citizen the two most important opportunities to participate in the life of the nation" (29). Consequently, the commission recommended establishing quotas in government jobs and educational institutions. It also suggested a more expansive role for the state in matters affecting the backward classes such as greater financial assistance by the state and central government assistance to state governments to aid the other backward classes (62–65).[22]

The Indian Constitution, given the socialist orientation of Congress Party elites, had introduced a new category called the "other backward classes" (which did not include the scheduled castes). The Kaka Kalelkar Commission saw caste as the basis of backwardness. The Mandal Commission also stressed the relationship of caste to backwardness, but it saw caste as maintaining the backwardness of some groups through politics (how this happens is not made clear in the report, except through some oblique references to Marxist notions of domination). With this in mind, it emphasized the role that the state could play, through quotas for government jobs, in promoting upward mobility for the backward castes.

The Mandal Commission and Uttar Pradesh Politics

The acceptance of the recommendations of the Mandal Commission by V. P. Singh's government had a large impact on the party system in Uttar Pradesh for a number of reasons. Forward castes have historically controlled the instruments of the state. As a result, they were likely to be more sensitive about quotas for backward castes. Quotas for backward castes would limit the access of forward castes to the state government, a government that played a key role in preserving their economic status (Frankel 1989). The forward castes' opposition to quotas was intensified by the fact that, unlike the situation in states such as Tamil Nadu and Karnataka, the private sector in UP was not developed enough to create jobs by itself. As a result, the state was still the chief employer (Backward Classes Commission 1980, xx).

Mobilization of Support in Assembly Segments

The Mandal Commission report played an important role in the mobilization efforts of political parties and the formation of cross-*jati* coalitions in the 1993 assembly elections. Within each assembly segment, under an SMSP electoral system, pluralities can only be attained by building alliances across *jatis*.[23] These coalitions of *jatis* were built around voter perceptions of state policy. Candidates of all parties stressed the importance of control over the state government, downplayed local issues, and stressed state policy and the politics of caste. In 1993, the emphasis as far as the latter is concerned focused on how the state could protect a set of castes rather than any particular *jati*. This conclusion is borne out by observations of the mobilization efforts of candidates. The campaigns of the various parties were followed in four constituencies—Dixir, Lalganj, Mahilabad, and Sahranpur—during the run-up to the 1993 assembly elections.

In Lalganj, an assembly segment dominated by *thakurs* (even though Azamgarh District, in which the constituency falls, is *yadav* dominated), the three major parties (Janata Dal, Congress, and BJP) all nominated candidates from the *thakur* subcaste. Similarly, in Dixir (a reserved constituency) the three main candidates all belonged to the same *jati—kuri*.[24] In Saharanpur, the two main competitors, the JD and the BJP, nominated candidates who were from the forward castes.[25]

The issues raised by each candidate focused on forward and backward caste coalitions and stressed both what the policy stance of his or her party would be if it came to power in Lucknow (the state capital) and how the party differed from other parties.[26] In Lalganj, the JD candidate focused on the development work he had done in the assembly segment. Addressing Muslims, he made repeated references to the JD's work on their behalf. In Saharanpur, the JD candidate stressed the relevance of the Mandal Commission. The findings of the commission, according to the candidate, were the only antidote to the Congress and the BJP. Even though the candidate was from the upper castes, he used the logic of the Mandal Commission to build a coalition among Muslims, *yadavs,* and *harijans.*

The group appeals made by BJP candidates in 1993 did not rely on explicitly religious messages such as referring to the building of a temple at Ayodhya on the ruins of the Babri Masjid, which had been destroyed in 1992. BJP supporters in Lalganj used an explicit caste appeal by shouting "BJP ko layenege, brahmanvad fellayange!" (We will bring in the BJP and spread brahman rule!). The caste basis of the party was reflected in Dixir as well, where, even though the BJP candidate had been a minister in the preceding BJP government, very few backward caste members, or *dalits,* were working for the party. This approach was adopted despite the fact that the candidate himself belonged to the scheduled castes, suggesting quite clearly that the residents of Dixir understood whose interests the BJP represented.

In Dixir, the SP candidate stressed that his party was the one that had initiated and championed the welfare of backward castes and *harijans.* He asked people to vote for him to preserve social justice and ensure that the recommendations of the Mandal Commission were adopted. In Mahilabad, the SP candidate asked for votes not for himself but for Mulayam Singh Yadav, who was advanced as the messiah of the downtrodden. The SP candidates, in fact, asked the voters to help elect Mulayam Singh Yadav as chief minister of Uttar Pradesh. Muslims, the largest group in the assembly segment, were appealed to with the argument that Mulayam Singh Yadav was the only leader who could save them from communalism. The candidate made caste-specific appeals as well. In the *yadav* areas, he made his appeal on the grounds that Mulayam Singh Yadav was a *yadav;* in *chamar* areas, he said "vote for me, as I am a *chamar.*" To the others, who did not belong to either caste, he suggested that for *dalits* to maintain their self-respect they must not be exploited by upper castes such as brahmans and *thakurs.* In a telling remark on the expected role of the state government, he pledged that if Mulayam Singh Yadav became the chief minister he would take the key of the *khazana* (treasury) from Mulayam Singh Yadav. The major concerns of the BSP candidates also related to caste. One stressed that *dalits* and backward castes should unite to deal with the brahmanical order. He also emphasized that since the backward castes were a majority in the state they should form a coalition to take power in Lucknow and overthrow the older order.[27]

The larger role advocated for the state in protecting particular castes and religions is apparent when the attitudes of political activists in Uttar Pradesh are contrasted with those in other states. In 1993, local activists from the various political parties were identified and interviewed in six states. The opinion of elites from Uttar Pradesh were compared with those from Andhra Pradesh, Gujarat, Kerala, Maharashtra, and West Bengal. Significant differences between the attitudes of Uttar Pradesh elites and those of elites in other states emerged. The prominent role of caste in Uttar Pradesh, and its relationship to the state government, are most apparent with respect to the attitudes of activists regarding the regulation of personal laws (in other words, the separate civil code for most religions). Sixty-one percent of the activists in Uttar Pradesh wanted a larger role for the state in regulating caste activities, whereas only 43 percent felt similarly in the other states. Similar results obtain when activists were asked whether the state should regulate personal laws, with 64 percent of the activists in Uttar Pradesh answering in the affirmative compared to only 42 percent in the other states. Given the positions adopted by the political parties on matters of caste, with specific parties advocating state policy to protect particular castes, this comes as no surprise.

Respondents were also asked what factor was most important in winning an election in their areas. Party activists in Uttar Pradesh and the other states had similar views on the relative influence of party loyalty, national issues, candidate personality, muscle power, and money. There were clear differences, however, in their opinions as to the influence of caste and religion. In Uttar Pradesh, 37 and 33 percent of local activists, respectively, said that caste and religion were important for electoral success, whereas only 8 and 12 percent from the other states thought caste and religion mattered. Consistent with the substantive focus of campaigns in Dixir, Lalganj, Mahilabad, and Saharanpur, 60 percent of the respondents in Uttar Pradesh thought that local issues were not significant. None of the candidates in the four assembly segments whose speeches and mobilization efforts were analyzed addressed local concerns in the 1993 elections. Most of the candidates instead focused on what their parties, if in power in the state government, could do for voters.

Congress and the Dilemma of a Catchall Party

Together with the interest in state government policy that came to dominate the preferences of voters and the positions adopted by political parties, the adoption of the Mandal Commission report and the concomitant divide between forward and backward castes brought into sharp focus the dilemma that the Congress, like other catchall parties, faced.[28] The Congress Party historically had garnered a majority of the forward and backward caste votes. The adoption of the recommendations of the Mandal Commission report placed the Congress Party in a difficult position. It could not take a stand against adopting the measures, as that would cause it to lose what support it had among the backward castes in Uttar Pradesh and perhaps across the rest of the nation.[29] Nor could it come out openly in favor of the report, for it would then lose the support of the forward castes, who were key party supporters and also constituted a significant portion of its officeholders (Hasan 1989).

The immediate beneficiary of the announcement that the recommendations of the Mandal Commission would be adopted was the SP, which has clearly become the party of choice among most of the backward castes.[30] The forward castes, on the other hand, began supporting the BJP. Following the V. P. Singh government's announcement that it would adopt the recommendations of the Mandal Commission, there were protests by forward caste students. The *Organiser,* a BJP paper, editorialized against the commission's report (Jaffrelot 1996, 415). The forward castes in Uttar Pradesh, as a consequence, perceived the BJP as representing their interests. The BJP responded to these developments by making more strident its message that it would create a Hindu state in which there would be no special treatment for minorities and by undertaking a *Rath Yatra* (pilgrimage on a chariot).[31] Though planned earlier, the *Rath Yatra* was spurred on by the acceptance of the Mandal Commission report. L. K. Advani, the BJP president, said that "the Mandal episode certainly put pressure on me in my constituency" (Jaffrelot 1996, 415).

Meanwhile, in the aftermath of the Congress's electoral debacle in 1991 the BSP increased its efforts to mobilize the scheduled costs and managed to draw their support. This deprived the Congress Party of the support of one of its key constitutencies. As a result, the Congress, the centrist party, dropped out as a major competitor. Its collapse spelled the death knell of the catchall party system in Uttar Pradesh, which moved from a system dominated by a catchall party to one clearly based on caste.[32]

Thus, the weak role of local government, the electoral rules (SMSP), and the presence of many *jatis* in a constituency have had an impact on how parties mobilize support. Political parties under the SMSP system needed to build coalitions of *jatis* to win elections.[33] Because the state, not local, governments exercise the most power in areas of primary concern to voters, coalitions among *jatis,* as the evaluation of the campaigns in four constituencies revealed, are built around the policy adopted by the state government and which party can best direct the resources of the state toward particular communities.

Mass Attitudes, State Policy, and the Emergence of a Cleavage-Based Party System

The transformation of the party system in Uttar Pradesh from one dominated by a catchall Congress Party to one rooted in social cleavages was complete by the time of the 1993 assembly elections. A postelection survey was conducted following the 1993 state assembly elections using a sample of 1,000 respondents, who were selected from voter lists using a stratified random sample, with the proportion of Muslims in a district forming the key category for stratification. The sample was divided into four categories: members of the forward castes, backward castes, and scheduled castes, and Muslims. The respondents were asked which party they voted for in the election. A majority of the forward caste members voted for the BJP (67 percent), whereas the backward (54 percent) and scheduled caste (50 percent) respondents expressed their preference for the SP/BSP alliance. This is a clear change from the 1989 election, when a majority among the forward and backward castes still preferred the Congress Party, though similar to the results regarding the 1991 election.

Voters were subsequently asked why they voted the way they did. The open-ended responses were recoded to yield five different categories describing why a respondent voted the way he or she did: peer group pressure from family members, friends, and other caste members; the party best represented group interests; a focus on a particular leader as a basis for the vote; issue based reasons; and, finally, preferences for a particular party. A plurality of respondents, regardless of their caste (about 30 percent of each among the forward, backward, and scheduled castes) chose reasons having to do with the programs, policies, or positions of the party for which they voted. This suggests that voters expressed clear preferences for political parties, not candidates or leaders (less than 10 percent in each caste saw the leader as an adequate basis on which to make a vote choice). Approximately 20 percent in each caste group voted the way they did because a particular party promoted their group interests. A similar proportion of the respondents based their votes on issues. These findings indicate that voters in Uttar Pradesh, no matter what caste, base their vote choices on the party, its policies, the issues that concerned them, and whether the party favored their group.

Respondents were also asked detailed questions about whether castes should vote as one bloc and whether other castes in their area voted that way. The reason for asking both sets of questions was that an individual may be unwilling to admit openly that a caste should express its political preferences, but he or she may be more open on the question of whether other castes voted that way. Replies to these questions were combined to generate a scale. The pervasive influence of caste was felt across all groups. A majority of forward, backward, and scheduled caste members said that caste does have a role to play in the political process: only 42, 38, and 22 percent of the forward, backward, and scheduled castes, respectively, suggested that caste should have no influence on voter choice.[34]

Respondents were further asked to identify the major problems facing their areas. This, too, was an open-ended question. The various responses were categorized as problems associated with unemployment, prices, social problems, other economic problems, and infrastructure-related issues. Given that caste has been associated with class, we expected that different castes would not hold similar perceptions on the problems in their areas. Surprisingly, there were no significant differences among the castes on a whole range of issues. Forty percent of each caste pointed to economic problems as the key issues; about 12 percent identified religious and social problems.

This finding is buttressed by a preelection survey conducted in 1996. In that survey, a different set of questions was asked. First, respondents were asked whether they were better or worse off compared to the previous year. There were no significant differences among forward and backward castes on this question: 27 percent of the forward and 24 percent of the backward castes said that they were much better off, while 60 percent of the forward and 51 percent of the backward castes said that they were doing better. Instead of asking an open-ended question, as in the 1993 study, the respondents in the 1996 survey were asked to identify the problems they faced. Specific problems were presented to the respondents, and they were asked whether that issue was a very serious problem, somewhat serious problem, not a serious problem, or no problem at all. On a whole range of issues such as poverty and prices, forward and backward caste respondents had similar perceptions about the extent of these problems. Among the backward castes, 84 and 81 percent saw unemployment, poverty, and prices as very serious problems. Forward caste members had similar perceptions, with 75 and 81 percent, respectively, describing the same three issues as very serious problems. This finding indicates that respondents from all castes, despite their class differences, have similar attitudes on a range of economic issues.

Differences among the castes, however, appear when respondents were asked about the seriousness of the problems in areas where the state government plays a key role, such as the day to day supply of food, the quality of schools and colleges, and health services.[35] In these areas, members of the forward castes were less likely to see serious problems: 28, 31, and 42 percent of them saw the day to day supply of food, schools, and health, respectively, as serious issues. Those who identified themselves as backward caste members had very different perceptions, with 49, 51, and 68 percent pointing to the seriousness of the day to day supply of food, schools, and health, respectively.

It could be argued that this difference between castes merely reflects their different class positions. This is, however, not the case. The two sets of issues—those dealing with unemployment, prices, and poverty and those that addressed the daily supply of food, the quality of schools and colleges, and health services—were combined to yield a single scale. At one end were arrayed those who perceived the two sets of issues as not being a problem; at the other are found those who thought that both sets represented serious problems. The scales were then regressed against caste and economic status (class position measured as a combination of income and education) of the respondents. The results (see table 24) indicate that the caste of a respondent influenced his or her perception of the seriousness of some problems but not others. In areas in which the state does not play a key role (poverty and prices), caste did not affect perceptions of the seriousness of a problem, while in areas in which the state does play a role (schools, supply of food, and health services) the caste of a respondent had a positive and significant impact on whether a problem was seen as serious. Members of the backward castes were more likely to perceive the latter problems as serious, even after controlling for class.

Thus, it appears that the caste basis of the party system, the role played by preferences regarding state policy, and the influence of perceptions about the social basis of political parties all structured the vote choice in Uttar Pradesh in 1993. This assessment is tested through a regression in which the dependent variable is vote choice among Hindus between the BJP and the SP/BSP coalition for the 1993 state assembly elections (see table 25). The choice between the parties can be explained by a number of factors. Explanations for the BJP's success have focused on the religiosity of the respondents, with the assumption that those who are more religious will support the BJP. An index of religiosity was constructed by combining responses to questions about how often a respondent attended religious gatherings, went to temple, and prayed. Another important variable used to explain the vote for the BJP is the share of a district's population that is Muslim, as the BJP, it is argued, will get more support in assembly segments with more Muslims. Two controls related to caste were added. The first was whether a respondent was willing to use caste as a basis for his or her vote; the second was whether the respondent was self-identified as belonging to the forward or backward castes.

A series of variables capturing perceptions of the performance of the BJP government, which was in power in Uttar Pradesh between 1991 and 1993, and respondent assessments of the policy positions of political parties was also included in the model. Respondents were asked to assess the state government's performance, with the expectation that those who

TABLE 24.   Caste, Class, and Issue Perceptions in Uttar Pradesh (OLS estimates)

	Economic Issues	Political Issues
Caste	−0.178	−1.591*
Caste standard error	0.22	0.200
Class	−0.082	−0.179
Class standard error	0.06	0.06
Constant	0.238	2.38*
R^2	0.005	0.14
F	1.49	45.99*
N	574	568

Source: 1996 preelection survey
*Significant at 0.01

TABLE 25.   Basis for Vote Choice between the BJP and the SP in Uttar Pradesh, 1993 (logistic regression)

Variable	Coefficient	Standard Error
Religiosity	0.0447	0.1764
Class	0.1155	0.1550
Proportion of Hindus	−0.0939	0.2540
Performance of BJP government	−1.1131*	0.2308
BJP favors forward castes	−0.8117**	0.4352
Government favors backward castes	1.1091*	0.5731
Government should protect Hindus	1.2124*	0.2996
Government should protect Muslims	−1.2831*	0.2960
Backward Caste	−1.295*	0.2763
Forward Caste	2.137*	0.3805
Caste important in voting decisions	−0.3962	0.2583
Constant	4.0878	

Source: 1993 Uttar Pradesh postelection survey
*Significant to 0.05   **Significant to 0.1
−2 log likelihood = 403.55964
N = 361
88.29 percent predicted

thought that the government had not performed well in the past were less likely to vote for it again. For the 1993 state assembly elections, this variable took on added significance, as it was during the watch of the BJP government (in 1992) that the mosque at Ayodhya was destroyed by those who thought it was built over a Hindu temple on the site believed to be the birthplace of the god Ram. To address party positioning, the survey elicited answers on whether the BJP favored any particular caste group. The responses were recoded to yield a categorical variable, which took on the values 1 if the BJP favored forward castes and 0 otherwise. Questions on the role of the government in protecting certain groups were posed—in particular, whether the government favored the backward castes (an important question given the role played by the Mandal Commission in the election campaign of 1993)—while two others inquired whether the respondent felt that the government should protect Hindus and Muslims.

The regression results, reported in table 25, suggest that a respondent's caste was indeed salient in determining the vote choice between the BJP and the SP/BSP in the 1993 state assembly elections. None of the variables noted in the literature as influencing the vote for the BJP, such as religiosity or the proportion of Muslims, was found to have an influence on vote choice for the BJP after controlling for caste and perceptions of government policy. All of the variables reporting the perception of voters about the government and the position of political parties were significant.

As noted earlier, the Mandal issue was critical in these elections. Not surprisingly, those who felt that the government favored the backward castes were more likely to vote for the BJP. Respondents who observed that the government needed to protect the interests of Hindus voted for the BJP, whereas those who thought that Muslims needed protection preferred the SP/BSP alliance. Finally, the negative coefficient on the variable reporting whether the BJP was perceived as favoring forward castes (and the greater likelihood of those who were inclined in that direction to vote for the BJP) is a clear indication that perceptions of a party's position play an important role in determining a voter's preference. These results suggest that perceptions of state policy are critical in determining the social basis of the party system and the decision of those among the backward and forward castes to vote for the SP and the BJP, respectively. The political expression of forwardness and backwardness, insofar as it is reflected in support for either the BJP or the SP, is clearly linked to voters' perceptions regarding the role of the state government.[36]

Similar results were obtained in a postelection survey based on the

1996 state assembly elections.[37] A different set of questions were posed in this survey instrument.[38] Respondents were asked what the aims of the major parties in the state were, what groups the parties represented, and why he or she voted for a particular party. Respondents were also asked why quotas were introduced—whether the motivation was merely political or there was some broader justification for the policy. They were further asked whether they voted for economic self-interest or political power. Finally, the survey requested that they identify their caste as either forward or backward.

As the question regarding the main aim of the major parties in the state was open ended, the responses were recoded to yield five categories: religious, caste, economic, political, and other concerns. The BJP was seen as protecting a religious order, while the SP and BSP were seen as favoring particular castes. Forty-five percent of the backward and 48 percent of the forward caste respondents said that the BJP's aim was promoting and protecting Hindus. A similar proportion of both castes said that the SP favored a particular caste. The BSP's caste orientations were even more apparent, as two-thirds of the forward and backward caste respondents said that the BSP's chief goal was advocating the interests of a particular caste. Fifty percent among the forward and 40 percent among the backward castes said that the Congress's main goal, on the other hand, was politics.

A second open-ended question asked respondents to identify which groups supported the main parties. When asked who supported the BJP, most respondents pointed to the forward castes (37 percent) and Hindus (42 percent). The SP was perceived as advancing the interests of the backward castes (60 percent) and *dalits* (27 percent). The BSP was seen clearly as a *dalit* party, with 82 percent of the respondents noting that the BSP advocated the needs of *dalits.* No major differences were found across castes: both forward and backward caste respondents had a clear sense of what each of the parties stood for and which group supported which party. This finding offers definitive evidence that the party system was rooted in specific cleavages in Uttar Pradesh in 1997. This is quite unlike the situation under the catchall Congress system, when the support basis of each party was never as clear.

This old pattern still holds true as far as the Congress Party is concerned. There was no clear sense of what the party represented: 27 percent of the respondents said that Congress favored the *dalits,* while 29 percent thought it favored the forward castes. Less than 1 percent thought the Congress Party advocated the interests of the backward castes. To make matters worse for the party, more members of the forward (36 percent) than the backward castes (19 percent) felt that Congress Party protected the *dalits*. At the same time, a much larger proportion among the backward (39 percent) than the forward castes (19 percent) said that Congress Party favored the forward castes. In other words, the backward castes see Congress as a party of the forward castes and the forward castes see the Congress as a party of the backward castes and *dalits*. This is the clearest evidence of the consequences of the dilemma faced by the Congress Party—when it did not take a stand on the backward/forward issue, its ambiguous position left the party with no consistent base of support. Instead, each caste group believes that Congress favors the other group.

Economic considerations do not help discriminate between BJP and SP voters, as most respondents picked economic interest as the reason for their vote choices. To comprehend why a respondent voted for a particular party, the survey provided them with a set of alternatives, focusing on issues of rights and economic interest: would the party provide people of their caste/status with representation in society, a voice, political rights, or an improved economic situation? Respondents could also offer any other reason they felt was more appropriate. An overwhelming majority, 77 percent, said they voted for the party that would protect their economic interests. These results suggest not only that respondents know which party represents which caste but that their support for a party is rooted in something other than the politics of voice or respect. The key variable is the perception of how best to ensure economic well-being and which party can provide it. Given the major role played by the state, an improvement in one's economic situation can only be achieved when a party supporting the respondent's caste controls the state government.

The emergence of a party system rooted in caste cleavages, then, is a direct consequence of the influence of state policy and competitive party politics. The economic and sociological distinctions between the forward and backward castes provided the possibility for the creation of a cleavage-based party system in UP. These cleavages formed the basis of the party system largely because state rather than local government exercises most of the power and authority. Once the national government adopted a clear policy on the backward castes and political parties took clearly defined positions supporting the concerns of either the forward or backward castes, the emergence of a cleavage-based party system in Uttar Pradesh was possible. Caste now clearly influences Uttar Pradesh politics at the state level, something it had not been able to do so definitively in the past.

Chapter 7

State Policy, Party Politics, and the Rise of the BJP

Alongside the decline of the Congress Party and the emergence of a cleavage-based party system in Uttar Pradesh, another key development in contemporary Indian electoral politics is the electoral success of the BJP. In addition to the forward castes, who voted for the BJP because of its stance on the Mandal Commission, the middle classes, too, were mobilized by the BJP. The Indian middle class has grown with economic development. As its interests were not promoted by the Congress, it was mobilizable by other political parties. The BJP, by shifting its economic platform to embrace a reduced role for the state, managed to draw middle-class support. Meanwhile, the separation of national and state elections and the Congress's explicit linkage of central government policy to electoral considerations, in conjunction with the role ascribed to the nation-state in economic development, led some voters to develop preferences over national policy. The BJP, by positioning itself as a national party, also managed to draw the support of voters who were dissatisfied with the performance of the central government.

Placing the BJP's electoral success in the context of state policy and electoral politics differs from conventional interpretations, which see the BJP's strong showing in the 1991 and 1996 national elections in terms of the rise of Hindu religious sentiments in India.[1] There is little evidence, however, that Hindus are either more religious than before or more willing to express their religiosity in the political arena. In the absence of such evidence, it is difficult to attribute the electoral success of the BJP to a mobilization of Hindus along religious lines. An alternative suggests that it is not religiosity per se but religious nationalism that lies at the base of the BJP's success. But why did religious nationalism—which has been a plank of the BJP since independence—become so important in the 1990s? This chapter claims that the BJP has been electorally successful because it was able to forge a coalition between the middle class, the forward castes, religious groups, and those voters who had preferences over the policies of the national government.

The middle class was mobilizable because of Congress Party politics. The Congress was the chief architect of the developmental state in India. Over time, the distinction between the party and the state had become less meaningful. The Congress limited access to the government to its supporters—large landlords, capitalists, and the political-bureaucratic combine (Bardhan 1984). The BJP, by questioning the excessive power of the state and showing a willingness to get the state out of the economy in 1991, drew the support of the middle classes, which had historically been excluded from the Congress-run government. Hence, the electoral success of the BJP lay not only in mobilizing the religious groups but in its ability to put together a viable coalition of religious Hindus and those disaffected by state economic policy. At the same time, as was noted earlier, with the emergence of electoral competition the Congress Party had increased the role not only of the state but of the national government. As the national government's policies increasingly became the focus of voter attention, the BJP's religious nationalist theme became a vote getter, as it enabled the BJP to draw support, across constituencies, from those concerned with national policy. Additionally, as discussed in the previous chapter, the adoption of quotas for backward castes led the forward castes to begin supporting the BJP in larger numbers than before. This chapter will provide evidence for this argument through an examination of the social basis of support for the Jana Sangh, the pre-1980 incarnation of the BJP, in the 1967 elections and for the BJP in the 1991 and 1996 elections.

Religiosity and Attitudes toward Other Religions in India

Both the 1989 and 1991 postelection surveys asked detailed questions about religiosity and attitudes toward other religions. In 1989, 46 percent of Hindus said they prayed every day; in the 1991 survey, 50 percent gave a similar response. The difference is not statistically significant and is within the margin of error. Even if the difference is taken seriously, it is too small to account for the doubling of support received by the BJP in the 1991 elections compared to those of 1989.

The surveys did yield interesting similarities among Hindus and Muslims on a range of issues concerning religious matters. A similar proportion of Hindus and Muslims (48 percent) said that their religion differed from other religions. A third of all respondents felt that people were becoming more religious, while another third thought that people were becoming less religious. Respondents were asked whether in their localities and states, as well as nationwide, relations among the different religions were consensual, conflictual, or had elements of both. Hindus and Muslims had strikingly identical perceptions of the extent of religious conflict in their localities (more than 70 percent of Hindus and Muslims thought relations among different religions at this level were consensual), in their states (slightly more than 20 percent of respondents of both religions identified the relations as consensual), and nationally (less than 10 percent of Hindus and Muslims perceived the relations to be consensual).[2] A difference between the religions did emerge when respondents were asked whether religion and politics go together. Only about a third of the Muslim respondents (34 percent) said that religion and politics went together, whereas just over half of the Hindus (51 percent) expressed similar opinions. What about backward and forward caste Hindus? Do they express identical preferences in response to these questions? Strikingly, there was almost no difference among Hindus, from either backward or forward castes, on these questions.

Economic and Religious Attitudes of Party Activists, 1993

To assess the relative importance of economic and religious considerations for the BJP, data from a 1993 study of local political elites were analyzed. Local elites from the major parties were identified and interviewed in seven states: Andhra Pradesh, Bihar, Kerala, Maharashtra, Madhya Pradesh, Uttar Pradesh, and West Bengal. Respondents were asked a wide range of questions concerning the role of the state, including whether the government should take more or less action in controlling trade and industry; in expanding the private sector and denationalizing industry; in regulating personal laws, religious matters, and caste activities; and in distributing food, providing law and order, and controlling corruption. The answers to the first two sets of questions—both of which address the state's role in economic matters—were combined to produce a scale of those who favored economic liberalization and those who did not. Forty-one percent of BJP activists were in favor of more liberalization, compared to 27 and 24 percent of Congress and other party activists, respectively. Thirty-seven and 44 percent of Congress and other party activists, respectively, and less than a fifth (18 percent) of the BJP activists advocated greater state control.

This attitudinal difference among political elites of the various parties on economic issues persists even when one controls for the religious orientations of the respondents. The 10 items dealing with the role of the state were standardized and combined to yield four principal categories: an economic orientation, which was a combination of responses to questions on state control over trade and industry; a social variable, which consolidated responses to questions concerning the regulation of religious matters, personal laws, and caste activities; responses to denationalization and the encouragement of privatization, which were merged into one category; and variables on corruption and law and order. Table 26 indicates that there are significant differences between the parties on some of these four categories. BJP activists were more likely to favor less state intervention in trade and a more active role for the state in denationalizing and privatizing industry. BJP activists also favored less of a role for the state in regulating personal laws, religious matters, and caste activities. Those associated with the Congress appear in the center of the political spectrum on all issues. Activists of other parties took positions to the left of the centrist Congress.

In addition, BJP activists differed from Congress and other party activists as far as religiosity and elite perceptions of other religions were concerned. Whereas 59 percent of BJP activists were likely to pray, go to temple, or attend religious meetings on a more or less regular basis, that was not so true for those affiliated with other parties: only 20 percent of the Congress and other party activists were similarly inclined. This sharp contrast persists when respondents were asked whether their religion differs from other religions. Among Hindu respondents, members of party elites associated with the BJP were most likely to see their religion as distinct from other religions (a majority of them thought so). In contrast, only 9 percent of Hindu Congress Party activists thought Hinduism was different from other religions.

TABLE 26.   Mean Scores of Party Activists on the Extent of State Intervention

Party	Economy	Social Issues	Liberalization	Other
Congress	−0.1619	0.1773	−0.0139	−0.028
BJP	0.5225	−0.3389	0.3196	0.0538
Other party	−0.03398	0.1641	−0.2706	0.1641

Source: 1993 elite survey
$N = 456$

To determine whether economic considerations influenced the attitudes of the BJP activists independent of religious and social considerations, a logistic regression model was estimated. The independent variables included not only respondent attitudes about the role of the state but also the respondents' religiosity and their perceptions of how much their religion differed from others. In recognition of the national orientation of the BJP, the final attitudinal variable in the model was whether national issues influenced election outcomes in their constituencies. Since the BJP is considered a forward caste party, the caste of the respondents was included as a control (Brass 1993). The results, reported in table 27, indicate that, even after controlling for religious orientation, religiosity, and caste, attitudes about the economy still distinguish BJP activists from those of other parties. And, of course, BJP activists are more likely to point to the impact of national issues on elections in their constituencies.

Even though economic and religious concerns are central in distinguishing BJP activists from those of other political parties, they represent independent dimensions of elite attitudes. A factor plot (see fig. 16) reveals that economic matters lie on a dimension that is clearly distinct from the religious concerns of the BJP. This factor plot was derived from a factor

TABLE 27.   Religion, Economics, and BJP Activists
(logistic regression)

Variable	Coefficient	Standard Error
Economic issues	0.3053*	0.0762
Social issues	0.0593	0.0593
Liberalization	−0.1877*	0.0859
Religion different	0.7644*	0.1555
Religiosity	−1.5091*	0.2283
Upper caste or not	−0.0122	0.2617
Other castes	0.0023	0.0790
National issues	−0.4455*	0.2088
Constant	0.3806	0.5095

Source: 1993 Elite survey
Note: Logistic regression is used to distinguish BJP activists'
attitudes from those of other party activists.
*Significant at 0.01
−2 log likelihood = 506.83801
78.62 percent predicted
$N = 407$

analysis of six variables (app. D). The variables forming the religious dimension are: the religiosity of the respondent *(reltype)*, whether religion and politics go together *(relpolt)*, and whether the respondent's religion (Hinduism) was perceived as different from other religions *(reldiff)*. The economic dimension was comprised of three variables: the extent of state control over trade *(trade)*, the extent of state control over industry *(industry)*, and whether the respondent favored greater encouragement to the private sector and advocated denationalization *(laissez)*. Figure 16 suggests quite clearly that among BJP activists the economy and religious orientation lie on different dimensions. Hence, economic issues cannot be treated as part of the same issue dimension as religious orientation.

The BJP, then, had a definite position on the role of the state in the economy—one that is not reducible to its religious orientation. Its advocacy of less state intervention (tables 26 and 27) gives the party an identity on economic matters that differs from that of other political parties. This distinct economic position is new to the BJP; earlier the party did not have a clear and distinct position on economic matters. The origins of the Jana Sangh (the precursor of the BJP) lay, instead, in the opposition of religious groups to the secular policies of the developmental state.

Secularism and the Emergence of the BJP

At independence, the governing regime in India believed that religion was a force that would thwart the process of nation building, that is, that religion would stand in the way of citizens developing a primary identification with the nation-state. An important component of this vision was a belief in the need to create a citizen identity that saw traditional social identities such as religion as inimical to the creation of a viable nation-state. Religion was perceived to be a backward-looking ideology, an element of traditional society that had to be shed so that citizens would owe primary allegiance to the nation-state. According to Subrata Kumar Mitra, Nehru "had no inclination to give institutional shape to what he saw as a vestige of tradition destined to obliteration through the operation of the inexorable laws of history" (1993, 756).

A segment of the Congress Party at independence was willing to accommodate the social policy agenda of Hindu religious groups. The creation of a legal code to govern social policy, however, sparked a debate among Hindu traditionalists and secularists within the ruling Congress Party (Graham 1990). In particular, conflict emerged over the Hindu Code

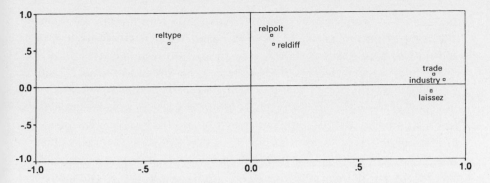

Fig. 16.   Economic and religious attitudes of BJP activists (factor plot).
Appendix D provides the details of the factor analysis.

Bill, which was intended to provide "for a unified system of law governing Hindu marriage" and "was going to give women rights that they had not had previously enjoyed. Many orthodox Hindus, some within the Congress, were opposed to the measure and its passage through the Constituent Assembly was continually delayed" (19). Nevertheless, in the end the bill passed, signaling to religious groups that the secular position had prevailed.

Evidence for the unwillingness of Congress to accommodate Hindu religious groups within its fold also comes from the efforts of the Rashtriya Swayamsevak Sangh, an openly Hindu organization, to create a role for itself within Congress at the local level.[3] Despite initial sympathy to these overtures, Congress reversed its position and decided not to allow its members to hold joint membership with the RSS. The division between the Hindu traditionalists and liberal secularists within the Congress was highlighted in the election for party president in 1951—an election contested between the more traditional Purshottamdas Tandon and a more secular J. B. Kripilani. Nehru's support for Kripilani, as well as his decision to force Purshottamdas Tandon to resign once he was elected, was a clear indication that powerful national leaders, of which Nehru was the most prominent, would ensure the dominance of the secularist position within the Congress Party.

This intraparty division ultimately led to the formation of a political party that promoted itself as the protector of the interests of the Hindus— the Jana Sangh. Its main architects were former Congressmen who rejected the Congress's secular policy preferences (Brass 1965; Graham 1990). According to Myron Weiner, the "issues which occupied the attention and interests of the members of [the Jana Sangh] . . . were essentially not economic" (1957, 212). The Jana Sangh was more concerned with cultural questions: "their opposition to the Hindu Code Bill, and their charge of favoritism toward Muslims by the government—these were the key issues . . . not land reform and other economic questions" (213). The emergence of the Jana Sangh, then, was closely associated with the secular state policy that was supported by the Congress Party. Though the Congress was willing to absorb economic groups with different interests, it was unwilling to accommodate a religious party. The close ties between the Jana Sangh and the RSS, however, placed limits on the party's ability to mobilize support among all segments of Indian society.

Unlike the Congress Party, the BJP's support rests in large part on the RSS, an association that, though closely associated with the BJP, is independent of the party. The link between the BJP and the RSS provides the BJP with an advantage as well as a disadvantage. Since the party is lent organizational support by the RSS, it is assured of an electoral presence insofar as the RSS can always mobilize support for the BJP (provided the BJP does not stray too far from the RSS's policy preferences).[4] Congress does not have a similar associational base and hence can be eliminated completely as an electoral presence (as happened in Uttar Pradesh). BJP's ties to the RSS, however, also put the party at a disadvantage. As long as the party relies on the RSS, it cannot take a policy position distant from that of the RSS. In other words, it would be difficult for the BJP to become a centrist party like the Congress.

The Economic Policies of the Jana Sangh and BJP, 1951–91

For much of the period since its inception, the BJP (and before that the Jana Sangh) followed the economic policy line of the Congress. The Jana Sangh supported a mixed economy in the 1950s and 1960s and Gandhian socialism in the early 1980s. In 1991, the party repositioned itself as a fierce critic of state intervention in the economy. In 1951, it supported land reform and called for the abolition of Jagirdari and Zamindari (the British land tenure system) "without compensation" (Bharatiya Jana Sangh 1973, 51). With regard to the industrial sector, the party stood for "public ownership of industries especially catering to the essential defence needs of the country" (52). In 1957, a year after the Congress's adoption of a socialist vision of society, the Jana Sangh repeated its stance that there was a need to avoid "individualistic capitalism as well as state capitalism" (85). In 1967 the Jana Sangh continued to advocate a "mixed economy . . . [and contended that] the controversy going on at present between the public sector and the private sector [was] meaningless" (166). The party also supported nationalizing industries as long as the "decision [to do so was] taken not on a political basis but on the basis of recommendations by a judicial commission to be appointed for this purpose" (166). Like the Congress, the Jana Sangh declared a national war on poverty in 1971. It advocated full employment, nationalization of foreign banks, a more profitable public sector, and an independent central monetary authority. The unwillingness of the Jana Sangh to adopt a more laissez-faire economic program during this period was most apparent in its reluctance to form a preelectoral coalition with the economically conservative party, the Swatantra. According to Hampton Davey, the "Jana Sangh leaders had reservations about the unabashed economic conservatism of Swatantra" (1972, 707).[5]

The Jana Sangh continued its support for an interventionist economic policy through the early 1980s, with the party—by then renamed the BJP—deciding to adopt Gandhian socialism in 1980. Among others, Atal Bihari Vajpayee, a BJP leader, actively advocated Gandhian socialism and positive secularism (Jaffrelot 1996, 316).[6] The promotion of Gandhian socialism by the BJP had immediate consequences for the party, especially in its relationship with the association that provided it with organizational strength—the RSS. In the 1984 election, after the adoption of Gandhian socialism (Gandhism, to the RSS, implied the appeasement of minorities), the BJP managed to get only 7 percent of the total votes cast and won two seats to the Lok Sabha. In 1986, the RSS ideologue, Nanaji Deshmukh, and the RSS chief, Balasaheb Deoras, "openly dissociated themselves from the BJP when . . . they declared that there was no electoral alternative to the Congress (I) at the national level" (Malik and Singh 1992, 323). The appointment of L. K. Advani, who had close associations with the RSS, as the party's president went a long way toward appeasing the RSS. The subsequent alliance of the BJP with the militant Hindu party in Maharashtra, the Shiv Sena, and its open advocacy of a Hindu state with Ram Rajya (a reference to a mythical age when the god Ram was king and there was peace and prosperity in the land) brought the RSS back to supporting the BJP.

For the 1991 elections, however, the BJP declared that "we will debureaucratise the economy to maximise production" (Ahuja and Paul 1992,

177) and upon election "[will] liberate the economy from the clutches of bureaucratic control" (182). The BJP wanted the state to "retreat from commercial activities and instead, concentrate on basic functions such as maintain law and order, justice, welfare programme, infrastructure, etc." (181). The party also promised "a healthy investment environment so that entrepreneurs [will] find [the] domestic market more attractive and challenging" and pledged to "debureaucratise the industry, [and] cut down the plethora of controls which have mushroomed over the years and which breed corruption and dampen enterprise"; it would also "clear projects promptly and quickly" (183).

The BJP's attack on the developmental state resonated with a segment of the population in 1991 because the economic and political policies adopted by the Congress Party following the fiscal and political crisis of the 1980s had not accommodated their interests. During the late 1980s and early 1990s, the BJP began to draw support from the upper and lower middle classes belonging to the "modern" sector of the economy (Jaffrelot 1996, 432). The middle classes supported the BJP because of the political economy of Congress rule. The Jana Sangh had been able to draw on this group in a limited fashion in the 1960s as well. In that period, the Jana Sangh was electorally successful in Madhya Pradesh because of the economic policies of the Congress, particularly the Compulsory Deposit Scheme (all those who paid agricultural, income, or sales tax; salaried workers; and urban landlords had to deposit sums with the government to help the latter avert a fiscal crisis), which isolated the middle classes (174–75). The Jana Sangh exploited "discontent with Nehru's economic policy among certain sections of the middle and upper classes" (183). Why couldn't the BJP continue this line of thinking and build support for itself?

Crisis in the Developmental State

The Congress, the prime promoter of the developmental state, dominated the electoral landscape continuously from 1947 to 1967. The party's provision of transfer payments, notably subsidies to various sectors, and the generation of employment through an expansive state sector allowed it to attract the support of most social groups. This control over the state, especially in the context of soft budget constraints, made it possible for the Congress to get broad-based support. These policies, however, also gave rise to the conditions under which this coalition could no longer be held together, namely, a fiscal and political crisis.

The large coalition that the Congress had built began to come apart during the mid-1960s due to the combination of a fiscal crisis caused by a series of bad harvests and a political crisis associated with succession struggles within the Congress. The Jana Sangh was unable to capitalize on these events for a couple of reasons. First, its platform was not very different from that of the Congress: thus, the Jana Sangh lacked a distinct identity on economic matters. Second, the Congress used state resources to keep together the large multiclass coalition of supporters that had supported it (Chhibber 1995). The selective allocation of these state subsidies helped ensure support for the Congress through the mid-1980s but raised the government of India's average budgetary deficit. The deficit as a proportion of GNP in the years following the fiscal crisis (between 1970 and 1987) was more than double the average deficit in the years preceding the crisis (between 1960 and 1970). By 1990–91, these government expenditures were a major reason why the fiscal deficit of the Indian government stood at over 8 percent of GDP (*Economic Times,* 28 February 1993).

Under Indira Gandhi, the Congress Party also increased its political control over the instruments of state, and the bureaucracy and the judiciary gradually lost their independence (Rudolph and Rudolph 1987). The dominant groups in this developmental party-state were the large landlords, capitalists, and members of the political-bureaucratic complex, all of whom appropriated state resources for themselves (Bardhan 1984). Opposition to this state came from the middle classes, especially small businessmen and farmers who did not have access to the political and economic resources provided by the Congress-controlled national government. The other development associated with the Indira and Rajiv Gandhi regimes, as was observed in chapter 4, was the larger role that the national government came to play in the affairs of the states and localities, made possible by a general expansion of the role of the state and the separation of national and state elections.

The middle classes were mobilized by the BJP, which tapped into their discontent by advocating a reduced role for the state in the economy.[7] The BJP's laissez-faire program allowed it to capture the political and economic right on the political spectrum. Unlike 1967, when there was a party, the Swatantra, on the economic right, the BJP occupied that position exclusively in 1991. Coincidentally, in 1991 the BJP managed to draw a proportion of votes similar to what the Jana Sangh and Swatantra combined had garnered in 1967 (almost a fifth of the total votes cast). Likewise, in 1996, too, the BJP managed to garner only a fifth of the total votes cast. In 1998 the proportion of votes received by the BJP reached a quarter.

The Social Basis of Support for the BJP: 1960s and 1990s

By advocating less state intervention, the BJP was able to attract the support of the middle class, which in 1991 was more likely to support the BJP than the Congress, especially when compared with 1967. The 1967 election had been preceded by a period of infighting in the Congress, a war with Pakistan in 1965, a series of bad harvests, and a fiscal crisis, which had led to a devaluation of the rupee. The 1991 national elections followed a period of disarray within the Congress organization and perhaps the most serious fiscal crisis the government of India had faced.

As the results in table 28 indicate, the vote for the erstwhile Jana Sangh (in contrast to the Congress) in 1967 was not influenced by respondents' occupations when controlling for other factors.[8] The variable that was most likely to influence the decision to vote for the Jana Sangh in 1967 was caste, with members of the forward castes more likely to vote for the party. In addition, those belonging to the preindependence generation were more likely to vote for the Jana Sangh. Additionally, the Jana Sangh was also clearly a regional party. The state a respondent lived in exercised an independent and significant influence on his or her support for the party. None of the other variables—such as urban residence, educational level, or occupation—helped discriminate Jana Sangh voters from those of the Congress Party.

By the time of the 1991 election study, the political picture had changed. The 1991 postelection study asked more direct questions about respondents' religious practices and attitudes. For instance, they were queried about whether they had friends, acquaintances, or relatives of other religions. The assumption was that, if an individual had such contacts, that person was less likely to be "communal," that is, against other religions. Respondents' religiosity was determined by asking them how often they prayed, went to temple, and attended religious meetings.

As the results presented in table 29 suggest, occupation is significant in determining whether an individual votes for the BJP or the Congress. The religiosity of a voter does not have a significant impact on the vote for the BJP. Religiosity, however, did distinguish BJP activists from those of other parties. The difference between the elite and the masses on this score is consonant with the observation that elites often take more extreme positions than those of other voters. Whether an individual knew someone from another religion did affect a respondent's decision to vote for the BJP. Caste was still important, with forward caste voters more likely to vote for the BJP.

TABLE 28.   The Social Basis of Support for the Jana Sangh, 1967

Variable	Coefficient	Standard Error
Caste	−0.2752*	0.1178
Education level	−0.191	0.3252
Economic status	−0.4392	0.2962
Age	0.0472	0.0894
Preindependence cohort	−1.1631*	0.5382
Rural/urban	0.6761	0.4235
Hindi heartland	−3.0206*	0.6577
Occupation	0.5556	0.6251
Constant	4.571	1.4949

Source: 1967 postelection survey
*Significant at 0.01
−2 log likelihood = 306.281
87.99 percent predicted
N = 457

TABLE 29.   The Social Basis of Support for the BJP, 1991 (logistic regression)

Variable	Coefficient	Standard Error
Caste	−0.3128*	0.048
Education level	−0.0076	0.104
Economic status	0.0642	0.061
Age	−0.4434*	0.1317
Religiosity	−0.093	0.0654
Know people from other religions	0.2251*	0.0888
Hindi heartland	0.2484*	0.1242
Rural/urban	0.1336	0.0641
Occupation	0.4946*	0.1763
Constant	−0.7032*	0.3582

Source: 1991 postelection survey
*Significant at 0.05
−2 log likelihood = 1,799.093
64.84 percent predicted
N = 1,425

There were two other important shifts from 1967 to 1991 in determining who transferred their support from the Congress Party to the BJP. First, the residence of the respondent became more critical, with more urban respondents likely to vote for the BJP in 1991 than was the case in 1967. More important, however, was the fact that respondents in what may be considered middle-class occupations were more likely to support the BJP than the Congress. The support of these groups, which have also grown in size as the country has become more urban and industrial, may also explain why the BJP has become more electorally competitive. Some of this support was due to the fact that Rajiv Gandhi had raised the hopes of the middle classes by promising economic and political changes he did not deliver (Weiner 1987).[9]

Religious Nationalism and the BJP

The data presented in this chapter suggest a clear class basis to support for the BJP rooted in electoral competition over state policy. This argument runs somewhat counter to claims that it is religious nationalism that lies at the core of the BJP's electoral success. The viability of the thesis presented in this chapter, relative to the religious nationalism plank, was tested using a 1993 mass survey conducted in conjunction with the elite survey of 1993. The focus of this survey was Indian secularism and the attitudes of Hindus and Muslims toward each other and toward key political questions. An analysis of the data reveals that the class thesis holds its own even when controlling for attitudes toward the nature of the Indian state. Respondents were asked whether they thought one owed loyalty to one's religion or the country; whether India was a Hindu state or not; and whether the government preferred Muslims and backward castes. Controlling for these variables, as well as age, sex, place of residence (city or village and state), respondents who were better educated and had a higher income were more likely to vote for the BJP. The estimates of the coefficients, based on a logistic regression analysis, for whether India is a Hindu state and owing primary responsibility to one's religion were also significant. In other words, the religious nationalism thesis holds it own, but the influence of class on who supports the BJP is still positive and significant.

The coefficients on education (0.42) and income (0.62) were significant at the 0.05 level, as was the coefficient on whether India should be a Hindu state or not (0.78). The logistic regression correctly predicted 79.2 percent of the cases with a log likelihood of 534.095. The analysis, based on 562 cases, provides clear evidence that those who are better educated and have higher incomes are more likely to vote for the BJP even when controlling for a variable (whether India should be a Hindu state or not) approximating religious nationalism.

1996—Does the Pattern Persist?

Continued middle-class support for the BJP is evident from an analysis of data drawn from a 1996 postelection survey. In addition to demographic variables such as gender, educational level, caste (backward or forward), age, income, and whether a respondent resided in the Hindi heartland (the region of the country where a version of Hindi was widely understood and spoken) or not, respondents were asked to classify their occupations. Those who said they belonged to white-collar occupations were distinguished from others who were either in blue-collar or agricultural work. Consistent with the explanation provided above, the expectation is that white-collar respondents would be more likely to vote for the BJP.

Three key attitudinal variables were included in the model. The first was whether an individual favored greater or lesser ownership of business by the government, under the assumption that those who favored greater individual ownership would vote for the BJP. The second was whether an individual was favorably inclined toward having Muslims as neighbors; assuming that those who did not want Muslims as neighbors would be likely to vote for the BJP, given its Hindu orientation. A final variable included in the model was the extent of confidence in the government in Delhi. This variable is important for a number of reasons. First, the government in power at the center before the 1996 elections was the Congress. Second, since the regime of Indira Gandhi the central government had come to play an even larger role in the economy and the national government had become more closely identified with the political party in power.[10] Third, as noted in chapter 4, the separation of national and state elections made the policies of the national government a focus of voter preference. The expectation was that those who expressed less confidence in the national government were more likely to vote for the BJP.

The dependent variable in the regression (see table 30) is whether a voter preferred the BJP to any other political party. The results support of a number of key hypotheses on who votes for the BJP, namely, the forward castes and those who do not want Muslims as neighbors. In 1996, the BJP still continued to draw more support from those in white-collar occupations. Further, those who prefer individual to state ownership of business are more likely to vote for the BJP. Finally, the degree of confidence in the national government also influences whether a respondent voted for the BJP, with those who had less confidence in the national government opting for the BJP.

This chapter has suggested that the electoral success of the religious party in India can be understood only in the context of party politics and the policies of the developmental state. The validity of this argument is bolstered by the lack of evidence to suggest that Indians—whether Hindus or Muslims—are becoming more religious or that there is increased religious conflict in the localities. Since there is little evidence that Hindus are becoming more religious, an explanation for the rise of the BJP as a powerful electoral force cannot hinge on asserting that the BJP mobilizes only those who are religious. Instead, the success of the party is ultimately attributable to its ability to mobilize those groups whose interests were no longer represented by the Congress such as the middle and upper classes and those working in the private sector. The BJP was able to mobilize these groups because of the policies adopted by the Congress-led developmental state. The policies formulated by the developmental state—most

TABLE 30.   Profile of BJP Support in the 1996 Elections (logistic regression)

Variable	Coefficient	Standard Error
Gender	–0.169	0.179
Educational level	0.009	0.032
Age	0.002	0.007
Family income	–0.766*	0.037
Private or government ownership	–0.053*	0.024
Confidence in Central Government	0.296*	0.085
Occupation		
White collar	0.309*	0.139
Others	–0.330*	0.129
Caste: forward or backward	–0.634*	0.166
Muslims acceptable as neighbors	–0.519*	0.158
Constant	0.981	0.647

Source: 1996 World Values survey
*Significant at 0.05
–2 log likelihood = 1,102.2779
71.32 percent predicted
N = 876

notably secularism and economic intervention—provided an opportunity for the BJP to build coalitions between religious groups and the middle classes. The policy responses of the developmental state to fiscal and political crises provided the catalyst for elites of religious parties to act as brokers and bring together religious groups and laissez-faire economic interests to form a powerful electoral force. Unlike the Congress, however, the BJP is constrained by its relationship with the RSS. While the latter ensures a minimal level of support for the BJP, it also prevents the party from reneging completely on its emphasis on Hinduism. Since a fair proportion of support for the party is built around state policy and the policy positions of other parties, support for the BJP is necessarily fluid.

Chapter 8

The Centrality of Parties to Indian Politics: The Politics of Economic Reform and Collective Violence

The emergence of links between social cleavages and party systems in India can be attributed to electoral competition over the policies of an activist state in the absence of associational life. Political parties in India were able to exercise this influence because in the absence of associational life they provide a key link between state and society. As a result, political parties have come to play a disproportionately large role in Indian political life. This centrality of political parties not only offers a different interpretation for the Congress Party's electoral decline but it also has clear implications for the path that economic reform, which India undertook in 1991, would take. Furthermore, the centrality of parties provides a link between collective violence and the democratic process in India.

This chapter begins with the observation that numerous studies of Indian politics have pointed to the role played by political parties in influencing outcomes in diverse areas such as social and economic policy and ethnic conflict. Most of this literature, however, does not ask why parties have come to play such a prominent role in Indian political life. After offering an answer to the question of why parties are so central, the chapter discusses the influence of party centrality on the electoral decline of the Congress, examines the nature and extent of economic reform, and offers an explanation for the coexistence of democracy and collective violence.

Party Centrality

Diverse analysts have noted that political parties are central to such facets of Indian political life as the problem of governability, ethnic conflict and separatist movements, the implementation of economic policy, and theoretical conceptualizations of the nature of the Indian state and Indian democracy.

Kohli (1990) links the crisis of governability in India to the organizational decline of the Congress. As the Congress atrophied organizationally, politicians found it increasingly difficult to reach a consensus. Problems of governability emerged as policy making became more complex. These problems were compounded by the "control of the state . . . [becoming] the goal for the competitive energies of many. . . . [I]n the absence of effective mediating institutions like parties, rapid politicization typically exacerbate[d] problems of governability" (30). Kohli quite correctly emphasizes assessing the role of political parties in discussing problems of governability in India but does not ask why politics, especially as it is expressed through political parties, is so critical.

Parties have been cited as the causes of caste and ethnic conflict. Brass (1990) argues that "issues of political control at both the local level and between the center and the states . . . affect the course of ethnic conflicts." Moreover, "shifting political alignments at the local level and the national level have interpenetrated and profoundly affected the formation of and disintegration of ethnic coalitions and the course of ethnic conflicts in the states and localities of the country" (205).

The emergence of separatist movements in Assam and Punjab has been attributed to party politics. In Assam, Dasgupta (1988) argues, the movement was concerned with "the control of resources within the state and access to national resources by those who consider themselves authentic Assamese" (154). The Assamese movement, especially after 1972, was led by "students, professionals and literary people" (159). Politicians in Assam, especially Congress politicians, used the leverage of the national government to pursue divisive policies. When Congress was unable to absorb these different interests, the party lost power, and group conflict spilled out into the open. The crisis in Punjab in the 1980s is similarly attributed to Congress Party politics by Brass (1988), who argues that "party politics . . . normally tended to moderate Hindu-Sikh political polarization and to work against the entrenchment of communal divisions" (180). Congress politics ended up disrupting this pattern. The Congress Party's electoral decline in the aftermath of the 1977 elections led the party to pursue policies that divided the Akali Dal and ultimately led to political violence in Punjab (Wallace 1988; Brass 1988).

Party politics and the changing nature of the party system also have direct consequences for the implementation of economic and social policy in India. Increased electoral competition has made it difficult for the central government to reduce budgetary deficits caused by excessive government loans and subsidies (Chhibber 1995). At the state level, the emergence of multiparty coalition governments has similarly resulted in larger budgetary deficits (Dutta 1996). These deficit-financed expenditures crowd out public investment in the infrastructure as well as private investments, both of which are key to further economic development. The success of antipoverty programs in West Bengal has been tied by Kohli (1987) and Echeverri-Ghent (1993) to the role played by political parties, particularly the Communist Party of India (Marxist). Likewise, Mitra (1992) notes that, in contrast to class models, the "allocation of developmental benefits in the local political arena is not the result of social dominance but is the outcome of a complex process based on bargaining and political competition" (410). Basu (1992) shows how women's issues in West Bengal were made subservient to the political and electoral considerations of the CPI(M). Taken together, these observations support the claim that party politics has penetrated many spheres of social and economic life in India.

Discussions of the nature of the Indian state and Indian democracy also rely on the centrality of party. Neo-Marxist theorists of the postcolonial state have stressed the importance of the party in overdeveloped states where state structures are far more developed because of their colonial legacies (Alavi 1973). Bardhan (1984) proposed understanding economic development in India and the Indian state in terms of the power wielded, among others, by the political-bureaucratic nexus. Lijphart's (1996) discussion of the successes and failures of consociationalism in India focuses solely on compromises reached among party elites.

What is striking about all these explanations is that diverse phenomena such as economic policy, ethnic conflict, and the problem of governability are all attributed to party politics. What is missing from most analyses, however, is *why political parties play such a pivotal role in political and economic developments*. The key role played by political parties in India is intriguing because political parties in other democracies are seen as at best relevant, but mostly ineffectual, in influencing policy outcomes, especially in the areas of economic and social policy (and much less as far as issues of governability are concerned). Corporatists argue that in many policy areas, such as the realms of macroeconomics and social welfare, bargaining among interest groups has been the primary mechanism for setting policy (Lehmbruch and Schmitter 1982). Political parties and their electoral considerations were of limited significance in this process. In a similar vein, Gourevitch (1986) points to the key role played by coalitions of major socioeconomic blocs in determining public policy. In this scheme, parties or party systems do not have a major role to play in the construction of public policy. Hibbs (1987) tried to resurrect a role for political parties in determining policy outcomes, especially among social-democratic parties. Research on the OECD countries has, however, shown that even in the context of rational expectations the ability of parties to affect economic policy is at best temporary (Alesina 1987, 1989; Alesina, Cohen, and Roubini 1992; Alesina and Roubini 1992). Social policy is also increasingly seen as resulting from corporatist bargains between labor and capital, which are mostly unrelated to the actual workings of party politics (Berger 1981). Putnam (1993), in a study of political and economic development in Italy, places social capital, not political parties, at the center of his analysis. Mainwaring and Scully (1995) observe that political parties have not been especially salient in parts of Latin America, whereas the power of the bureaucracy in Japan is well documented (Chalmers-Johnson 1991).

A survey of the analysis of Indian politics, however, yields a different result. If anything, political parties are seen to play a more important role now than ever before, influencing everything from social policy (such as antipoverty programs and women's issues) to economic programs and political conflict (ethnic and caste conflict as well as religious divisions). Political parties are central to Indian political and economic life because in the absence of associational life and the presence of an activist state they came to provide one key link between state and society. Placing political parties at the center of political life, as a preeminent link between state and society, also enables one to develop an understanding of the electoral decline of the Congress Party and the nature and extent of economic reform and to hazard an answer to a key paradox of Indian democracy: the coexistence of collective violence and democratic governance.

Explaining Changes in Indian Party Politics

Contemporary accounts of changes in the Indian party system have focused on the electoral decline of the Congress party and the end of the Congress system. The party's electoral success over the years has been attributed to its ability to represent—and, more importantly, contain—the various social divisions that pervade Indian society through its centrist policies (Kothari 1964; Manor 1964; Rudolph 1987). Not surprisingly, then, explanations of the party's decline have focused on why the Congress could no longer contain within its fold the various social divisions that characterize Indian society and hence was no longer viable. The answers offered have focused on reasons internal to the Congress's organization, Congress's relationship to the state, and the influence of social forces such as religion and caste.

Consistent with explanations of party decline in other contexts, a set of answers rooted in reasons internal to political parties has been offered to this question.[1] These explanations include attributing the inability of Congress to hold its "catchall" coalition together to the organizational decay of the Congress and the excessive influence of its national leaders, particularly Indira Gandhi.[2] The "organizational" argument stresses the absence of intraparty elections since 1972 as a main cause for the Congress's decline. The absence of intraparty elections and the preeminent role played by the leader led to the erosion of an organizational base that had been seen as key to the earlier electoral success of the party. While the absence of organizational elections and the quirks of individual leaders do seem to have prevented a viable Congress response to emerging electoral challenges at times, these accounts do not fully explain the emergence of challenges to the Congress Party. Further, upon closer examination Congress appears not to have been a well-organized political party even in the period of one-party dominance (see chapter 3).

The relationship between organization and electoral success is tenuous as well. Political parties that have succeeded Congress—the Telugu Desam in Andhra Pradesh, the All-India Anna Dravida Munnetra Kazhgam in Tamil Nadu, the Samajwadi Party in Uttar Pradesh, the Janata Dal in Bihar—do not have well-established party organizations. Kohli's description of local politics likewise points to the poor organization of the major competing parties in cities such as Belgaum (1990). The two best organized parties in India, the Bharatiya Janata Party and the Communist Party of India (Marxist), have enjoyed only limited electoral success during most of the period since independence. Insofar as many political parties in India are electorally successful despite little or no organization, one must question whether the Congress Party's electoral decline can really be attributed to organizational decline.

Related explanations have stressed the subservience of the party to the prime minister as being central to the decline of the party. As the party came to be dominated by one person, Indira Gandhi, she sought to make personal political survival coincident with the fortunes of the party (Kochanek 1976; Hart 1976). Regional and local leaders whose mobilizational skills Congress depended on were sidelined. No opposition was brooked within the party, and, according to this explanation, the open intraparty competition that had characterized the party in the Nehru era, and was ostensibly central to Congress's electoral dominance, was destroyed.

Can centralization of authority within the party explain its electoral decline? It has been generally acknowledged that Indira Gandhi was overwhelmingly motivated by the desire to retain power. If reelection, which is necessary for retaining power, was Indira Gandhi's most important concern, why did she continue to pursue policies, such as destroying the Congress's organization, that would lead to electoral suicide? Further, if leadership is so critical to party decline, why is Congress's decline less noticeable in some states than in others? In Bihar and Uttar Pradesh, the party is literally a shadow of its former self, whereas in other states such as Maharashtra, Andhra Pradesh, and Orissa it still has a significant electoral presence. Moreover, as Kohli (1994) points out, centralization is not limited to Congress or the national leaders within the Congress Party. State chief ministers also centralize power regardless of their party. The electoral decline of the Congress thus cannot be seen as resulting from the overcentralization of power within the party or the erratic actions of prime ministers or chief ministers alone. The reasons for its decline must be sought elsewhere.

The party's control over the state offers perhaps a more satisfying account of its decline. Extensive political corruption in India suggests that politicians are most interested in lining their pockets and hence are not as concerned with voter demands as they should be. Voters have tended, as a result, to punish ruling parties. This explanation has merit as a description of corruption itself but cannot account completely for regional and national variations in party decline. It fails to explain why Congress has been completely obliterated in some states but not in others, given that there is little evidence that the degree of nonperformance by parties or corruption varies by state. A corruption- or performance-based account of Congress's decline is not sufficient to account for the BJP's position as the leading national party or the emergence of state-specific party systems.

The Congress Party's electoral decline, it has been argued in the preceding chapters, may be understood by placing electoral competition within the context of state-society relations, especially the ability of political parties to forge links between social groups and party systems. As these links emerged they had the largest impact on the ability of the Congress Party to continue its catchall politics, a politics that had been critical to its electoral dominance.

The argument offered in this book provides an alternative explanation for the electoral decline of the Congress Party. The Congress Party had built support for itself by pursuing catchall politics, a catchall politics helped along by the absence of associational life. This mode of mobilizing support for the Congress Party could be sustained as long as competing political parties could not put together an alternative way of organizing political support. Once other political parties could divide society differently (the most effective way of doing this was through state policy as we saw in chapter 6), the Congress Party found it difficult to defend its catchall politics.

In addition to the electoral decline of the Congress and the emergence of a cleavage-based party system, contemporary Indian politics is marked by an increased turnout in state-level elections. Mobilization and turnout have increased for state elections since 1991 (Yadav 1996). This development is understandable when a catchall party is replaced by political parties rooted in social cleavages. As the catchall party begins to lose support, other parties begin to mobilize support more actively. As ethnically based political parties become politically salient, they, unlike the Congress, take policy positions closer to the interests of a particular group. For instance, in Uttar Pradesh the positions adopted by the BJP, SP, and BSP are closer to the preferences of the forward, backward, and scheduled castes, respectively, than the centrist position of the Congress Party. As political parties closer to voters' policy preferences become political contenders, voters are more likely to draw benefits when their party comes to power. As a result, turnout goes up. With increasing power in the hands of state governments and a weakening of the central government's authority, turnout for state assembly elections increases; this trend is most noticeable after 1991.

It is also conceivable that the absence of associational life may account for the low rates of incumbency in India. Most incumbents who run for reelection are not returned to Parliament, or even the state assembly, in the next election (incumbency rates in India are around 25 percent). The low incumbency rate may be due to the absence of associations, which can play a key role in assisting an incumbent's reelection efforts. Associations help mobilize voters by defining issues that are salient to the voters. In political societies where associational life is weak, candidates and parties have to mobilize voters directly. Since candidates and parties are unable to reach every individual voter directly they remain vulnerable to better mobilization by an opponent. The influence of interest groups on incumbency rates is clearest in the United States, where increases in

184 Democracy without Associations

incumbency rates, after World War II, were accompanied by greater activity by interest groups.

Political Parties and Economic Reform: India

The current phase of economic reform in India began in 1991–92 when the government faced a fiscal crisis: a serious credit squeeze, a sharp drop in foreign exchange reserves, 12 percent inflation, a major reduction in foreign lending, and fiscal deficits. As a result, GDP growth dropped to 0.8 percent. Recovery measures were instituted, aided by government policies liberalizing the economy. As a consequence, the balance of payments was improved, credit was reestablished, the fiscal deficit was reduced, and the economy was restabilized. The government introduced a variety of measures to open up the economy, deregulating foreign trade to some extent, reducing tariffs, and welcoming new investments, foreign and domestic. A whole new regime of reforms continued to be adopted. By 1992–93, the annual GDP growth rate for India had increased to 5 percent, and it rose to more than 6 percent in succeeding years (Joshi and Little 1996, 17). With the defeat of the Rao Congress government in 1996 and the transition to the left of center United Front government, there has been an apparent slowing of the reform process, although by the end of 1996 the growth rate stood at 6.5 percent.

At first blush, this round of economic reform has been successful. The central government had tried to introduce economic reform earlier. There was a sporadic relaxation of controls under Indira Gandhi and a more concerted effort to liberalize under Rajiv Gandhi, which evoked opposition from the Congress rank and file, leftist intellectuals, the working class, and certain rural groups. This negative reaction caused Rajiv, in the late 1980s, to abandon reform policies and return to his "socialist rhetoric" (Kohli 1990, 307–38). In the end, however, there is consensus among the parties on the desirability of reform—the parties hold the same position on whether to cut government expenditures or not—namely, that there shall be no cuts.

The reason for this convergence is not difficult to fathom. The Indian party system developed in the context of a state that had decided to be the engine of the social and economic transformation of India. As the state became the focus for the distribution of resources and began to play an ever increasing role, political parties began to mobilize support around the distribution of state resources. Once the parties had gone down that route, they found it exceedingly difficult to change their distributive policies, especially in the amount of subsidies directed to food and agriculture. Most food subsidies went to the urban sector to keep the price of food low and appease the powerful agricultural lobby, whose interests were largely represented by the state-level Congress parties. Not surprisingly, in its attempts to deal with fiscal crises no central government has been able to make changes in central government expenditure patterns. Despite the government's need to reduce expenditures in the face of a fiscal crisis, the amount of food subsidies actually went up in 1991–92 (*Times of India,* 2 January 1992). The same is true of the fertilizer subsidy, where the government had to retreat from it's "more economically rational" policy pronouncements. In its first budget proposals after the 1991 elections, the Congress (I) government proposed to reduce fertilizer subsidies by Rs 4 billion by raising fertilizer prices. Facing pressure from the agricultural sector and the state parties, the government reduced its scheduled price increase from 40 to 30 percent. It also gave "total exemption from the hike in fertiliser prices to small and marginal farmers [and] offered some relief to big land owners" (*Times of India,* 2 January 1992). Opposition to fertilizer policy reform came from both Congress and non-Congress states. The Congress-led government in Karnataka, for instance, "decided to . . . sell the stock [of fertilizer] procured prior to the presentation of the Union Budget at the old rates *against* the centre's direction" (*Times of India,* 14 August 1991; emphasis added). The Karnataka government also continued to provide subsidies to the fertilizer sector. For instance, in its 1993–94 budget, the Karnataka government allocated a subsidy of Rs 260 million to complex fertilizers alone (*Deccan Herald,* 23 February 1993). Opposition to fertilizer pricing was also voiced by the Gujarat, Rajasthan, and Uttar Pradesh state governments on the grounds that it would be difficult for them to monitor these policies (*Times of India,* 14 August 1991).

A Government of India discussion paper on subsidies noted that subsidies on merit goods, such as primary education, health, etc., accounted for 0.72 percent of GDP, whereas subsidies allocated to nonmerit goods like fertilizer and food amounted to 3.79 percent of GDP in 1994–95 (Ministry of Finance, *Government Subsidies in India,* 6–7). Merit goods were also less than a third of the total subsidies allocated by state governments in 1993–94 (9). Since 1991, the beginning of the economic reform, subsidies on food have increased from Rs 2.8 billion in 1991–92 to Rs 6.06 billion in 1996–97. Similarly, fertilizer subsidies increased to Rs 7.2 billion in 1996–97 from Rs 5.2 billion in 1991–92 (20).

The weakness of the government in fiscal management is quite apparent when its finances are examined. For instance, during 1995–96 the monetized deficit was higher than in any year since 1991–92, and the conventional budget deficit had increased to 0.9 percent of GDP from 0.1 percent in 1994–95. Similarly, large revenue deficits persisted, which also altered the nature of the gross fiscal deficit. "Revenue deficit as a ratio of the gross fiscal deficit in fact increased from 31.5 per cent, on an average, during the latter half of the 'eighties to 49.8 per cent during the period 1991–95 and rose further to 52.1 per cent in 1995–96, notwithstanding the decline in revenue deficit relative to GDP to 3.1 per cent in 1995–96 (Revised Estimates) from 3.3 per cent in 1994–95" (RBI Annual Report 1997). These large deficits, especially on the revenue side, have led to severe constraints on budgeted capital expenditures, which declined, on average, from 2.8 percent of GDP during 1985–90 to 1.8 percent during 1991–95 and 1.3 percent in 1995–96.[3]

These patterns are consistent with the observation that as political parties increased their role the state and its resources became ever more the locus of political struggle, thereby transforming party politics and the economic reform process. In India, as was observed in chapter 5, the emergence of political competition was an important force behind the increase in government expenditures. Insofar as a ruling party, whether Congress or any other, uses state resources to shore up support for itself, as political parties often do in competitive electoral democracies, the resources available for development-related expenditures are reduced. In India, for instance, the redirection of resources toward subsidies affected economic growth because fewer resources were available for investment in the infrastructure. The lack of infrastructural development led to industrial stagnation beginning in the mid-1960s and lasted for about two decades. It is also hampering the government's ability to attract investment in the industrial sector, and the lack of infrastructural development is a key hindrance to India's efforts to develop.

This use of state resources to mobilize support for a political party also limits its political options. In particular, this book suggests that if a political party uses the instruments of state to mobilize support for itself in a competitive electoral environment it will be extremely difficult for the party to introduce policy reform. Any such reform, especially a rationalization of government expenditures, would require that the party modify its strategy of mobilizing support through targeted government expenditures. In the face of electoral competition, it is even more imperative for the party to maintain that support basis, thereby constraining the party's ability to undertake a radical reallocation of those resources. To do so would be to deprive itself of its primary source of support (absent a well-developed organization). Finally, political parties in India have little incentive to introduce comprehensive distributive reform given the absence of electoral competition based on parties with different ideological positions. Political parties in India, especially state-level parties, contest elections to provide supporters with access to the state. Insofar as that remains the sole concern of parties, economic rationalization of government expenditures may be long off.

As far as regulatory policies are concerned, Congress and the ruling coalitions have been able to undertake some radical measures. The major change has been that entry restrictions on industry have been eased significantly and tariffs lowered. No exit policy for these companies has yet been announced. In other words, companies (domestic and foreign) may enter the market, but once in it they are not allowed to leave. These regulatory changes, allowing easy entry, were possible because altering regulatory policies is far less politically costly for Congress, as producer groups that were most affected by entry are a smaller proportion of the total electorate than even those who may face the consequences of exit. There is some evidence that changes in the government's regulatory practices, or entry rules, are politically determined. Take the petrochemical industry, for instance. The initial policy announced by the prime minister suggested the delicensing of the industry, and the government's measures were "understood by experts to mean that no licensing was required for petrochemicals." However, the "detailed notification . . . issued by the government [a few days later] . . . added on a lot of items" that were still under the license regime (*Times of India,* 3 August 1991), ostensibly to benefit one group of industrialists over another. Changes in some regulatory policies are a direct result of electoral pressures. Take the cotton industry. In the face of rising domestic prices of cotton yarn and to increase the availability of cotton to the domestic handloom weavers, the government suspended export of cotton from India, leading to losses in market share for the industry and less foreign exchange for the country. Some industry advocates suggested that the prime minister was "trying to win some sympathy in AP [Andhra Pradesh] which has a large handloom sector" because the prime minister was going to contest an election in Andhra Pradesh in the coming months (*Times of India,* 21 September 1991).

Moreover, insofar as control over state office and the use of that office for maintaining support was the raison d'être of state parties, fiscal reform at the state level should be far more problematic. The fiscal position of the state governments has not shown improvement, especially where expenditure restraints are concerned. The Reserve Bank of India, in its annual report in 1996, pointed to the persistence of large revenue deficits, a rising interest burden, increasing distortions in the pattern of expenditures, and minuscule growth in nontax revenues in the states. Thus, "the persistence of revenue deficit and the concomitant rise in fiscal deficits would result in an outstanding debt amounting to Rs.2,43,160 crore or 19.5 per cent of GDP as at end-March 1997" (RBI Annual Report 1996).

Even as far as regulatory reform is concerned, state governments have not undertaken appropriate measures. Many industrialists have noted that at the state level there is no sign of liberalization (*India Today,* 31 July 1992). Additionally, a comprehensive study of reform in seven states completed by the National Council for Applied Economic Research (NCAER) observed that only in two states, Maharashtra and Gujarat, has liberalization made any headway (NCAER 1994).

The Paradox of the Coexistence of Collective Violence and Democracy

A long-standing paradox of Indian politics is the extent of collective violence that accompanies a vibrant democracy (Weiner 1989). An indicator of collective violence is the number of riots that take place in a given year. From 1967 to 1993, years for which data are currently available, the number of riots in the 15 largest states more than doubled, from 41,923 to 91,174, reaching a high of more than 100,000 in 1983 (fig. 17). This increase is, of course, not consistent across all states. Some, such as Bihar, Uttar Pradesh, and West Bengal, have averaged more than 10,000 riots a year, whereas other, such as Haryana, have had far fewer (fig. 18). These averages, however, conceal a lot. For most states, Andhra Pradesh, Bihar, Gujarat, Haryana, Karnataka, Kerala, Maharashtra, Madhya Pradesh, and Tamil Nadu, the number of riots over the years has increased, though with some variance as the number of riots in a year fluctuates somewhat. In Rajasthan, by contrast, the number of riots has increased almost monotonically. The number of riots in Assam has remained pretty much the same, although there was a spike in the early 1980s. The number of

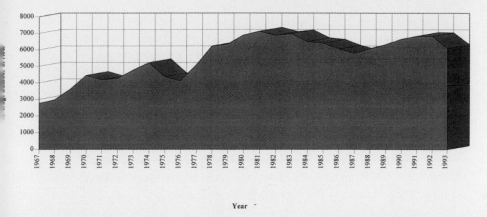

Fig. 17.   Average number of riots in the major Indian states, 1967–93.
(Data from Bureau of Police Research and Development, various issues.)

riots has gone down in Uttar Pradesh and West Bengal, with the decline in
West Bengal the most noticeable and consistent.

What explains this alteration in the number of riots? Tambiah (1990)
attributes the coexistence of democracy and collective violence to the way
mass politics is conducted in India. He observes that the "reliance on
crowds opens the door to the invention and propagation of collective slogans and collective ideologies" and as "ethnicity is the most potent ener-
gizer . . . it is also an umbrella under which personal, familial, commercial,
and other local scores are sought to be settled" (758). If this is indeed the
case, why do riots take place on some occasions and not on others, and are
these riots really local? Basu (1995) argues, in a fine-grained analysis of a
riot in the town of Bijnor in western Uttar Pradesh, that the role played by
a weak state, a state government controlled by politicians, and the electoral considerations of the BJP cannot be discarded when attempting to
account for a riot. Riots, Basu goes on to argue, are not merely local but
tied to the role played by the state and political leaders. In a similar vein,
Brass (1997) notes that the weak state is critical in explaining why some
events escalate to riots and others do not and "when full-fledged riots
develop, the local politicians and authorities are often either incompetent
or they themselves desire the riots to take place" (9).

While party politics is seen as critical in the making of individual riots,
does it have an influence on the overall level of riots in a state and across

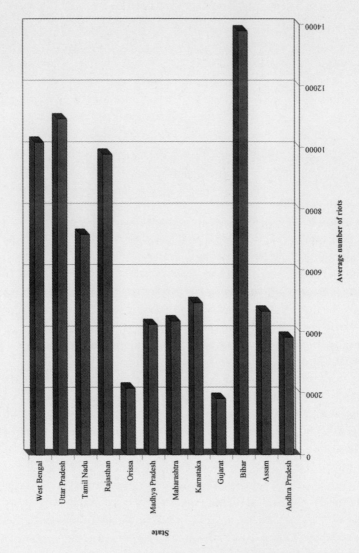

Fig. 18. Average number of riots in the major Indian states, 1967–93. (Data from Bureau of Police Research and Development, various issues.)

The Centrality of Parties to Indian Politics 191

the nation? To examine the validity of the political hypotheses concerning the reasons for riots, a regression model was estimated in which the occurrence of riots was associated with party politics, in particular cabinet instability in a state. Cabinet instability was taken as a key independent variable for two reasons. Greater cabinet instability implies that there is a breakdown of political authority in a state in that particular year.[4] Hence, the state should be weaker. Second, higher cabinet instability may also suggest that the political situation is in flux. Consequently, the various political parties and politicians in a state would seek to destabilize the existing government by raising the specter of violence and/or establishing their "authority" in a locality. In Hyderabad, for instance, riots accompanied factional conflict within the Congress ministry and ended suddenly once a new ministry was appointed (Varshney 1997, esp. 11).

The results of the analysis reported in table 31 relates the number of riots in a state to key economic, law and order, and political variables. The economic variables include both macromeasures of a state's economy and state government expenditures. Three macroeconomic indicators are used: the gross domestic product of a state attributable to registered manufacturing and agriculture and the per capita income of the state. The proportion of registered manufacturing provides a measure of the extent of industrial development in a state and is included in the regression on the

TABLE 31.   Riots in the Indian States, 1967–93 (cross-sectional time-series Poisson regression)

Variable	Coefficient	Robust Standard Error
Number of murders	0.0010930	0.0000761
State domestic product—manufacturing	0.0851102*	0.0384315
State domestic product—agriculture	0.0327070	0.0571014
State expenditures—education	0.1943265	0.2187640
State expenditures—nondevelopment	−0.1331764	0.1718727
State per capita income	−0.0012168*	0.0003515
State cabinet instability	0.0043754*	0.0017488
Constant	7.566*	1.5239160

Source: Bureau of Police Research and Development, various issues; Reserve Bank of India Bulletin, various issues; Asian Recorder, various issues
  *Significant at 0.05
  Chi-squared = 77.44
  Probability > chi-square = 0.00
  $N = 159$

assumption that more industrialized states should see a greater number of riots. More agricultural states, on the other hand, should see a lower incidence of riots. The per capita income of a state is a final macrolevel control, as richer states should be less prone to collective violence. In addition to these macrolevel variables, government expenditures are included in the analysis, and they are predictors of the preferences of the state government. Two key state expenditures are included. The first is the amount a state spends on education, on the assumption that states that spend more on education, such as Kerala, are concerned with the social upliftment of the residents of the state. The amount of nondevelopmental expenditure, on the other hand, measures the monies spent by a state on administration, police, and so on. The general law and order situation is reflected in the number of murders in a state, and the states and years in which there are more murders are the ones in which one should expect more riots. The extent of cabinet instability reflects the political situation in a state. The regression, a cross-sectional time-series random effects Poisson estimation, supports the contention that the political situation in a state is associated with the number of riots.[5] Two other variables are significant. Registered manufacturing has a positive and significant coefficient, suggesting that the number of riots is positively associated with it. The opposite holds for per capita income, which is negatively related to the number of riots.

Why is it that collective violence is linked to party politics, both inter- and intraparty competition? Two kinds of explanation may be offered, both relying on the central role played by political parties in Indian political life. The first explanation is based on the links between social cleavages and the party system, and the second focuses on the centrality of party to issues of governance.

The Indian party system has come increasingly to rest on social cleavages. This by itself is not unusual. In many parts of the world, as in Western Europe, parties are rooted in social cleavages. The clearer links between social cleavages and party systems can lead to greater collective violence. Political parties are the key link between society and the state. As the party system comes to be rooted in social cleavages, political conflict between parties translates into conflict among groups and vice versa. Second, political parties are central to governance in India, especially with the politicization of the bureaucracy and the judiciary. In times of cabinet instability and elections, it is not clear, then, who carries the authority of the state.[6] This enables the mobilization of "gangs" by political parties and local political aspirants, and violent conflict ensues.

In sum, then, the role played by political parties in providing a key link between state and society has had a series of consequences for Indian politics, consequences that extend well beyond electoral politics and party system change. Key facets of economic reform in India, especially the reform of government expenditures, are held hostage to electoral considerations. The continued persistence of riots in the various state can also be attributed to party politics.

Chapter 9

Forming Links between Social Cleavages and Party Systems: Algeria and Spain

So far we have noted that weak associational life and the large role played by a state allowed political parties to structure the relationship between social cleavages and the party system in India. While the analysis has been limited to the Indian case, the argument is applicable in a number of different settings. In Algeria, in the local elections of 1990 a religious party, the FIS, won a majority, replacing the FLN, which was not only the party that brought independence to Algeria but represented most Algerians. In Spain in the 1990s, a catchall party system, which had characterized much of Spanish politics since the transition to democracy was transformed into one rooted in social cleavages. The state plays a large and active role in the social and economic life of Algeria and Spain. Both countries are also characterized by weak associational life. Spain, for which survey data are available, also has a low level of associational life (second only to that of India). In Algeria, the one-party state ruled by the FLN prevented the emergence of associational life outside the party. In Algeria, then, the success of the FIS can be tied to the intraparty politics of the FLN and the policy positions adopted by the FIS. In Spain, too, the transformation of the party system into one rooted in social cleavages is associated with party competition. This chapter will first examine the electoral success of the religious party in Algeria and then turn its attention to the emergence of a class-based party system in Spain.

The Electoral Success of a Religious Party in Algeria

In Algeria, the response of the FLN to a fiscal crisis and the policy position adopted by the FIS are central in accounting for the electoral fortunes of the FIS. Algeria, soon after it attained independence from the French in 1962, established a state that would play a key role in the social and economic transformation of the nation. The state was controlled by the party that had brought independence—the FLN, which ushered in state-led development. The overwhelming role played by the party prevented the emergence of any autonomous associational life. Whatever associational life did exist, such as trade unions, was associated with the party-state. The FLN ruled mostly unchallenged until it announced local elections in 1991. In the aftermath of those elections, a religious party, the FIS, emerged as the largest party.

Economic development financed and regulated by the state had sustained widespread endorsement of the FLN for much of the period since independence and created interests around government expenditures and policies. The FLN's use of economic policy to garner support, however, created the possibility for an opposition party to mobilize support along economic dimensions once, facing a fiscal crisis, the FLN could no longer pursue the policies that had allowed it to retain the support of most Algerians. A sharp drop in oil prices on the international market and an accompanying fiscal crisis exacerbated conflicts over who would draw benefits from government expenditures. The FIS, seizing the opportunity that the elections afforded, managed to win over voters whose interests had been systematically ignored in the FLN's response to budgetary deficits. Thus, the middle classes deserted the FLN and supported the FIS.

An early indicator of the decline of the FLN and the appeal of the FIS came with the local elections of 1990. In that election, the first multiparty election held in Algeria, voters went to the polls to elect 48 provisional assemblies and 1,541 town councils. The FLN gained a majority in only 487 of the municipalities and 14 *wilayas,* or provincial governments, and received only 28.13 percent of the vote. The FIS emerged as the far more popular party, winning control over 853 municipalities and 32 *wilayas* and obtaining 54.25 percent of the votes cast (Iratni and Tahi 1991, 471). A similar trend was observed after the first round of parliamentary elections in December 1991. The FIS polled twice as many votes (24.5 percent) as the FLN (12.2 percent) and won 188 of the 231 seats (out of a total of 430 seats) that were decided at the end of that round. Fearing the FIS's ascension to power, the army canceled the second round of parliamentary elections and tightened its control over Algerian political life.

An important reason for the electoral success of the FIS in the local elections was the support it obtained from those of the middle class who had previously endorsed the FLN. In particular, Algerians associated with the small business sector, low-level bureaucrats and administrators, and the educated segment of the population voted for the FIS. The FIS was able to draw the support of these groups because the postcolonial settlement, of which these groups were an integral part, proved politically unviable in the context of the fiscal and political crises of the late 1980s. The FLN responded to the fiscal crisis by signaling a partial opening of the market and a downsizing of the public sector. The proposed liberalization, ironically, led to increased financial and political corruption and larger transaction costs for small businesses. Public sector reform, especially the dismantling of state-owned corporations, generated opposition from public sector employees. The elections of 1990 provided an opportunity for these groups to exit the FLN and extend their support to the FIS. Evidence that it was those associated with the small business sector, public sector employees, and the educated segments of society who supported the FIS in the 1990 election will be provided by an analysis of aggregate election returns and census data.[1]

The Period of One-Party Dominance

In Algeria, one-party rule was established soon after independence, with the FLN drawing support from most groups (Knauss 1987; Lazreg 1976; Tlemcani 1986). The petite bourgeoisie, along with a small nascent capitalist class, supported the Ben Bella regime, even though emphasis was placed on state-led development, for they benefited economically by "acquir[ing] small factories or . . . establish[ing] new industrial enterprises" through their association with "influential officials and local notables" (Bennoune 1989, 162). The support of these business groups enabled the adoption of a state-led development strategy without much organized opposition from segments of society most likely to resist expansion of the role of the state in the economy. The coup that put Boumedienne in power was a response to Ben Bella's heavy-handed treatment of the military. The coup did not lead to any other significant policy changes.

The Boumedienne regime also pursued economic policies that satisfied the interests of most segments of Algerian society. The regime continued to draw support from the small capitalist class, as it protected the interests of the private sector (Bennoune 1989, 162; Ruedy 1992). Between 1966 and 1971, 930 private enterprises were established in Algeria, compared to only 245 between 1955 and 1965 (Bennoune 1989, 168). The size of the private sector, whose interests lay in downstream industry, light industrial establishments, and internal trade (128), increased by 50 percent between 1969 and 1977 (170). As downstream industries were

dependent upon the activity of larger state enterprises, the economic interests of the capitalist class were tied to the state sector, thereby introducing
a political element into the relationship between the owners of light industrial establishments and the larger state-run enterprises. Similarly, price
and tariff controls introduced and enforced by the regime added a political element to internal trade.

Boumedienne's regime was able to pursue this strategy of state-led
industrialization in which the heavy industrial sector was controlled by the
state because of the oil revenues available to the regime in this period.
These oil revenues also enabled the FLN to draw support from other segments of society through expenditures on social services, especially education and food subsidies. In 1971, for instance, the FLN regime invested
almost 30 percent of its total revenue in education and an equal sum in
social services and infrastructural development. These disbursements
helped the party maintain its populist and egalitarian image. The populist
image of the FLN was further enhanced by the adoption of autogestion,
which established a detailed system of worker self-management and profit
sharing in each enterprise. Autogestion allowed the regime to draw the
support of the working class by giving it a key role in the nation's development (Ruedy 1992, 199). The organization of socialist management
enterprises and the relative security of employment in the state sector,
which employed many Algerians, prevented the formation of broad social
protest movements (Leca 1990, 160).

The FLN maintained its populist image among a majority of Algerians as long as it could deliver access to consumer and social goods (Lamchichi 1991, 104–5) and provide an avenue for employment through the
state sector. These expenditure-driven policies were dependent on revenues from hydrocarbon sales. The latter financed employment, paid
salaries, and permitted the import of consumer goods (212). As long as
hydrocarbon sales generated increasing revenues, the FLN could achieve
a social compromise among competing interests in Algeria: it could pursue
state-led industrialization, allow private interests to develop downstream
industry, allocate subsidies for consumer goods, and provide employment
in the state sector. Employment in the state sector was often extended
without concern about whether such a policy of hiring was economically
viable. For instance, SONATRACH (the national oil company) increased
the number of workers it employed threefold while its production levels
remained stagnant (Leca 1990). Hence, the social consensus forged by the
FLN was largely due to a redistributive economy, which could be successfully reproduced only in the period of increasing oil revenues. As long as

the consensus could be maintained, it lent credence to the FLN's claims that it represented all Algerian interests, and the FLN could be seen as a party that, though centralized, was composed of "heterogeneous groups with different outlooks" and represented "contradictory class interests" (Ruedy 1992, 262).

The Fiscal Crisis

A drop in oil prices in the early 1980s led to a revenue shortfall for the Algerian government. The volume of exports of crude petroleum, indexed with 1985 as the base year, fell from 188 in 1978 to 110 in 1982 and went no higher than 110 until 1990. Revenue from petroleum exports went from 6.03 billion dinars in 1973 to 17.8 billion and reached a high of 56.0 billion in 1981. As oil prices dropped, revenue from petroleum exports fell to 45.3 billion dinars in 1983. Yet government expenditures kept going up in this period. In 1981, the government's recurrent expenditure was 36.1 billion dinars, and in 1983, despite a shortfall in petroleum revenue, the government's recurrent expenditure rose to 50.4 billion. The increase in government expenditures continued through 1990, when they reached 84.0 billion dinars.

Given this discrepancy between revenue and expenditure, the government incurred a budgetary deficit in the 1980s. The rise of oil prices in 1973 had allowed the government financial flexibility, and it had run a small surplus in its accounts. The drop in oil prices and the lack of fiscal discipline led to a deficit in government accounts from 1986 onward (fig. 19). In this period, because of continued high levels of recurrent government expenditures, the ratio of Algeria's external debt to GNP also shot up from 32.4 percent of GNP in 1985 to almost 53 percent in 1990 (EIU Country Profile 1986/87–1991/92). The debt service ratio also increased from 26 percent in 1981 to 96.5 percent in 1988, and the national debt almost doubled from 1979 to 1987 (Bennoune 1989, 300). Not only did the national debt increase but real growth in per capita GDP fell, and during much of the five years preceding the end of the 1980s (except 1989) the Algerian economy experienced a drop in per capita GDP (fig. 20).

The FLN's Response to the Fiscal Crisis

The fiscal crisis accompanied the accession to power of Chadli Benjedid, who succeeded Boumedienne upon the latter's death in 1978. In order to deal with high levels of recurrent expenditures and lower oil revenues, the

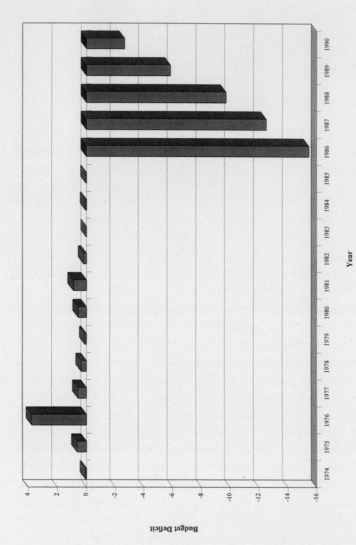

Fig. 19. The Algerian budget deficit as a proportion of government revenue, 1974–90. (Data from EIU Country Reports, various issues.)

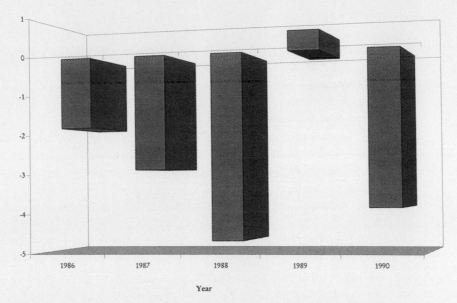

Fig. 20. Changes in Algeria's real per capita GDP, 1986–90. (Data from EIU Country Reports, various issues.)

Chadli regime introduced economic reforms in the early 1980s. The reforms, which were to overturn the centralized industry-based socialist program and reorient the economy toward market-based principles, had two important components: the encouragement of private interests and a downsizing of the large public sector firms that had come to dominate Algerian society. Despite the original intentions of the government, these reforms did not lead to less state intervention in the economy.

After 1979, private interests were indeed encouraged, but the development of these interests, as expected in politically dominated markets, was even more closely tied to the state, for "the new bourgeoisie [was], closely linked to conservative elements within the government, the party and the army" (Bennoune 1989, 268). Most members of the bourgeoisie also sought out a "powerful protector within the regime, either through marriage alliance or through association-corruption" (270). Not surprisingly, "the so-called 'liberalisation' had been accompanied by the deterioration of the political and administrative economy as a whole. Indeed, bureaucratic red tape had become so stifling that it was almost impossible for both public and private sectors to operate normally . . . [and] corruption and nepotism [became] mechanisms of the state so that private investors

[were] compelled to associate with highly placed officials" (271). Liberalization was occurring in Algeria but through an alliance of large industrialists and state actors—an alliance based on payoffs, bribes, threats, promises, and trades (Richards and Waterbury 1990, 420).

Whatever privatization took place in Algeria was also occurring firmly within the ambit of state authority. A Chamber of Commerce was created to encourage private companies, but the "revived Chamber of Commerce [was] . . . directed by the state which employ[ed] chamber officials" (EIU Country Report 1987, 4:12). Not only was the Chamber of Commerce in state hands, but every project that entailed any investment in the Algerian economy had to be approved by an official, and all private investment, even in this period of liberalization, was monitored by a government agency—the Office for the National Coordination of Private Investment (OSCIP), which was created in 1983 under the Ministry of Planning (Lamchichi 1991, 223). Given the continued regulatory role played by the state, the private sector "did not grow as rapidly as expected . . . due to the difficulty of operating in an environment dominated by massive state corporations and administrative bureaucracies" (Ruedy 1992, 234).

In addition, most of the benefits from whatever liberalization did occur were cornered by "a small coterie of businessmen and officials [who were] . . . seen to be enriching themselves on the proceeds of liberalisation" (EIU Country Report 1986, 2:12).[2] The subsequent increase in political corruption in Algeria in the 1980s (Bennoune 1989; Dillman 1992) further raised transaction costs for members of the middle classes, who were less able to capture rents compared to the large industrialists largely due to their relative lack of political influence.

Similarly, the segmentation of the public sector did not result in "decentralised decision-making" but rather led to making "the ministry the supreme arbiter and the co-ordinator of a chaotic situation. Instead of the announced decentralisation of decision-making, the restructuring of enterprises resulted in a creeping centralisation of power" (Bennoune 1989, 276). Not surprisingly, "efforts to restructure the private sector [were] popular with company managers and younger technocrats, but . . . received a less enthusiastic response from lower paid workers" (EIU Country Report 1988, 4:7). The dismantling of state corporations also led to rising unemployment and a drop in industrial output. As a result of these policy changes, low-level government workers no longer saw the FLN as a protector of their interests. The Algerian public sector split into two camps: the upper-level public sector managers who supported the reforms and a lower level of poorly paid public employees.[3]

In sum, despite government pronouncements about encouraging private enterprise, the Algerian economy was still characterized by a very large regulatory role played by the state in which the party played a central role. In the context of a fiscal crisis, the regulatory role of the state limited opportunities mostly to those with access to the state, which was either through the FLN or the military, for the state no longer had the resources necessary to support the economic interests of all classes as it had done in the past. The interests of the small business sector, because of the increasing political and financial corruption and limited avenues open to the state, were isolated by the FLN-led regime. Similarly, public sector workers were not supportive of the regime's efforts to downsize the public sector.

The Fiscal Crisis and Distributive Policies

To address the fiscal crisis, the Algerian government made changes in its expenditure patterns as well. "Drastic cuts in per capita spending on health, education and housing" were introduced (Porteous 1991, 16). These cuts, in conjunction with the inflationary pressure and curbs on imports caused by the large budgetary deficit of the government, led to large price increases, up to 40 percent in some cases (Rummel 1992, 58). The impact of inflation, curbs on imports, and subsidy cuts were felt by most of the vulnerable segments of Algerian society, despite the government's attempts to continue to provide subsidies for most items of mass consumption. In 1985, in spite of the government's commitment "to austerity . . . it was unable to cut subsidies on education, books, cereals and other staples" (EIU Country Report 1985, 1:13). In 1986, the minister of finance, A. Khellef, declared that subsidies on foodstuffs would remain at the current level and the government would not heed calls to cut them (EIU Country Report 1986, 2:11).

While the price rise affected most segments of Algerian society, members of the middle classes, especially in the salaried sector, most of whom are either government workers or employed by the small business sector, were most affected by these policy changes. Government policies on subsidy allocations, taxation, and housing all had an appreciable impact on the middle classes. First, as far as subsidies were concerned, the FLN regime reduced "across-the-board subsidies to producers and consumers

. . . in favor of targeted subsidies to exporters and to basic needs for the poorest consumers" (Pfiefer 1992, 172). In addition, in order to raise revenue in early 1990 the government introduced new taxes. The burden of these taxes was borne differentially by the middle classes. The regime introduced a .25 dinar per liter increase in the supergrade petrol price, a new tax on property between .25 and 4 percent, and higher taxes on consumer goods such as satellite dishes and alcohol (EIU Country Report 1990, 1:13).

A similar trend can be observed in the housing policy adopted by the FLN regime. In the mid-1980s, facing a housing crisis, the government decided that even if new public programs were going to be introduced access to lodging would be limited to those families whose income did not exceed a certain prespecified ceiling (Semmoud 1986, 135). This had a differential impact on the middle classes, especially among those in the salaried class whose incomes were higher than the limit set by the government, and consequently they did not have access to private property (Semmoud 1986).

The middle classes, not surprisingly, were dissatisfied with the FLN, as it became quite clear that, given the regulatory policy response of the FLN to the fiscal crisis, the regime was more concerned with meeting the interests of the large capitalists, the military, and the upper echelons of the bureaucracy. Changes in subsidy allocations, taxation rates, and housing policy further isolated the middle classes. The benefits that a few in Algeria garnered from the liberalization program and the disproportionate impact of policy changes on the middle classes also belied any claims the FLN may have made about its egalitarian nature and its role as a representative of the concerns of all Algerians. In other words, the FLN's response to the fiscal crisis created a crisis of confidence because the regime had built its reputation on a policy of dispensing public goods to all segments of Algerian society.

Reactions to economic dislocation were directed against the party because the party-state had been the chief provider of economic goods. The less ability the party had to distribute resources, the more riots over economic problems turned into reactions against the party-state and its policies. The party became the focus of discontent due to the growing sense of exasperation with arbitrary government among most Algerians and a concomitant demand for a form of government based on the rule of law (Roberts 1992, 436). Increased corruption, which had manifested itself after Boumedienne 's death, led most Algerians to become "increasingly concerned with the FLN's tightened grip on power and the pervasiveness of corruption" (Dillman 1992, 36). Many "Algerians were also repulsed by the networks of patronage that granted so many benefits to those who [had] access to them, while excluding those who have no choice but to live hopeless lives. The immediate consequence[s] of such a system were . . . complete withdrawal from and disinterest in public life . . . [and] total hatred [of] the State and its symbols" (Zoubir 1992, 88). This violence against the state undermined the ability of the FLN to project itself as the sole defender of the integrity of the Algerian nation. Consequent to the riots, segments of society that were more concerned with the problem of order—often the educated segment of society—withdrew their support for the FLN.[4]

The FIS, seizing this opportunity, promoted an economic message critical of a planned economy. The planned economy was seen as a source of oppression which retarded and discouraged private initiative (Al-Ahnaf, Botiveau, and Frégosi 1991, 156). The FIS advocated less state intervention in the economy; it affirmed its opposition to socialism, its support for the privatization of all sectors of the economy, and a return of all nationalized property (Faath 1992).[5] In the area of industry the FIS was for the promotion of small and medium-sized industry, limited state intervention, and protection of the private sector (Lamchichi 1992, 216; Al-Ahnaf, Botiveau, and Frégosi 1991, 181). In the commercial sphere, the FIS wanted to abolish the current monopolies, encourage competition, and allow private societies to enter the financial markets so that investment would be encouraged and the property of the people protected. These economic policies were pursued by the FIS with the aim of establishing a "bazaar" economy based on merchant interests (Lakehel 1989, 234). This is not to say that the FLN was against privatization but rather that its position on liberalization was far less credible because of the general political and economic crisis faced by Algerian society under its watch.

Besides advocating less state intervention, the FIS also favored the preservation of the public sector (Lamchichi 1992, 216). While this simultaneous support for the public sector and a bazaar economy has been noted to be contradictory in purely economic terms (Lamchichi 1992), the policy position of the FIS was politically rational. As public sector employees were disaffected by the FLN's policies of breaking up the public sector by adopting a policy that would preserve the public sector, those employees could be mobilized to vote for the FIS. The call for an election afforded the FIS an opportunity to mobilize the support of groups disaffected with the economic policies of the FLN.

Hence, the electoral success of the FIS was made possible by the exit of specific social groups from the FLN. These groups exited the FLN because the party pursued economic policies that met the interests of rent-seeking coalitions embedded within the party. These policies, which led to increased political and financial corruption and a selective disbursement of public expenditures, excluded the interests of the middle classes. The FIS, which was better organized through its network of mosques and its delivery of social services, also incorporated economic policies, such as less state intervention and a vision of national order, that appealed to groups whose interests were no longer protected by the FLN.

Without a doubt, the FIS's electoral success was tied to its superior organization (compared to that of other parties that advocated religion and less state intervention such as the Parti National Algérien and the Parti du Renouveau Algérien), its ability to use the network of mosques to propagate its message, and the national appeal of its leadership. Superior organization by itself, however, cannot account for the sectional basis of the FIS's success. The exit of specific groups from the FLN was necessary before the FIS's organizational skills could be translated into votes.

The Middle Classes and the FIS: 1990 Local Elections

To determine whether it was the middle classes that exited the FLN and voted for the FIS, election returns from the local Algerian elections of 1990 were analyzed in conjunction with census data. Election data were available for 216 (of the 1,526) communes distributed in almost every section of the country.[6] These communes were in two *wilaya* in the northeast, three in the northcentral region, four in the northwest, and three in the south. This distribution of communes enabled us to discern voting patterns in Berber-dominated communes, wealthy urban and coastal sectors, and rural areas in the south.

From the census data those demographic data were selected that could be expected to influence voting for either the FLN or the FIS.[7] To assess the independent impact of each of these demographic variables on the vote for the FLN and the FIS, controlling for the others, a regression model was estimated. The dependent variable was the number of seats that the FLN or the FIS won in each commune. The independent variables were log transformations of the census data on social categories. Since persons associated with the small business sector and low-level government workers were more likely to exit the FLN and vote for the FIS, these two groups were combined into one category. A similar transformation was done for persons between the ages of 25 and 34 (who were most likely to vote for the FIS) and those above 50 (who, because of their socialization during the war of independence and the years immediately afterward, we would expect to support the FLN). All other variables were kept as reported in the census. As table 32 indicates, the communes in which the FIS did significantly better than the FLN were those in which there was a high proportion of French and Arabic speakers, single people, members of the small business sector and low-level government workers, and younger people—especially persons between the ages of 25 and 35 (table 32).

The robustness of the conclusion that it was these groups that supported the FIS is reflected in the fact that in a regression estimated with the number of seats won by the FIS and the FLN as the dependent variables, and keeping the same independent variables, the signs of the regression coefficients reversed.[8] FIS support was higher where there were higher proportions of French and Arabic speakers, single people, small business sector and low-level government workers, and people between the ages of 25 and 35. The FLN did do well, as expected, in areas with more administrators and people over 50—communes in which the FIS did poorly. Interestingly, the proportion of those who were unemployed and with homes with electricity (a surrogate for urban areas) did not have a significant influence on support for either the FIS or the FLN.[9]

Middle-class support for the FIS was also noted by observers of the elections. The FIS drew support from "elements of the traditional bourgeoisie and traders" (EIU Country Report 1990, 3:12). The FLN, too, was aware of exit by the petite bourgeoisie from the party. To address this exit by the small business sector in the local elections, the FLN introduced policy changes after the elections. These changes retained government subsidies to various sectors but introduced "reforms to the commercial register" that would "allow people to enter business and stop controls on what a shopkeeper could sell" (21).[10] Similarly, support by the educated segment for the FIS was noted in *Algérie Actualité* by journalists who visited the FIS communes in coastal towns. They found that the "new APC Presidents to be moderate and well educated professionals who professed not only Islamist values but also a firm conviction that the FIS was the only way to overcome FLN mismanagement" (13) and that "Algeria's Islamists, in particular those supporting the FIS, [were] educated and, in some ways, moderate in their political views. Many are of middle class background . . ." (Entelis 1992, 78).

In Algeria, then, as in India, the electoral success of a religious party was rooted in its ability to forge a coalition between the middle classes and the religious. This coalition was viable only because the policies of the developmental state were closely associated with the ruling political parties, the FLN and the Congress. The FLN and Congress exercised great

TABLE 32.   The Social Basis of Support for the Algerian FIS and FLN, 1990 (OLS estimates)

Social Group	FIS	FLN
French and Arabic speakers	2.09*	−0.87*
	(0.55)	(0.35)
Uneducated	0.23	0.15
	(0.29)	(0.19)
Urban dwellers	0.12	−0.03
	(0.18)	(0.12)
Single	1.73*	−0.83**
	(0.72)	(0.47)
Small business/low-level government	1.42*	−0.55**
	(0.51)	(0.33)
Over 50	−6.88*	2.94*
	(1.06)	(0.68)
Age 25–35	4.00*	−0.71
	(1.38)	(0.89)
Administrators	−1.07	0.59**
	(0.50)	(0.32)
Constant	−12.42*	−0.22
	(2.69)	(1.73)
Regression Statistics		
Adjusted R^2	0.57	0.19
Standard error	2.25	1.45
F	36.48	7.13
Significance of F	0.00	0.00
$N = 212$		

Source: El Moudjahid, 19–27 June 1990; Algeria 1977.

Note: Figures are unstandardized regression coefficients; standard errors are in parentheses. The estimates were derived from separate regressions, one with the number of seats won by the FIS as the dependent variable and the other with the number of seats won by the FLN as the dependent variable. The independent variables are log transformations of the number of people in the specified social group residing in a commune.

*Significant at 0.05   **Significant at 0.1

influence over state policy. Both parties were coterminous with the state because historically both had projected themselves as the parties that *were* the nation and both were central in linking state to society. In Spain, too, where the socialists projected themselves as the national party, party centrality was key in accounting for the emergence of a cleavage-based party system in the 1990s.

Social Cleavages and the Party System in Spain

Spain began its transition to democracy in the context of a state that played a large role in the social and economic life of most Spaniards and the virtual absence of associational life. In the absence of these associations, politicians were able to temper the influence of social cleavages as catchall parties dominated the electoral landscape. Social cleavages have never been seen as principal determinants of the vote in Spain (Barnes et al. 1985; Caciagli 1986; Gunther et al. 1986; Linz and Montero 1986; Gunther 1991; Justel 1992; Gunther and Montero 1994). The weak link between social divisions and political parties was attributed mostly to the absence of associational life that allowed parties to develop and sustain "catchall" electoral strategies (McDonough et. al. 1988). The Unión de Centro Democrático (UCD) and the Partido Socialista Obrero Español (PSOE) drew support across most social divisions (Caciagli 1986; Gunther et al. 1986; Puhle 1986; Tezanos 1989).[11] Studies of the party system in this period consistently noted that social class and other variables that measure social differences had almost no influence on the vote.[12] Analysis of the 1979 survey data displayed that only two "social cleavages were significantly related to voting behavior—trade union membership and religiosity" (Gunther, 1991, p. 51). None of the other social cleavages were considered to be significant in structuring party politics in Spain. Gunther noted that "the social bases of partisanship [were] weak and (for all parties except the AP) declining in importance between 1979 and 1982" (1991, 50) "and the social profile of PSOE support hardly differed from that of the rest of society" (Puhle 1986, 325). Analyses of the 1986 and 1989 elections further corroborated the view that social cleavages could not explain voting patterns; Justel (1992, 54) observes that social class in particular did not have any statistical significance in explaining the vote for different political parties.

By 1992, as Chhibber and Torcal (1997) note, the PSOE no longer drew support across different social strata and social class had become salient in defining electoral support for the party. Table 33 displays the results of a logistic regression model drawn from a survey conducted immediately after the 1996 elections, in conjunction with the World Values Survey, in which social status is the key independent variable. The dependent variable is whether a respondent voted for the PSOE (1) or voted for the PP (0). The most relevant finding of this table is the significant influence of social class on vote for either the PSOE or the PP, even when controlling for a number of variables such as ideology, religiosity (a measure of church attendance that varies from more frequent to no attendance), occupation (a nominal variable included in the model as a categorical variable), and habitat (an ordinal variable that reports the size of the town a respondent lived in). Age, sex, religiosity, and the wealth of a province are sociodemographic variables that do not appear to have a statistically significant influence on voting for either party. The results of this regression clearly demonstrate that social class is significant in defining support for the PSOE. The heterogeneous social composition of support that characterized the PSOE appears to have disappeared (table 33).

Why has a catchall party system, which characterized Spanish electoral politics for much of the period since the transition to democracy, transformed itself into a cleavage-based party system. The emergence of class as a salient factor is endogenous to party politics and the economic and fiscal policies adopted by the PSOE government. In contrast to the early and mid-1980s, the programmatic positions adopted by the two main parties on economic and fiscal policy since 1989 have differed quite substantially. These differences were also exacerbated by the distributive policies implemented by the socialist government, which clearly favored some segments of society over others. These two factors led to a clear class basis to public perceptions of the parties and the vote.

Party Economic and Social Programs

Over the last few years, the Spanish economy, especially fiscal policy and public expenditures, has emerged at the center of much of the political debate in Spain. This debate constitutes a significant shift from the debates at the end of the 1970s and the first half of the 1980s. The deep economic crisis and its most conspicuous consequence—the high rate of unemployment (21.7 percent) of the 1990s could be cited as a reason for the politicization of this issue in the 1990s. But, while unemployment was equally salient at the end of the 1970s and during the 1982 elections, political discourse in that period focused more on the modernization of the economy.

In sharp contrast, by the end of the 1980s the positions of the major parties on economic matters were clearly distinct. Interparty debate is now focused around economic concerns and the redistribution of wealth. Also, the solutions offered by the two major parties to the contemporary economic crisis differ significantly.

In 1982, the deep economic crisis did not receive as much attention as the consolidation of democracy, the territorial organization of the state, education, and the precarious situation of some public services. The programmatic orientation of both the PSOE and the Alianza Popular (AP) reflected their central concern with these issues. The strategy of the PSOE

TABLE 33.   The Social Basis of Support for the Spanish PSOE, 1996 (logistic regression estimates)

Variable	Coefficient	Standard Error
Professional	–0.0617	0.2753
White-collar worker	–0.0054	0.2713
Blue-collar worker	–0.1718	0.2107
Self-employed	–0.1457	0.3747
Retired	–0.1335	0.2712
Housewife	0.0522	0.2339
Student	0.0614	0.3086
Unemployed	0.1876	0.2365
Financial satisfaction	0.0741*	0.0394
Country run by socialists	0.1246	0.1761
Attends religious services	0.1417*	0.0439
Gender	0.2239	0.1983
Government response to poverty	–0.1219	0.1643
Size of town	0.0265	0.0404
Left-right self-placement	–1.0611*	0.0624
Age group	0.0007	0.0758
Material/postmaterial	–0.1193	0.1361
Competition good	0.0456	0.0311
Class	–0.2981*	0.0666
Confidence in government	–0.3208*	0.1231
Interaction of class and performance	–0.0172	0.0370
Constant	3.7823	0.9268

Source: 1996 World Values Survey
*Significant at 0.05
$N = 1,136$
–2 log likelihood = 950.785
86.44 percent predicted

was to resolve the crisis by advocating a general modernization of the economy (PSOE 1982, 21). The party proposed reducing inflation, maintaining the basic macroeconomic balances, reducing public debt, and promoting structural reforms. These policies were very similar to those proposed by the previous UCD government, the only difference being that the PSOE applied those policies more coherently and decisively (Maravall 1995, 121). The conservative party, then called Alianza Popular, also proposed control over the public deficit and increasing taxes. The economic concerns advocated by the AP were overshadowed, however, by conservative and religious social proposals dealing with education, family, and abortion.[13]

Between 1982 and 1986, the PSOE faced electoral competition only from a centrist party founded by former president Suarez, the Centro Democrático y Social (CDS), and the potential challenge of such "adventurous" political operations as the so-called Operacion Roca, the efforts of an important Catalan leader to form a center-liberal national political project. For the 1986 elections, the strategy of the PSOE focused on responding to these threats to its electoral dominance. The PSOE created a very ambiguous program full of vague promises but containing few specific proposals (*El País,* 1 June 1986). The central idea of the 1986 program was to continue the process of modernizing the economy and society, and the party's main political slogan was "On the Right Track" (PSOE 1986; *El País,* 21 June 1986). Only the conservatives, included in an electoral coalition called Coalición Popular (CP), provided a more elaborate economic program. The CP proposed some specific economic and fiscal measures such as a reduction in the rate of the money retained monthly for the income taxes (IRPF), lowering the fiscal burden for those with the lowest incomes, increased flexibility in the labor and finance markets, and the privatization of public companies. These economic proposals were not, however, at the core of the conservative program. Though less extreme in some of their positions, the conservatives still stressed moral issues, including support of the pro-life option, withdrawal of the pro-public education law passed by the socialists (LODE), and other concerns such as freedom of choice for doctors in hospitals. In 1986, then, economic considerations were still not at the center of the electoral campaign.

For the 1989 elections, however, party elites of both the socialist and conservative parties presented very different programs to the electorate. The PSOE paid hardly any attention to fiscal policy, which was practically reduced to two measures: fighting fiscal fraud and creating better fiscal treatment for those in the lowest income brackets. The PSOE stressed instead distributive measures such as raising retirement payments and extending unemployment insurance to a larger percentage of the unemployed (PSOE 1989; *El País,* 23 October 1989). Conservatives, on the other hand, proposed freezing all income taxes for two years and advocated a progressive decrease in the tax after this period, a reduction of the marginal tax rate in three brackets of income, reduction of public deficit by decreasing public consumption, and the privatization of some public companies. The conservatives were clearly supporting supply-side economics, with special attention paid to lowering the income tax rate and reducing public consumption (PP 1989, 58–63; *El País,* 26 October 1989). This was highlighted two days before the election when Jose Maria Aznar, a conservative leader, invited assistants at one of his political rallies "to fill in the income tax form before going to cast their ballots" (*El País,* 27 October 1989).

The conservatives, with Aznar as their new leader, also decided to present an image to the electorate of a renewed party with younger leaders. The PP dropped many of its earlier conservative concerns with social and moral matters such as abortion, family issues, and withdrawal of the education law—LODE (*El País,* 26 October 1989). The PP manifesto for the 1989 elections avoided references to family and abortion issues (PP 1989, 10–12). In 1989, then, the programs of both parties contained different sets of economic proposals, proposals that clearly contrasted with the manifestos of these parties in previous elections. The conservatives quite clearly favored a reduction in taxes, while the socialists focused upon specific redistributive measures.

Why did the socialists pursue a political strategy of moving to the left when occupation of the center had allowed them to dominate the Spanish electoral scene? The socialists changed their economic plank and stressed redistributive measures because, in the aftermath of the 1986 elections, the Izquierda Unida (IU), a leftist electoral coalition that included communists, doubled its vote share at the expense of the socialists. The IU increased its vote from 4.61 percent in 1986 to 9.23 percent in 1989, while the socialists saw their share of the vote reduced from 43.44 percent in 1986 to 40.32 percent in 1989. A serious challenge to the predominant position of the socialists also came from the unions. Politicized unions constituted growing extraparliamentary opposition to the PSOE. The increasing pressure of unions on the socialists reached its peak with the successful general strike of December 1988. The PSOE responded to this extraparliamentary pressure.

The socialist response shows that the party had to heed union demands because dominant catchall parties face dilemmas that are unique to them. Parties rooted more firmly in social cleavages know what the interests of their constituents are and advocate policies largely in consonance with the interests of their supporters. A dominant catchall party has no fixed social basis. Such parties are more likely to react to electoral and extraparliamentary pressures from many different groups, for they are not certain of retaining the support of any one group. Moreover, if a dominant catchall party loses the support of a significant segment of the population, it can no longer consider itself as catchall, a position essential to its self-image and electoral success. As the communists doubled their vote share and the trade unions struck, the socialists shifted to the left to make sure that certain social sectors did not abandon them. This shift was capitalized upon by the conservatives.

What were the reasons behind the strategic shift made by the conservatives? The conservatives in 1989 were endeavoring to deal with a series of electoral defeats that began in 1982. The PP elites realized that for them to win an election it would be necessary to capture voters located toward the center of the ideological spectrum. Attempts to capture the center focused on changing the perception of the electorate about the conservatives' ideology. The conservatives made a strategic choice to moderate their position on moral issues and stress a concrete and more liberal economic program. To meet these goals, the party forced the resignation of its leader, Manuel Fraga, who was a principal advocate of conservative positions on moral issues. In 1989, at the tenth national party congress, new party elites, led by Aznar, emerged after some years of intraparty conflict following the resignation of Fraga. These elites believed that creation of a coherent economic program would serve to end internal conflicts, stabilize the new leadership, and ensure electoral success (Gangas 1994).

The adoption of distributive policies as the centerpiece of an economic policy by the PSOE gave the PP the opportunity it needed, and the PSOE came to be clearly distinguished from the more economically conservative PP. The contrasting policies offered by both parties provided cues to the Spanish voters that the parties were pursuing clearly defined and different economic policies. By itself, perhaps this strategic shift would not have provoked identification of different sectors of the society with these parties, but the socialists also alienated the middle and upper classes and favored pensioners and the unemployed by using its control over the Spanish state to actively distribute resources to the latter.

PSOE Government Economic Policies from 1989 Onward

After 1989, the socialist government embarked upon a series of distributive measures. It raised unemployment coverage, increasing the number of beneficiaries by almost two-thirds. This reform led to an increase in the number of unemployed with total coverage—which went up from 449,000 in 1989 to 700,000 in 1992 (Instituto Nacional de Estadística 1992). This larger coverage led to a jump of almost 25 percent in government expenditures on unemployment benefits in four years. Additionally, a law was passed in Parliament to cover people who had never even made contributions to their pension funds (Law 26/1990 of 20 December 1990), and, in accordance with this law, another law (22/1991 of 28 June 1991) was approved, allocating 65 billion pesetas in credit to finance pension shortfalls. The number of citizens who received some type of pension rose from 5,942,800 in 1989 to 6,422,600 in 1992 (Instituto Nacional de Estadística 1992).

As a result, social expenditures increased dramatically in this period. The OECD estimates that there was an increase in social expenditures of over 50 percent in the three years prior to 1992—from 69.6 billion pesetas in 1988 to 119.7 billion pesetas in 1992 (from 17 to 20 percent of gross domestic product).[14] The PSOE could not meet these expenditures through budgetary deficits because of the restrictions imposed by Spain's having joined the Exchange Rate Mechanism (ERM) of the European Economic Community in 1988. To meet the requirements of the ERM— one of which was limits on budget deficits—the Spanish government acquired the extra resources by raising taxes. In 1991, the value-added tax (VAT) was raised from 12 to 13 percent and excise duties on oils and tobacco were increased. In July 1992, the government increased the VAT by an additional 2 percent, to 15 percent. The personal income tax was raised as well, by an average of 2 percent for all but the lowest categories, while the withholding tax rate also went up. To fund its social expenditures, employer social security contributions were raised from 5.2 to 6.2 percent. In addition, companies were to assume part of the sick leave payments borne by the social security system. By 1992, the public deficit had reached 5 percent of GDP, reversing the trend observed in the previous period (1985 to 1989), during which the deficit had been reduced from 6.9 to 2.7 percent. To deal with this deficit, the "tax burden on households and business was increased, public sector investment was contained and the downward trend in interest rates was reversed" (OECD 1992–93, 81–87).

The Algerian and Spanish cases have further illustrated the general applicability of the framework advanced in this book to explain contemporary trends in Indian party politics. In Algeria, the electoral success of the FIS is endogenous to party politics. The policies adopted the ruling FLN in the context of a state that played a large role in the social and economic life of Algeria set the political conditions for the rise of the FIS. Similarly, in Spain, as the governing PSOE, a catchall party, responded to electoral pressures and altered state policy, this allowed the conservative PP to mobilize support among the upper classes. This led, in turn, to the transformation of the cleavage-based party system to one rooted in specific social cleavages—class in the Spanish case.

Chapter 10

Conclusion: Rethinking Party Systems and Social Cleavages

Understanding the relationship between social cleavages and party systems has undergone a transformation since the theory was first posited by Lipset and Rokkan (1967). In its initial formulation, the links between social cleavages and party systems were seen as emerging from the national and industrial revolutions that characterized Europe in the beginning of the twentieth century. This argument, which was widely accepted, relied on a sociological determinism in which these social cleavages emerged independently of the actions of agents. In other words, once the social transformation of Western Europe had taken place the social structure that emerged almost axiomatically structured the party system.

To address the issue of agency, alternative strands of thinking emerged by asking: what is a social cleavage? Could any social category be perceived as a social cleavage or is it that only some social characteristics take on a form that can divide society? The answer to this question has taken on two broad forms: one stresses the role of organizations and the other the state. A social characteristic, it is argued, could only be transformed into a social cleavage when it developed its own independent organization (Bartolini and Mair 1990). In other words, of the many possible cleavages only those with independent organizations representing them emerge as salient in structuring the party systems. Why, however, do organizations form around some social divisions not others? Another line of thinking that sees the emergence of social cleavages as a result of intentional action posits the state, not organizations, as a source for the formation of social cleavages (Brass 1985).

States, however, are not unitary actors, and state institutions such as electoral laws are seen as playing an important role in determining which social divisions are transformed into social cleavages and which cleavages will form the basis of the party system. Electoral laws have this influence, as they determine not only the incentives faced by politicians and voters but who coordinates with whom (Cox 1997).

The argument developed in this book offers a different perspective than the current understandings of how social cleavages come to be linked to party systems. It argues that in cases in which there is weak associational life (i.e., no independent organization exists around key social characteristics) the politicization of social cleavages and their links to the party system are a consequence of electoral competition over state policy. This is especially the case when the state plays an active role in the social and economic life of a nation. At what level these cleavages form the basis of the party system, however, is indeed influenced by institutions such as electoral laws, but electoral competition over state policy is key in determining which social cleavages will form the basis of a party system. In other words, the only social cleavages that come to structure the party system are those concerned directly with state policy, but only those aspects of state policy that are the basis of electoral competition.

This explanation of the formation of links between social cleavages and party systems is thus different from current explanations of the same phenomenon. It differs from the Lipset and Rokkan formulations and Bartolini and Mair's reconceptualization of that framework in that those assessments were limited to countries with well-developed associations. The argument developed here has focused on cases in which there is weak associational life and in the process has offered a more general theory, linked to theories of the state and society, on how the nature of electoral competition can generate the links between political parties and social cleavages. At the same time, by introducing political parties as agents trying to mobilize support from voters on a set of issues, the explanation offers a more agent-based account than theories that link the state to the formation of identities. It notes that state policy may indeed be important but that the concerns of actors, such as political parties, can play an important role in the transformation of some social characteristics into social cleavages that come to structure the party system. The argument presented in this book also departs from the current emphasis on electoral laws. While acknowledging the role of electoral laws, it also suggests that some aspects of state policy can lead voters to develop cross-local preferences and that those may overshadow local concerns generated by electoral laws that require a local mobilization of voters. Hence, while electoral laws are indeed important, the role played by the state cannot be overlooked, for it can influence the extent and level of voter and candidate coordination. These claims are substantiated through a detailed examination of the emergence of cleavage-based parties in India and their comparative significance sustained by a close look at the transformation of party systems in Algeria and Spain.

India

The Indian case is instructive on the matter of how social cleavages come to structure the party system. When India adopted universal franchise for its first elections, held in 1952, the electoral system was SMSP. Indian society was at that time characterized, as it had been for a very long time, by *jatis,* social groups with clearly defined local hierarchies and rules of commensality. The SMSP electoral system requires candidates and parties to build support locally. In most constituencies, two candidates/parties draw most of the votes. As no one *jati* is numerically preponderant in any constituency and in no constituency are there only two *jatis,* to win a plurality of the vote candidates and parties have to build support across castes. At the local level, then, more than one *jati* can vote for a party, causing a party (especially Congress, which dominated the electoral scene for almost half a century) at the state level to appear as a catchall party. The Congress maintained its catchall nature by controlling the instruments of the state, a state that was seen as the engine of social and economic transformation. The absence of active associational life helped the party retain its catchall image, as there were no state or national groups that could constrain the party to adopt either statewide or national positions that would inhibit its ability to appear as a catchall party. In other SMSP systems, such as that of the United States, the presence of active associational life forces political parties to take national positions, and the two parties do not appear as catchall to their voters.

The Congress Party in India retained its electoral dominance for a multitude of reasons. Congress had a mandate as the party that had brought independence, its leaders were charismatic, and it used policy and state resources to shore up its electoral support. As the party's electoral success was not tied to its organizational strength, it did not face any imperatives to build and sustain an effective organization. The party was held together by those who controlled the executive office, and, as most financial and political power was vested in the central government, the prime minister became the undisputed authority in the party.

The role played by the state, state institutions (especially federalism), and weak associational life influenced the nature of the party system in India. While the large role played by the state and weak associational life created conditions for the dominance of a centrist party, they also generated circumstances under which cleavage-based parties, centered around state policy, could emerge. The active role played by the state had provided the central government with a large role in the economic and social life of the nation. The central government shared some of its power and authority with state governments. Local governments, on the other hand, had no autonomy and were politically and financially dependent upon the state governments. As the state governments played an important role in setting policy and in the distribution and collection of resources, the national Congress Party was less a national organization than a collection of state-level Congress parties, each of which represented interests unique to its region.

These structural features influenced the nature of party system change as they laid out the strategic possibilities for opposition parties to mobilize support. The first set of conflicts to emerge were within the Congress Party—between the state-level and national parties. This conflict became public in the early 1960s when there was a leadership crisis. The succession struggles that followed the deaths of two prime ministers led to a weakening of central authority, and the national party fell into the hands of state leaders. This limited the ability of the national party to control intraparty conflict in the states. As a result of the defections that followed, Congress suffered a serious setback in the national elections of 1967. Most of the opposition parties that emerged during this period were state specific.

The Congress, under Indira Gandhi, adopted a series of measures to address these concerns. The national elections that followed in 1971 were distinct insofar as for the first time state and national elections were separated. The electoral success of Indira Gandhi's Congress (R), not the Congress (O), also made it clear that an organization was not necessary for electoral success. The events of 1967 also made it apparent that for the national party to maintain itself in power it was important that state governments be controlled either by Congress or a party that was favorable to Congress. As a consequence, the national government increased its intervention in state politics; initiated a partisan disbursement of economic resources; and created a larger role for the state in the economic life of the nation.

After 1967, the electoral fortunes of parties rose and fell according to the shifting support they received from voters, and the predominant feature of electoral politics in this era was exit. Electoral competition did not result from the mobilization of new groups in the electoral process (there is almost no evidence to support that position) but from the defection of groups from one party to another. Congress remained competitive in many areas, but it declined completely in states such as Uttar Pradesh.

A prominent reason for the decline of the Congress in Uttar Pradesh is the emergence of a cleavage-based party system there. Congress, until 1989, was a catchall party insofar as members of the forward, backward, and scheduled castes voted for it. The adoption of the Mandal Commission report in 1990 led to a division between backward and forward castes in UP, as the various *jatis* came together under the label of either forward or backward caste. This was no doubt buttressed by the fact that there are enough forward caste voters to have an impact in Uttar Pradesh, but the mobilization efforts of political parties were the key variable in generating the cleavage basis of the party system, especially as the demand for quotas did not come from a backward caste association.

In addition to drawing the support of the forward castes, the BJP was electorally successful because it was able to forge a coalition between the middle class and religious groups. The BJP, an advocate of a mixed economy through the 1970s and Gandhian socialism in the early 1980s, emerged as an ardent critic of state intervention in 1990. This programmatic shift enabled the BJP to garner support from the middle class. The middle class was "mobilizable" because of Congress Party politics. Congress, the dominant party, was the chief architect of the development state in India. Over time, the distinction between the party and the state had become less meaningful. Congress, the party that controlled the state, limited access to the state to its supporters, the large landlords, capitalists, and the political-bureaucratic combine. By questioning the excessive "power of the state" and demonstrating a willingness to "get the state out of the economy," the BJP in 1991 drew the support of middle-class voters whose interests were no longer represented within the Congress party-state. The electoral success of the BJP hence lay not in mobilizing the "'religious" but in its ability to put together a viable coalition between religious Hindus and those disaffected by state economic policy.

In addition to the forward castes and the middle classes, those Indians who had preferences over national policy also voted for the BJP. The BJP was able to mobilize the latter because of the close association of the Congress Party with the nation-state. The Congress Party, as we observed earlier, saw itself as synonymous with the state. Over the years the distinction between the state and the party eroded to the point where one could not be distinguished from the other. This opened the door for the BJP to garner support by linking the Congress Party's policies to an alternative nationalist vision. Even though the Jana Sangh (the predecessor to the BJP) had offered a Hindu nationalist vision, it was not able to use it successfully to garner support for itself because the Congress Party and the state could be distinguished from each other. Once the Congress Party, for electoral considerations, had tied itself closely to the state, the BJP's nationalist vision had more resonance among a segment of voters insofar as particular policies, such as a common civil code, could be couched in more nationalist terms. The BJP's advocacy of a common civil code gained currency only after the Congress Party had taken a stand against a common civil code in 1985–86.

The transformation of the party system in India offers a number of comparative suggestions. First, party politics and party systems do not develop outside state structures, particularly electoral laws, federalism, and the role played by the state in the economy. Second, the relationship of social cleavages to party systems is not axiomatic, as is suggested. In nations where the state comes to play a key role and associational life is weak, parties can influence the creation of links between social cleavages and the party system. Third, parties face a unique dilemma as far as their relationship to their social bases is concerned. If a party relies on an association, as the BJP does on the RSS, it is assured of a degree of support but it cannot adopt policies counter to the interests of its social base. Catchall parties can draw support from many segments of society, but they can also lose support rapidly, as Congress did in Uttar Pradesh. Fourth, the study of party politics would be enhanced, as would that of state-society relations, if parties were placed within the state-society context and the state-society debates included a study of parties and party systems.

Algeria and Spain

The emergence of a cleavage-based party system in both Algeria and Spain can be understood, too, once we place electoral competition and party politics in the context of state-society relations. The state plays a large and active role in the social and economic lives of Algeria and Spain. Both countries are also characterized by weak associational life. In Algeria, the emergence of a cleavage-based party system after the local elections of 1990 was a direct result of the positions taken on the state's economic policy, especially on distributional issues, by the religious party—the FIS—and the governing FLN. Similarly, Spain, which had been characterized by a catchall party system from the transition of democracy to the early 1990s, developed a party system rooted in social cleavages, especially class.

This transformation occurred as a result of electoral competition between the PSOE and the PP, which was characterized by clearly different positions adopted by the parties on economic issues.

What remains unclear, however, is whether these cleavages sans organization can provide a stable basis for the party system much like the way the organized cleavages of Western Europe structured their party systems. Can electoral competition and political parties replace organizations as the basis for the formation of social cleavages? The answer to that question may depend on whether this process leads to the formation of a new identity. In the Indian case, whether the distinction between forward, backward, and scheduled castes can provide a stable basis for the party system may also rest on whether these identities, as a result of electoral competition over key facets of state policy, come to be salient organizing features of Indian society. The other question that remains unanswered is the effect on political life of a party system that makes some social divisions more salient than others. Will such a party system generate a more divisive political life than one in which social cleavages arise independent of political parties and associations representing these cleavages have an autonomous existence?

Appendixes

Appendix A

Survey Data from India Used in the Book

Year	Nature of Sample	Coverage	Sample Size	Principal Investigator
1966	Local elites	3 states: Gujarat, Maharashtra, and Uttar Pradesh	1,000	Samuel Eldersveld
1967	Party activists	All-India	1,000	CSDS
1967	Mass	All-India	2,240	CSDS
1971	Mass	All-India	4,922	CSDS
1980	Mass	All-India	3,900	CSDS
1989	Mass	6 States: Andhra Pradesh, Bihar, Madhya Pradesh, Maharashtra, Uttar Pradesh, and West Bengal	2,800	Author/OASES
1991	Mass	6 States: Andhra Pradesh, Bihar, Madhya Pradesh, Maharashtra, Uttar Pradesh, and West Benga	3,000	Author/OASES
1993	Party activists	7 States: Andhra Pradesh, Bihar, Kerala, Madhya Pradesh, Maharashtra, Uttar Pradesh, and West Bengal	600	Author/OASES
1993	Mass	Uttar Pradesh	1,000	Author/OASES
1993	Mass	7 States: Andhra Pradesh, Bihar, Kerala, Madhya Pradesh, Maharashtra, Uttar Pradesh, and West Bengal	1,000	Author/OASES
1996	Local Elites	Gujarat, Maharashtra, and Uttar Pradesh	500	Author/OASES
1996	Mass	Andhra Pradesh, Gujarat, Karnataka, Maharashtra, Uttar Pradesh, and West Bengal	2,500	Author/OASES
1996	Mass	All-India	2,000	Author/World Values Survey/ OASES

Appendix B

Central Disbursement of Resources to States

State	Years					
Andhra Pradesh	1972	1978	1980	1982	1983	
Assam	1972	1979	1980	1982	1984	
Bihar	1972	1973	1980	1983		
Gujarat	1971	1972	1973	1974	1980	
Haryana	1968	1972	1979	1982		
Karnataka	1972	1978	1980	1982		
Kerala	1970	1977	1979	1981	1982	
Madhya Pradesh	1972	1977	1980			
Maharashtra	1972	1975	1980	1982	1983	
Orissa	1972	1974	1976	1977	1980	
Punjab	1972	1983	1984			
Rajasthan	1971	1972	1973	1980	1981	
Tamil Nadu	1971	1977	1980			
Uttar Pradesh	1971	1973	1974	1976	1982	1984
West Bengal	1969	1971	1972	1977		

Appendix C

Values for Political Variable Used for Subsidy Allocation by the Center

Year	Value for EP
1951	.0000
1952	16.0000
1953	.0000
1954	.0000
1955	1.0000
1956	.0000
1957	16.0000
1958	.0000
1959	.0000
1960	1.0000
1961	1.0000
1962	16.0000
1963	.0000
1964	.0000
1965	1.0000
1966	.0000
1967	16.0000
1968	1.0000
1969	4.0000
1970	1.0000
1971	16.0000
1972	11.0000
1973	.0000
1974	2.0000
1975	1.0000
1976	.0000
1977	16.0000
1978	4.0000
1979	16.0000
1980	12.0000
1981	.0000
1982	3.0000
1983	3.0000
1984	.0000
1985	4.0000

Appendix D

Factor Analysis Statistics (varimax rotation)

Kaiser-Meyer-Olkin measure of sampling adequacy = .69809

Bartlett test of sphericity = 195.66573, significance = .00000

VARIMAX rotation 1 for extraction 1 in analysis 1 – Kaiser normalization

VARIMAX converged in three iterations

Rotated Factor Matrix:

	Factor 1	Factor 2
LAISSEZ	.84066	–.09281
RELPOLT	.09695	.68860
RELDIFF	.10486	.56741
RELTYPE	–.37922	.59042
TRADE	.85283	.13455
INDST	.90241	.06225

Factor Transformation Matrix:

	Factor 1	Factor 2
Factor 1	.99999	–.00383
Factor 2	.00383	.99999

Notes

Chapter 1

1. Vidhan Sabhas are state assemblies. There were some notable exceptions to Congress's electoral dominance in the states—the best known of which is Kerala. In 1957, the Communist Party of India came to power in Kerala. That regime lasted two years, until 1959, when president's rule was imposed on the state, and in the elections that followed, in 1960, Congress was returned to power.

2. The electoral success of the party was rooted in the "Congress system," which characterized Indian party politics for almost half a century. In its most prominent exposition, Congress was a *"party of consensus"*(Kothari 1964, 1162). The dominant party—the Congress—represented a plurality, and it was prepared to absorb groups and movements from outside the party, which thus enabled it to represent a "historical consensus . . . [and] the present consensus" (1165). The catchall and centrist nature of the Indian party system and the consensus represented by the Congress Party appear to have come undone with the electoral success of state-based, religious, and caste-based political parties.

3. The Lok Sabha is the lower house of Parliament. Congress has indeed faced electoral challenges before. In 1967, the party was unable to form a government in eight states and commanded a bare majority in the Lok Sabha. In the national elections that followed in 1971 and in the state assembly elections of 1972, Congress returned to power with overwhelming majorities nationally and in the states. In 1977, it did not win elections to the Lok Sabha and was defeated in the state elections that followed in seven states. The party was, however, able to regain its majority in Parliament as well as in most state assemblies after the elections of 1980. There is general agreement that there is little possibility that Congress would be able to repeat its performance of 1980 in any upcoming election (Gould and Ganguly 1993; Mehta 1997).

4. The Congress was out of power twice earlier. In 1977, a preelectoral coalition defeated Congress in the national elections. In 1989, Congress was the largest party in Parliament, but a coalition government, of which the BJP was an important constituent, was formed at the center.

5. The number of parties, N, is calculated using the widely accepted formula first advocated by Laakso and Taagepera (1979). N is the inverse of the Hersfindhal concentration index and is measured as $1/\Sigma p_i^2$, where p_i can be the proportion of the popular votes received by party i in an election or the proportion of seats in the legislature controlled by party i. For details on N and other mea-

sures, see Chhibber and Kollman (1998). In figure 2, the number of effective parties was calculated using the proportion of seats in the Lok Sabha won by the various parties.

6. The BJP, with 20 percent, however, got fewer votes than the Congress, which garnered 28 percent of the vote.

7. The meaning and origins of caste are a source of intense debate. In this book, two widely accepted notions of caste are used. The first is the distinction between forward, backward, and scheduled castes. The origins of this tripartite division lie in the *varna* scheme, in which there are four caste categories: brahmans (priests), *kshatriyas* (warrior-rulers), *vaishyas* (traders), and *shudras* (manual and agricultural workers in service of the other three castes). The first three are considered to be the forward castes, with *shudras* classified as the backward castes. Those outside the *varna* scheme came to be classified as the scheduled costs. A clear exposition appears in Rao and Frankel 1989. A second understanding of caste sees it as equivalent to *jatis,* which are endogamous social groups that form a important basis of local social organization.

8. This is a new development in Uttar Pradesh politics. Brass (1990, 1993a, 1993b) notes that caste is not a salient political force at the state level.

9. The mechanism through which these social cleavages come to assert themselves, however, varies and includes reasons internal to the Congress's organization, its relationship to the state, and the influence of social forces such as religion and caste.

10. Though Lipset and Rokkan's "freezing hypothesis" has been questioned (Wolinetz 1979; Maguirre 1983; Pedersen 1983; Dalton et al. 1984; Shamir 1984; Ersson and Lane 1987), it is still one of the most powerful theories for explaining patterns of electoral and party system stability in Western democracies (Bartolini and Mair 1990).

11. Although this interpretation is not as deterministic about the relationship between social cleavages and party systems, it lacks a theory of agency. From this formulation, it is not clear why, despite the presence of many social differences, only some are institutionalized as the basis of the party system.

12. Only about 2 percent of Indians are members of caste or religious associations. Chapter 3 reports associational membership in caste and religious associations in more detail.

13. The party–social cleavage model also comes up against a broadly popular interpretation of Congress's electoral success. In this framework, Congress is seen as a catchall party not rooted in a particular set of caste or class interests. The party sat at the center of Indian politics and incorporated all interests, while the opposition was confined to acting as points of pressure (Kothari 1964; Morris-Jones 1964). If this is indeed the case, then the appropriate issue to be discussed is why groups were always turning to Congress instead of supporting the opposition either singly or in a coalition. Also, if Congress could shape and reshape its coalitional basis as the single-party-dominant model suggests, Congress would not exist as a sole representative of some interests and its electoral dominance could not be attributed to its ties to particular interests.

14. Caste, insofar as it is meaningful for marriage, finds expression as *jati.* Irawati Karve (1958) linked *jati* to endogamy. The subsequent kinship of *jati* mem-

bers existed in relation to territory, with the village and the linguistic region forming the territorial boundaries in most cases. For the many meanings of *jati*, see
Chatterjee 1996, 282–84.

15. Diverse studies, such as those of Brass (1983, 1988a), Sisson (1972), and
Weiner (1962a, 1962b) have noted the local nature of voter mobilization in India.

16. It appears that the entire "state-society" debate has bypassed theorists of
political parties. Most articles in a special volume of the *Journal of Theoretical Politics* dealing with party system change did not consider either the role of the state
or the complex set of state-society relations as influencing party system change.See,
in particular, Laver 1989, Mair 1989, Reiter 1989, Smith 1989, and Strom 1989.
Even longer historical studies of party system change, such as those by Aldrich
(1995) in a book entitled "*Why Parties? The Origin and Transformation of Party
Politics in America,*" do not consider either the state or society as significant in
influencing the various transformations the American party system has undergone.
Przeworski and Sprague's (1989) treatment of electoral socialism is in a similar
vein. There are a few exceptions—notably Shefter 1994, Finegold and Skocpol
1995, and Skocpol 1995. While they do examine the influence of the state on political parties, none of them relate state structures to either the electoral fortunes of
political parties or party system change. Mueller (1993) does address the relationship between civil society, the state, and political parties when addressing party
system change, but does not provide a causal relationship between party system
change, state structures. and associational life. None of them address the influence
of secondary associations on parties and party systems.

17. Of course, institutions are established by politicians given certain constraints—either domestic or international. Once established, however, these same
institutions constrain what politicians can do.

18. Ames (1987) does make a claim for the influence of some institutional considerations, but much of the literature (e.g., Fair 1978; Fiorina 1991; Frey and
Schnieder 1988; Kohno and Nishizawa 1990; Lewis-Beck 1989; and Tufte 1978)
tends to see political parties as operating outside the constraints imposed by state
structures and social institutions.

19. Students of party organization have rarely, if ever, examined the influence
of the state on party structure. Eldersveld (1982) and Panebianco (1988) have
made important arguments about party organizations but neither examines in any
systematic way the influence of state structures on party organization. There is,
however, a vast literature on the effect of electoral laws on the nature of the party
system. Lijphart (1994) provides a comprehensive review.

20. In some cases, instead of interacting with the state, residents can withdraw
from the state. For a prescient analysis for the conditions under which this can
happen see Bates 1981.

21. For the lasting influence of religiosity on structuring the Spanish party system, see Montero 1994.

22. In cases in which associational life is well developed and associations pre-
cede parties (as with Labour in England), political parties are dependent upon
these associations, and such parties, in some instances, will even commit electoral
suicide because of their dependence on secondary associations (Tsebelis 1990). In

countries in which associational life is weak and the state does not play a major role as a policymaker, parties compete with other associations in influencing policy. When the state plays a large role and associations are well developed, parties are not as relevant in either making economic policy or politicizing social differences. The welfare states of Scandinavia are a case in point (Esping-Anderson 1985).

23. A similar kind of lacuna can be found in the literature on state-society relations. With a few exceptions, political parties are considered somewhat epiphenomenal to the major conflicts between state and society. The absence of any systematic discussion of political parties or their role in influencing state-society relations in Migdal, Kohli, and Shue (1994) is representative of the state of the debate.

24. It is important to distinguish the active state from the strong state. Just because a state comes to play an active role does not imply that the state is strong. The strength of a state is a result of a myriad of factors, of which an active role may or may not be one. It is conceivable that a state may be so active that it becomes important for society to control it, and the resulting weakness of the state may result directly from the active role ascribed to it. The argument developed in this book stresses the large role played by the state in many facets of a nation's life.

25. For the role of the state and party in the development process, especially how Congress defined the economic agenda, see Frankel 1978, Kohli 1987a, Manor 1990, Parekh 1995, and Kaviraj 1996.

26. A detailed discussion of federalism in India is in chapter 2. For fiscal federalism, see Rao and Chelliah 1991, Gulati 1987, Bagchi 1991, and Bagchi et al. 1992. A fair bit of research has also been done on political federalism. In particular, see Dua 1981, Wood 1984, Weiner 1996.

27. Details on the formation of multicaste coalitions in constituencies can be found in chapter 3.

28. Given the weakness, or absence of, associational life, associations do not compete with political parties in policy making at the national level. Not surprisingly, major policy decisions in India are also taken without interest group debates, and implementation, too, is carried out mostly through individual contacts (Kochanek 1987). Even in the best known case of society having thwarted efforts by the national government to institutionalize land reform in the 1950s and 1960s, the farmers group did not lobby in the nation's capital but managed to gain control over the electoral process within the states, obtained majorities in state assemblies, and thereby prevented the implementation of land reform. The landed elite used the party—especially the party in the state—to thwart land reform. As there are no well-established associations in India and the state came to occupy a dominant position, political party has become *the* link between state and society.

29. The importance of access to state resources and the critical role played by political parties in that process is well documented for the Indian case (Weiner 1967, Rudolph 1987, Brass 1965, 1981a, 1981b, Frankel 1978).

30. In the United States, for instance, the labor movement can force elected representatives to take their interests into consideration. These associations have influence across electoral districts, and politicians have to respond to their

demands. In India, this is not the case, and politicians face little pressure from large state or national associations.

31. Voters could either support or oppose the policy proposed by a party. If a majority supported it the other party could come to power. If, on the other hand, many voters were indifferent to the policy it would have no effect on the outcome. The trick, then, is to find an issue that will exercise most voters.

32. The Congress's multicaste coalition could also be sundered by a regional appeal—such as that made by N. T. Rama Rao when he floated the Telugu Desam Party, whose electoral success was based on his ability to convince voters that the pride of the Telugu people was at stake if the Congress continued to rule.

33. All catchall parties do not react similarly. Facing restrictions imposed on Spain by the European Exchange Rate Mechanism in the late 1980s, the governing Spanish socialists, in the Partido Socialista Obrero Español, had to make reallocation decisions regarding taxation and social spending. The socialists opted to raise taxes and continue high levels of social spending. A party of the right, the Partido Popular, capitalized on the leftward shift of the socialists and, capturing the right, managed to emerge as the largest party after the 1996 elections. The PSOE, however, is still the second largest party in the Spanish Parliament and draws significant support from the lower classes.

34. While caste is indeed a local phenomenon, caste relations vary across the Indian states. Most prominently, caste relations in parts of northern India, particularly in Uttar Pradesh and Bihar, differ from those in other states. As Frankel (1989a) notes, it is only "within this area that the twice-born castes are fully articulated and represented . . . [and] the *varna* divide between the twice-born castes and the Shudras in the Hindi heartland areas has historically demarcated a rigid social hierarchy." In the south, however, "the *varna* structure by itself could not legitimize the secular stratification of wealth and power" (6). In other words, in parts of northern India caste as a ritual phenomenon overlapped almost completely the political and economic dominance of the upper castes, whereas in southern India the ritual status of brahmans was not accompanied by either political or economic power, which often lay in the hands of lower castes.

35. The dilemma faced by Congress over the Mandal Commission and the consequences that followed in Uttar Pradesh can also be explained through a simple spatial model. As the status quo on the issue of caste was set by another party, Congress was no longer able to take the median position, a position that was central to its catchall politics. Further, the state median for Uttar Pradesh (given the large number of forward castes with significant economic strength) in this case differed from the national median (in many states the backward castes have not only a substantial majority but economic resources). This is not the case in other policy areas such as agricultural pricing and aid to the poor. In the latter, the national and state medians do not differ substantially. Congress could take a median position nationally without fear that it would compromise its median position in a particular state.

36. State policy and party politics have played an important role in making some cleavages the basis of a party system in Spain (Chhibber and Torcal 1997). This differs from the analysis of Barnes et al. (1985), Gunther (1991), and Gunther

and Montero (1994), who adopt a bottom-up approach consistent with that of Lipset and Rokkan (1967). In that framework, social cleavages emerge out of associational life, as with trade unions giving rise to social democratic or socialist parties (Przeworski and Sprague 1988).

37. Rogowski (1995) offers a similar defense of consociationalism.

Chapter 2

1. It is often remarked that the Indian Constitution has been amended too often. Since the Constitution is a policy document as well, many of the amendments deal with policy matters. Almost half of all amendments to the Constitution have been policy related. Similar trends are seen in other constitutions that have a large policy emphasis. In the United States, Alabama has a policy-directed constitution, which also has been amended often (Lutz 1995).

2. The 44th Amendment, passed in 1978, added to the above "to minimize inequality in income, status, facilities and opportunities, amongst individuals and groups."

3. There are 21 Scheduled Caste Development Corporations functioning in states with a significant proportion of scheduled castes.

4. For the active role played by the state in agricultural transformation, see Herring 1987 and Kohli 1987. Basu (1990) offers a critical analysis of both positions.

5. The state also exercises a large coercive role in Indian society (Mathur 1992). Susanne Rudolph (1987) problematizes the notion of the state, especially in its applicability to the Indian subcontinent.

6. Reliance on a network of provincial leaders was an innovation introduced by Gandhi (Brown 1994).

7. Bednar, Eskridge, and Ferejohn (1997) provide a keen discussion of the political theory of federalism.

8. The political and fiscal relationship between the center and the states has been well explored. This section merely provides a brief overview of the salient features of the institutional relationship between the center and the states.

9. Austin (1966) provides a comprehensive treatment of why the Indian Constitution looks the way it does.

10. The 16th Amendment to the Constitution (adopted in 1963) also made it clear that advocacy of secession did not have protection under freedom of expression.

11. The prime minister, who appears only in Article 74 of the Constitution as the head of the Council of Ministers, exercises this authority over the president, as the latter is required, under the Constitution, to accept the advice of the cabinet. There are, however, constitutional provisions that limit how long Parliament can legislate on behalf of a state. Regardless, this act is a powerful tool in the hands of the center, which has used it often.

12. For instance, for the 1960–61 fiscal year the center's revenue receipts from direct and indirect taxes amounted to 56 percent of the total revenue raised by all

governments, state and national, while the center's share of capital receipts was 83 percent.

13. Articles 268 and 269 are concerned with "Duties Levied by the Union but Collected and Appropriated by the States" (such as some excise duties) and "Taxes Levied as Well as Collected by the Union, but Assigned to the States within Which They are Leviable"(such as taxes levied on interstate commerce).

14. It could be said that Nehru took a total, rather than partial, view of the resources of the center and the states. As a result, the Congress leadership did not deem it necessary to institutionalize center-state financial relations in more detail.

15. For a long period (until 1985), state governments relied on overdrafts from the Reserve Bank of India as short-term ways and means advances. The Overdraft Regulation Scheme put into practice by the Reserve Bank of India has hardened the soft budget constraints that states faced earlier.

16. Manor (1995), in a discussion of the role of chief ministers, makes a similar argument, noting that states have areas of autonomous power and authority.

17. The Montague-Chelmsford reforms of 1919 made a provision for a separate "local tax list" for exclusive utilization by local governments. This was, however, abolished under the Government of India Act of 1935 following Gandhi's reorganization of the Congress Party along provincial lines. The Indian Constitution is marked by the absence of a local tax list. This is especially important since all residual powers, that is, powers not expressly attributed to a level of government, are vested in the center. Datta (1993) offers a historical discussion of the development of urban government in India.

18. Rural Development is an independent ministry today.

19. This survey was carried out as part of a cross-national study of local government. The study in India was coordinated by Samuel Eldersveld.

20. Statistically these averages are different, with a difference of means test yielding a t-value of 8.15, significant at the 0.001 level.

21. The study was carried out by the Organisation for Socio-Economic Systems (OASES), with the author as the principal investigator.

22. Three states—Maharashtra, Gujarat, and West Bengal—account for two-thirds of all rural government revenue.

23. Ten million = 1 crore.

24. Village *panchayat* revenues are dependent upon the house tax; market tax; *octroi,* or terminal, tax; water fees; and grants-in-aid from higher levels of government. *Panchayat samitis,* in the absence of property taxes, can raise money from only a few sources; they do get a percentage of the land revenue; sugar, water, and other cesses; taxes on professions; surcharges or duties on the transfer of immovable property; tolls; the pilgrim tax; and grants-in-aid (Planning Commission 1957).

25. In Rajasthan, if a budgetary proposal exceeds Rs 5,000, it has to be sanctioned by the state government.

26. This contrasts sharply with the center's allocations to the states. Between 1952 and 1985, central grants to the states comprised 14 percent of the center's total expenditures on the current account. During the same period, over a third (36 percent) of the center's capital expenditures were in the form of loans to the states

and union territories (calculated by the author from various issues of Ministry of Finance, In *Economic and Functional Classification of the Budget*).

27. West Bengal may be an exception, especially after the Communist Party of India (Marxist) [CPI(M)] came to power in 1977. Webster (1992) provides an analysis of *panchayati raj* in West Bengal and attributes the role of PRIs in development in Bengal to the CPI(M). Kohli (1989a) also looks at how the role of local government is important in West Bengal.

28. Three states, Andhra Pradesh, Karnataka, and West Bengal, did make forays into *panchayati raj* in the 1980s. In Karnataka, all functions of development at the district and lower levels were transferred to *panchayati raj* institutions and the District and Rural Development Agency (DRDA) was merged with the Zilla Parishad. These reforms were overturned, however, a few years later. West Bengal did not go as far as Karnataka and kept the DRDA outside of the scope of *panchayati raj* institutions. Andhra Pradesh did not yield powers to *panchayati raj* bodies.

Chapter 3

1. For revisions within the framework of that model, see Kothari 1970 and Joshi and Desai 1987.

2. This is important, as a dominant paradigm of the study of contemporary Indian politics has been the organizational decay of the Congress. The baseline of comparison for these studies is the organization of the party in the 1950s and 1960s when, it is assumed, that the party had a well-functioning organization.

3. Mitra (1994) suggests that democratic politics, especially electoral mobilization along the lines of caste, has played an important role in changing the extant patterns of socioeconomic dominance that characterized rural and urban India.

4. In the 1991 postelection survey, respondents were asked to identify the most important *jati* in their area. A follow-up question asked them what made that *jati* important. Fifty-one percent said it was numerical preponderance that made the *jati* important, whereas only 16 percent pointed to ritual importance, and 19 percent thought wealth was the key to the significance of the *jati*. These results suggest quite unequivocally that with the advent of democracy, numbers play the largest role in determining the importance of a *jati*.

5. Parties, too, are careful in their associations with castes. When large castes are not homogeneous and if a party is too close to one, others in the area become alienated. "Political parties gain stability only by involving all major sections of the community" (Kothari 1970, 20). Beteille (1970) makes the similar observation that "parties in their turn try to create an appeal for every major group and not merely a single group" (293).

6. Mitra (1979) provides an incisive analysis of how local political coalitions were built across castes and two parties dominated the electoral landscape in a village in Orissa.

7. Using a different measure, the mode, Goyal and Hahn (1966) also calculated the number of parties as two for the elections of 1952, 1957, and 1962 in Kerala, Madhya Pradesh, Orissa, Punjab, and West Bengal.

8. The number of parties (N) was calculated using the formula advocated by Laasko and Taagepera (1989). Unlike figure 2, N in this case was calculated using the proportion of votes received by each of the parties in every constituency, and the number in the figure represents the average number of parties in the various constituencies for each election. However, the number of parties at the national level, that is, in Parliament, is not 2. This is due, in large part, to the persistent problem of party aggregation in India, where voters express a preference for locally competitive but nationally noncompetitive parties. See Chhibber and Kollman 1998 for the detailed argument.

9. Dasgupta (1970) provides a comprehensive assessment of the politics behind language in India. Laitin (1989) offers a game-theoretic perspective on the language issue in India, with the actors being the bureaucracy and politicians.

10. M. N. Srinivas observed that "the creation of linguistic States on 1st November 1956 in most parts of the country has strengthened the barriers between them" (1958, 571).

11. On the rare occasions when the Congress tried to introduce limits to the power of state-level politicians, these measures were resisted within the party. For instance, when the Bihar Pradesh Congress Committee in 1951 passed a resolution banning future members of the legislature from accepting nomination for seats in local bodies or serving as presidents and secretaries of the Provincial and District Congress Committees (and banning presidents and secretaries of Provincial and District Congress Committees from serving as members of local bodies) the national Congress Working Committee (which consisted of many state chief ministers) decided not to approve the resolution.

12. An exception is the Confederation of Indian Industry (CII), which emerged as a powerful lobbying agency in the 1990s.

13. For the many meanings of caste, see Kolenda 1986. The relationship between the caste system and politics is also discussed in Raheja 1988.

14. The Andhra Pradesh High Court had declared the government's order unconstitutional.

15. It could be asked why a *jati* is not considered equivalent to an association. An association, by definition, is a group that comes together to advance a common cause or interest. Similarly situated people do have the potential of forming an association, but whether they do or not does not follow from this occupation of similar positions. For example, working in a factory makes one a worker but not necessarily a member of a trade union, though being a worker is necessary to join a trade union.

16. Juergensmeyer (1991) provides a discussion of the development of the Radhasoamis. Jaffrelot (1994) examines the role of the Arya Samaj in the politics of British India.

17. Andersen and Damle (1986) offer a comprehensive historical overview of the rise and ideology of the RSS. For a keen discussion of the inroads made by the RSS in Kerala, see Jayaprasaad 1991.

18. A brief exploration of the relationship between the BJP and the RSS appears in chapter 7.

19. Class is a measure of the relative economic status of the respondents in the

election surveys. This economic classification was based on the reported income and education of the respondents. A preliminary factor analysis revealed that these two variables could be used in conjunction with one another. Family income was used as a measure of the financial status of the household. These two variables—education and income—were then standardized and added. Caste, in this formulation, does not refer to either *jati* or the fourfold *varna* category. Respondents were asked their caste, and the response was the respondent's *jati* (which is how most Indians understand caste). The various *jatis* were recoded to yield an analytically useful category. The reclassification was defined in an informal workshop held at UCLA during the summer of 1985. At that workshop, Ramashray Roy, Richard Sisson, William Vanderbok, and the author went through archival material on most of the *jatis* in each state and classified them into categories that reflected commonality of status in the state and also constituted meaningful social and analytic categories such as brahman, upper caste, merchant castes, middle castes, upwardly mobile castes, lower castes, and *harijans*. The upwardly mobile and lower castes constitute what are now known as the backward castes.

20. For instance, when Sukhadia was the chief minister of Rajasthan, Udaipur (Sukhadia's constituency) witnessed the development of such facilities as a university medical college, a railway training center, *ayurvedic* and polytechnical colleges, a zinc smelter, and so on. Communities could also benefit from an executive position acquired by one of their members. For instance, in Gujarat one *bariya* (a *jati*) who was a deputy minister in the Congress controlled the Gujarat government. "Under his leadership Congress has organized a new Kshatriya organization concerned with providing the community with educational opportunities. A boarding hostel was started in the town of Anand to provide free accommodations to members of the Kshatriya community" (Weiner 1967, 114–15). Patronage provided one of the building blocks of the Congress Party in much the same way that machines were the basis of party politics in the turn of the century United States. Weiner observed that "the active party membership increasingly viewed the Congress as a means of obtaining jobs for friends and relatives and of gaining access to the many services and material benefits which government at all levels can bestow" (34). Not surprisingly, "Congress party workers . . . [were] concerned with helping agriculturists solve their problems, particularly those problems which can be dealt with through government action. Party workers help them obtain such commodities as fertilisers, seeds, and cement" and also help them find employment (82). The Congress Party's electoral dominance lay, as in Kaira District, in "its control over government and quasi-governmental institutions in the district" (79). The relationship between legislators and constituencies in this period was also examined by Maheshwari (1976), Mohapatra (1971), Sisson and Shrader (1972), and Shrader and Sisson (1987).

21. Kothari (1961a) has argued that at the national level Nehru stymied the growth of the organization.

22. In Bihar, the rejected candidates offered themselves as independents (Majumdar 1956). The formation of the Kisan Mazdoor Praja Parishad (KMPP) was largely due to the efforts of Congress dissidents (Kochanek 1968).

23. Weiner (1962a, 1962b), too, associates factions within Congress with access

to state largesse. Brass (1983, 1988a, 1988b) shows how access to the state was influential in creating splits within a political party.

24. A district is an administrative subdivision within a state. District boundaries do not correspond with boundaries of constituencies (electoral districts).

25. A subsample of 450, from six states, Andhra Pradesh, Bihar, Uttar Pradesh, West Bengal, Maharashtra and Kerala, was used in the analysis to ensure comparison with a similar study conducted in 1993.

26. Party elites were asked the extent of their contacts with other party activists at levels lower and higher than them, whether they met rarely, occasionally, or often. The mean score of Congress activists for contacts with those lower than them was 2.38 (on a scale of 1 to 3, from low to high), whereas for the other parties it was 2.51. Statistically, the means were significantly different (the *t*-statistic of 4.16 is significant at the .05 level). A similar pattern obtained for contacts with those in higher positions in the party. Congress activists scored 2.14, while the other party activists averaged 2.27. This difference, too, was statistically significant (the *t*-statistic was 3.96).

27. Stanley Kochanek (1968) noted that perhaps the greatest failure of the party in the immediate postindependence period was its inability to build up a party organization.

28. Franda (1962) details the declining membership of the Congress Party through the 1950s and discusses the failed efforts to rejuvenate the organization during that period.

29. Factionalism is not unique to the Congress Party. The Communists faced the same dilemma, as did the Socialists, who were as faction ridden as other leftist parties such as the Revolutionary Socialist Party, the Forward Bloc, and the Peasants and Workers Party. The Swatantra Party did not even pretend to be cohesive, its founders contenting themselves with bringing together local opposition groups in a minimal program of opposition to the Nehru-inspired state socialism of the Congress.

30. The reasons offered for the variance in the nature of the party's organization by Dhebar were multifarious. They included the lack of political consciousness and psychological integration, inequality in the stature of senior leaders, and internal tensions resulting from caste and communal prejudices.

Chapter 4

1. For the "restoration" argument, see Weiner 1989. The 1984 national elections were an exception to this. Those elections followed the assassination of Indira Gandhi, and Congress won on a large sympathy wave.

2. Robins (1979) offers a comprehensive analysis of the relationship between seats and votes analysis for the 1967 elections.

3. Roy (1969) makes a similar observation.

4. Severe intraparty conflict within the BJP in Gujarat in 1996 also led to a fall of the BJP government there. The national party, despite numerous interventions, was unable to hold a majority together. The BJP's experience stands in contrast to that of Indira Gandhi, who in most cases of infighting within the Congress could

ensure that the party stayed in power. Indira Gandhi was successful only as long as the party she headed was in power in the central government. As in 1996 the BJP was not in power in Delhi, its ability to keep the BJP together was limited. Brass (1983) notes how a major source of conflict within the Congress Party in Uttar Pradesh was the tension between mambers of the Congress Party from the state and those in Delhi (272).

5. The selection of 'weak' leaders to head the Congress Party is a practice that has continued to date. Narasimha Rao became prime minister in 1991 as a compromise choice among the regional Congress leaders. Similarly, Sitaram Kesri emerged as Congress Party president in 1996 as the party was unwilling to elevate either of the two strong regional leaders, Arjun Singh and Sharad Pawar, to the post.

6. Punjab politics in the early 1980s provide another instance: the conflict over Zail Singh, who, as home minister in the central cabinet, kept interfering in Punjab politics. Zail Singh was a former chief minister of Punjab and had headed a faction of the Congress there. After his move to the central government, Darbara Singh became chief minister of Punjab. Darbara Singh's attempts to hold together the factionally divided Punjab party were thwarted by Zail Singh, who wished to further the interests of his faction. Darbara Singh, on the other hand, wanted to establish his own authority in the Punjab Congress Party and ensure that those who had close ties to him would benefit from Congress's control over the Punjab government. Darbara Singh, as Punjab chief minister, resisted this intervention by Zail Singh, for he saw Zail Singh as trying to usurp the chief minister's authority and promote the interests of his own faction.

7. This strategy worked in sustaining a large coalition and single-party dominance in Sweden for almost half a century. See Esping-Andersen 1990 for details.

8. The data in this paragraph are from the 1967 postelection survey.

9. Eldersveld and Ahmed (1978) offer an exhaustive study of the election based on the 1967 mass and elite surveys.

10. The extent of factional conflict in a state was determined from newspaper reports preceding the 1967 election.

11. Roy (1969) ascribes Congress's loss to the Bharatiya Kranti Dal (BKD) in Uttar Pradesh to defections from the Congress.

12. The clearest instance of this allegiance to a party being conditional upon its control over a "higher office" is the state elections that followed the national elections of 1977 and 1980. In both instances, the state elections, which were held after the national elections, witnessed the electoral success in the states of the party that was in power at the center, the Janata in 1977 and Congress in 1980.

13. Data were drawn from the 1967, 1971, and 1980 postelection surveys.

14. The notion of exit comes from Hirschman 1970.

15. The dominant Congress Party underwent three additional splits. The Congress (R) suffered its first major division in the 1977 elections at the end of Indira's two-year national emergency, which saw not only leaders of opposition parties but also leaders of the Congress (R) jailed for allegedly illegal activities or for what was believed to be their proclivity to act in a manner inimical to the public interest. In these elections, the Congress for Democracy led by Jagjivan Ram (the defense min-

ister of the incumbent Congress [R] government) joined the new national opposition coalition—the Janata Party—to contest the elections. The coalition soundly defeated the Congress (R), which won but two of 225 seats in the Hindi-speaking states of northern India. The Congress was also defeated in all 10 state elections held three months later. Subsequent to this severe electoral setback, which witnessed the prime minister and many of her ministerial colleagues going down in defeat, a segment of the party led by senior members formed a new Congress party—the Congress (U), named after its leader, Devraj Urs—and so contested the elections of 1980, winning 5.3 percent of the vote and 13 seats in contrast to 40 percent of the vote and 67 seats for the Congress (I), which stands for Indira. Yet another split occurred after the 1980 elections with the formation of the Congress (S). The Congress (U) met its demise with the death of its leader, while eventually the Congress (S) all but disappeared from the political landscape, winning but five seats in the Lok Sabha and only 1.6 percent of the popular vote in 1984.

16. The Congress contested 39 seats in Tamil Nadu in that election.

17. In the 1996 elections, Congress allied itself with the unpopular AI-ADMK and was wiped out in Tamil Nadu, though a party that broke away from the Congress, the Tamil Maanila Congress, did extremely well.

18. Data are from the *Reserve Bank of India Bulletin.* Calculations were done by the author.

19. This chapter will concern itself with the "political elements that constrain public policy, making the choice of 'control variables' . . . by administrative or political considerations, such as fear of military coup or political agitation" rather than with the "political elements in the choice of planning objectives" (Sen 1984, 21).

20. I would like to thank Mr. M. L. Tandon, a former official of the Ministry of Information and Broadcasting, for bringing this to my notice.

21. Justice A. S.Qureshi, a judge of the Gujarat High Court and a member of the ninth Finance Commission, dissented with the report of the commission, arguing against the excessive financial powers vested in the central government. Justice Qureshi noted that the Finance Commission was, in his opinion, constitutionally a permanent body and not one appointed afresh every five years. He argued that "all regular fiscal transfers form the Center to the States by way of grants are covered under Article 275 . . . [and] the Finance Commission alone has the jurisdiction, powers and authority to make regular transfers from the Center to the States under Article 275" (Finance Commission 1990, 49). He went on to add that it was in "total contravention of the Constitutional provisions [that] plan grants were given to the States by the Union Government through the Planning Commission" (49). The central government's discretionary grants to the states—grants the center feels are permissible under Article 282 of the Constitution—were also questioned. Justice Qureshi argued that Article 282 did not fall under the heading "Distribution of Revenues between the Union and the States" but under a separate heading, "Miscellaneous Financial Provisions" (49), Article 282 was also a virtual reproduction of "a similar provision contained in Section 150(2) of the Government of India Act, 1935" (50). The impetus behind those provisions was to grant special assistance to Bengal in 1943–44 during the Bengal famine. Since 1951, however, 84 per-

cent of transfers from the center to states have taken place outside the Finance Commission's ambit (51), and hence these provisions were unconstitutional. Without discussing the constitutional merits of Justice Qureshi's position, it is clear from this dissent as well that the central government has appropriated a large role for itself in its financial dealings with the states, some of which is constitutionally questionable.

22. The data in this section were drawn from the Lok Sabha Secretariat 1987.

23. The data in this section come from the Commission on Center-State Relations (1988).

24. Redirecting resources based on electoral considerations does not necessarily translate into electoral success. Politicians, having imperfect information about the outcome of an election, tend to undertake measures that, in their opinion, will increase the probability of their reelection. Electoral success does not necessarily follow from electorally driven resource disbursement, as George Bush discovered in the 1992 elections for the presidency in the United States. Despite his attempts to placate farmers and workers in the arms industry, Bush lost the election.

25. For instance, just before the 1977 national elections it was reported that "the disbursements by the Central and state Governments have been on a fairly large scale lately and . . . the Central Government has also been extending liberal assistance to the States" (*Hindu,* 11 February 1977).

26. For the theoretical reasons for using "pooled regression" and why it is appropriate for cross-sectional over-time data, see Stimson 1985.

27. In the mid-1960s, the center established a public sector Food Corporation of India. This agency procures food, and then the central government allocates it to deficit states from the central pool. The distribution of food by the center takes place through central allocations to fair price shops in each state, which sell food at prices set by the government. Food can also be distributed through dispersions to mills in the states or to the state governments directly. For our purposes, we need not distinguish between these categories, for the net effect of each is to ensure that there is enough food in the public distribution system in a state.

28. Punjab and Haryana were excluded from the analysis because they are food surplus states.

29. There is also a structural reason why the national party had to mobilize support for itself. In chapter 3, it was noted that coalitions have to be built locally. Further, the size of a parliamentary constituency is much larger than that for a state assembly. Candidates for the Lok and Vidhan Sabhas build their own coalitions. When the elections were separated, whatever need there was for candidates to coordinate their efforts also declined. Candidates contesting Lok Sabha elections, then, have to build their own coalitions.

30. Meyer and Malcolm (1993), using aggregate data, show the relationship between economic conditions and electoral outcomes. Their independent variables are so completely correlated that their conclusions are somewhat questionable. Chowdhury (1993) reports that there is evidence of a political business cycle in India. The data used for analysis are industrial output in the registered sector. This is such a small proportion of total output that it is difficult to draw national-level

conclusions, especially since most Indians still live in rural areas and most legislators come from them.

Chapter 5

1. While aggregate statistics point to a decline of the Congress, in fact the decline was not monotonic. The party's performance in most states showed fluctuation in the degree of support the party could garner.

2. The lower the vote difference between Congress and its major opponent in a state the more competitive the state. The vote difference measure is preferable to the average Index of Opposition Unity, which also went up, from 70 to 78, suggesting higher levels of competition with Congress. The Index of Opposition Unity (Butler, Roy, and Lahiri 1996) measures unity among opposition parties. The reason for using the vote difference as a measure of opposition strength instead of the index of opposition unity is that the latter hides some significant differences. For instance, the Index of Opposition Unity is 50 for the opposition party getting 20, 25, or 30 percent of the 40, 50, or 60 percent total opposition vote. In each of the cases, the winning party, say, the Congress, would have had 60, 50, or 40 percent of the vote and won the election. But an election in which the dominant party gets 60 percent of the vote is different from the one in which it gets 40 percent. In the former, one party dominates the electoral scene, while in the latter case it could be argued that it was not the strength of the Congress but divisions within the opposition that led to the Congress's victory.

3. This movement, which was once important, has almost disappeared from the political scene today.

4. The notion that previously unmobilized groups have provided the real opposition to Congress also rests on the assumption that Congress's social base has remained unchanged. A more accurate depiction may be that it is not unmobilized groups that are entering the electoral arena. Rather, some existing groups, given a particular policy or set of policies adopted by the state government, are now more readily mobilizable *as a larger group.* Chapter 6 discusses this in the case of Uttar Pradesh.

5. The highest turnout was in the national election of 1984, the election that followed the assassination of Indira Gandhi.

6. The lowering of the voting age in 1989 did bring in new voters, but it's impact on the party system is yet unclear.

7. The vote mobilized by a party measures the proportion of the total electorate that turned out for a party. An example may help clarify the difference between mobilization and vote share. Suppose Congress gets 40 percent of the total votes cast but only 50 percent of the electorate turned out to vote. While Congress's vote share is 40 percent, the party mobilized only 20 percent of the electorate (40 × 0.5).

8. This study focuses on cabinet offices in the states for two reasons. First, this book is based on the argument that state politics provides a basis for understand-

ing national politics. Second, enough good work has been done on the national cabinet. In particular, see Nicholson 1972, 1975; and Sisson 1981, 1985.

9. Mitra (1978) provides a formal model of cabinet instabilty in selected Indian states. This analysis differs insofar as it does not concern itself with the parties that form the cabinet.

10. An example will help clarify the method used. After 1967, the total number of events was 3,363 (adding the number of ministers added, resignations, reshuffles, and resignations of chief ministers). There were also 195 resignations of chief ministers. In other words, the probability of a chief minister resigning (of the total number of ways a cabinet may be changed) is 0.05 (195 divided by 3,363). The value assigned to the resignation of a chief minister should be higher than the value for adding a minister. The value given to a chief minister's resignation is thus 0.95 (unity less 0.05). For the addition of a minister, the same calculation yields 0.29.

11. Kochanek (1968) provides comprehensive evidence for the desire of state leaders for central intervention in order to maintain their own power.

12. It could be argued that the party coalesced into two factions because the simple majority rule for intraparty elections required a 50 percent plus one share of the party to win elections. Also, the two major candidates for party office positioned themselves in such a manner that they could prevent the entry of another candidate. For a theoretical statement of the latter proposition, see Shepsle and Cohen 1990.

13. Increased factionalism has been attributed to the centralization of power within the party. That could indeed be the case, but it does not change the outcome—the Congress prime minister was the one who had to resolve all factional conflicts in the state parties.

14. Mitra (1992) provides an insightful analysis of why midlevel elites are critical to Indian politics.

15. Graham (1973, 1993) makes a case for seeing the Congress Party as a rally in which leadership played a central role.

16. The influence of leadership evaluation on the vote is consistent across the many social divisions that characterize contemporary Indian society. With the exception of literates, where leadership did not influence the vote in 1980, the relationship between leadership evaluations and the Congress vote shows a pronounced increase over time for each social group.

17. A regression analysis finds that leadership evaluations are significantly associated with perceptions of the performance of the government even after controlling for the partisan orientation of the respondents for the 1971, 1980, and 1989 national elections.

18. The Bofors scandal is associated with the purchase of 155mm guns by the Indian military to bolster its artillery. Bofors is the name of the Swedish company whose guns were finally purchased. It has been alleged that senior Indian politicians, including Rajiv Gandhi, received kickbacks for the purchase of guns from Bofors.

19. A senior security official who worked closely with both Indira and Rajiv Gandhi, and wishes to remain unidentified, pointed out that with Indira Gandhi one knew who was in charge. Rajiv Gandhi, on the other hand, never exuded the same confidence.

20. The number used for comparing the effective number of parties was the average effective number of parties across the constituencies in a state.

Chapter 6

1. UP is a critical case for the argument advanced in the book. The state is characterized by the closest approximation of a stratified caste-system (Frankel 1989b, esp. 5–7). Evidence for the rigid caste hierarchy and prevalence of clear distinctions among *jatis* comes from the 1996 postelection survey. Seventeen percent of the respondents in UP did not have either friends or relatives from other castes. This contrasts sharply with other states, such as Maharashtra and Gujarat, where less than 2 percent responded similarly. There is another reason to focus on party politics in UP. The largest decline of the Congress Party has taken place in two Indian states, Bihar and Uttar Pradesh. Bihar and Uttar Pradesh together account for 139 of the 542 seats in the Lok Sabha. In both states, the Congress Party was dominant for much of the period following independence, and in both the party is no longer even competitive; it is a shadow of its former self. In Uttar Pradesh—the state that provided all of Congress's prime ministers except Narasimha Rao—Congress won five of the 85 seats to the Lok Sabha in the elections of 1991 and two in 1996. For the 1996 state assembly elections, Congress was a junior partner in an alliance with the Bahujan Samaj Party (BSP). In Bihar, Congress managed to get only one seat out of 54 in 1991 and two in 1996. The much discussed national decline of the party is also closely associated with the virtual decimation of the party in Bihar and Uttar Pradesh. These two states represent more than a quarter of the total electorate. In 1980, when Congress received 42.7 percent of the vote nationally, 9.4 percent of its 42.7 percent vote (or 22 percent of the Congress's total vote) came from Bihar and Uttar Pradesh. In 1991, when Congress managed only 36.5 percent of the vote (a drop of 6.2 percent over 1980), Congress garnered only 5.34 percent of the vote from Bihar and Uttar Pradesh. Of the 6.2 percent drop in the Congress's vote, a full 4 percent came from these two states (i.e., two-thirds of the Congress Party's drop in vote share between 1980 and 1991 is due to the party's poor performance in Bihar and Uttar Pradesh). In other words, one cannot understand Congress's national electoral decline without examining why the party has been almost completely obliterated in these two states.

2. In most of the discussion on the adoption of the Mandal Commission report and its aftermath, one fact is usually ignored. Before the adoption of the recommendations of the report by the V. P. Singh government in 1990, there was no popular agitation for quotas for backward castes in Uttar Pradesh or Bihar. There was no backward caste association asking for quotas. Unlike the situation in other democracies, as, for instance, with the environmental movement in Western Europe, where society pressures political parties for policy changes, there was no such social pressure on the Indian parties in 1990. This is not to say that quotas should or should not be adopted but simply that the decisions were made by political leaders without pressure from organized caste associations.

3. Not only Congress but even the Janata Party, which came to power in 1977, was a heterogenous catchall coalition (Hasan 1989a).

4. The class argument is made most forcefully by Frankel (1989) and Omvedt (1980, 1991).

5. Kothari (1964) provides a keen discussion of this process.

6. Brass's analysis of study of Aligarh District also reveals that most major political conflict was within the various forward caste *jatis* (1983, 224–31).

7. These proportions are so high because the votes received by all other parties and independent candidates were excluded from the calculation. The reason for doing so is to ensure comparison with the current party system. The dominant parties are the BJP (the successor of the Jan Sangh), the SP (a splinter group of and successor to the Socialists and the BKD), the BSP (which did not exist then), and the Congress.

8. Data are drawn from the 1989 postelection survey.

9. For the reasons for the electoral success and collapse of the Janata Dal, see Fickett 1993.

10. The emergence of these parties as powerful political forces also reduced the votes received by independents by 50 percent (from 15.5 percent in 1989 to 7.3 percent in 1991).

11. Brass (1993) notes that "the BJP extended its vote base significantly in 1991," but it was not clear at whose expense (261). The reason it is not clear from which party the BJP stole support is that the two major parties, the Congress and the Janata Dal, were catchall parties.

12. For a critical assessment of the relationship of caste to class, see Brass 1983, 1988a. Analysis of the 1971 and 1991 surveys reveals that the correlation between income and forward and backward caste is very low (0.2), and hence arguments about the one-to-one relationship between caste and class should be treated with some suspicion.

13. Ahmad and Saxena (1993) offer a discussion of land and political power in Uttar Pradesh.

14. Data were collected from the Reserve Bank of India *Bulletin.* In the other states, the average proportion of loans granted to local governments by the states was 4 percent. The difference between Uttar Pradesh and the other states was not statistically significant.

15. Nehru, true to the fabian line, in letters to the chief ministers, spoke of the need to improve the condition of the backward classes. Even though the commission submitted its report in 1955, Nehru made no reference to it in letters to the chief ministers in either 1955 or 1956 (Nehru 1985, vols. 3–4).

16. Article 16, Clause 4, grants the state the power to provide "for the reservation of appointments or positions in favor of any backward class of citizens, which in the opinion of the state, is not adequately represented in the services under the state." Article 15, Clause 5, says that the state can make special provisions "for the advancement of any socially and educationally backward classes of citizens or for the Scheduled Castes and Tribes."

17. At the outset, the report claims (Backward Classes Commission 1955, iv) that, for national solidarity, groups of any kind are detrimental to the fundamental organization of modern society. Modern societies recognize only individuals at one end and governments at the other.

18. This way of thinking also followed a modernization paradigm insofar as the discussion saw social backwardness as the cause of economic backwardness (Backward Classes Commission 1955, xiv, xv).

19. One way to address this problem, in the opinion of the commission, would be to limit salary differentials in government service.

20. Scheduled castes and tribes have 22.5 percent of the seats reserved for them.

21. The commission's reliance on the prevalence of caste associations to make its claims about the role of caste in Indian society is odd, especially in light of the data presented in chapter 2, where it is demonstrated quite clearly that most Indians do not belong to any caste association. According to the commission, this is the key to the perpetuation of the caste system and the inequalities associated with it.

22. For a trenchant critique of the Mandal Commission's methodology and its deep flaws, see Dharma Kumar 1993.

23. Parties are constrained to build cross-*jati* coalitions because of the nature of *jati* and the electoral system. For a detailed discussion of this, see chapter 3.

24. A reserved constituency is one in which only scheduled caste and tribe candidates can contest elections.

25. With a single exception, the party organizations of the political parties did not play a significant role in the campaign. In Lalganj, the JD campaign was organized by a few prominent individuals. There was no party organization to speak of, and the party made no direct contribution to the campaign. In the case of the BJP candidate, the party was definitely more involved in the campaign, but its role was limited to providing banners, posters, and audio cassettes. In Sahranpur, the JD campaign was also managed by a few personal friends of the candidate. In Mahilabad, even though the SP candidate was selected by Mulayam Singh Yadav, the SP did not play a role in the campaign, which was left to the candidate. The Congress campaign was unorganized in all four assembly segments, with the party giving no real direction. Even the BJP, ostensibly the best organized of all the parties, left its candidates to organize much of their campaigns themselves.

26. There was little difference among the parties on economic issues. Mulayam Singh Yadav stressed the lack of development in Uttar Pradesh during the previous BJP regime and promised all kinds of benefits to voters, such as pensions for widows and the handicapped and abolition of the sales tax (*Amar Ujaala,* 31 October 1993). The BJP, too, promised to abolish the sales tax—an issue close to the hearts of the traders in the state (*Amar Ujaala,* 4 November 1993). Congress promised economic development and stressed state largesse for agriculture in the form of higher procurement prices for sugarcane and paddy (*Aaj,* 12 November 1993).

27. A BSP member of the legislature reportedly said that the adoption of the Mandal Commission's recommendation and increased control over the state government would be beneficial to the scheduled castes, at least in reducing the number and severity of the atrocities committed against them (Lieten 1994).

28. A similar kind of dynamic influenced the decline of the catchall socialists in Spain in the 1990s. Details of the Spanish case appear in chapter 9.

29. Rajiv Gandhi also failed to take a position on quotas for the backward castes when the issue was raised in Andhra Pradesh. In Gujarat, though, he had used the adoption of quotas to remove a state chief minister from the chief ministership (Weiner 1987).

30. Wright (1995) provides a keen description of how Mulayam Singh Yadav capitalized on the dilemma faced by the Congress Party.

31. The actual *yatra,* from the south to the north, was undertaken by motorcade.

32. The BSP showed signs of becoming an electoral force as early as 1989. It was, however, only after the 1993 elections, when it was clear that Congress was a spent force, that the BSP emerged as a powerful political party in its own right.

33. If there were one numerically dominant caste, a party could target it, but since the population is more fragmented coalitions are necessary to succeed under the SMSP scheme.

34. Leiten (1994) observes that "elections in UP [have] gone the casteist way" (777).

35. The government plays a major role in the distribution of food. Most educational institutions in India are state run. Health services are provided by individual physicians, but most hospitals are the preserve of the government.

36. Leiten (1994) quotes a BSP activist who noted that Kanshi Ram (the leader of the BSP) was "fighting only for a share in the administration" (779).

37. By 1996, fissures had developed between the SP and the BSP. For the reasons for this, see Mishra 1995a and 1995b.

38. The survey was conducted in conjunction with the World Values Survey. An additional seven questions were posed to respondents in Uttar Pradesh. The short nature of the instrument limits the range of the analysis.

Chapter 7

1. Another explanation is more directly related to political considerations. Congress fanned religious politics by reopening the Ayodhya issue, which allowed Hindu fundamentalists to express far more vociferously their claim that the Babri Masjid in Ayodhya was built on the birth site of Lord Rama (Engineer 1994; Parikh 1993; Thakur 1993). Once Congress decided to play the religious card, it found itself in the position of defending an issue that was at odds with its earlier secular stance and the concerns of Muslims, who had historically been supporters of the Congress. But why did Congress's alienation of Muslims lead to the electoral success of the BJP?

2. This is not surprising; as noted earlier, the problem is not in the locality but at state and national levels.

3. This discussion draws heavily on Graham 1990.

4. The RSS has 3.8 million members in contrast to the BJP, which has only 300,000 (Malik and Singh 1992, 323).

5. Graham (1970) makes a similar claim about how the BJP's economic program differed from that of the Swatantra.

6. See Rudolph and Rudolph 1980 and Gould 1980. This move to the center alienated the party's supporters, and the party's political base also narrowed.

7. The economic liberalization introduced by Rajiv Gandhi did not change this relationship in any significant way. Any liberalization that Indira or Rajiv Gandhi introduced occurred within parameters laid out by the state. This point is made in

Kohli 1989. Greater economic opportunities were still available only to those with access to the state.

8. Occupation was coded as a dummy variable. Traders, the self-employed, low-level government employees, and those in middle- and low-level positions in the private sector were coded as 1; those in other occupations were coded as 0.

9. Kohli (1990) discusses why Rajiv Gandhi failed.

10. Brass (1993) makes a similar claim.

Chapter 8

1. See, in particular, Bell and Criddle 1989 and Kendrick and McCrone 1989.

2. This class of explanations has been extended to explain the rise of regional parties (Kohli 1987b) and the success of the BJP (Varshney 1993).

3. The deterioration would be even sharper if the accounting included only nondefense capital outlays.

4. For the measurement of the extent of cabinet instability, see chapter 5.

5. For event data, because of the nature of the distribution, a Poisson regression is the appropriate technique (Chatterji and Price 1991). A random effects estimation was used because the number of riots can also vary across states for state-specific reasons.

6. This was confirmed in interviews with district magistrates in two districts in Tamil Nadu and Karnataka who were acting as returning officers for state elections.

Chapter 9

1. The argument developed in this chapter extends earlier explanations of the FLN's decline and the success of the FIS. It has been previously argued that the success of the FIS "stems primarily from the failures of the FLN regime" (Zoubir 1992, 94), that the FIS managed to draw the support of those who were tired of the FLN (Mortimer 1991), and that the vote of June 1990 "was largely a vote against a discredited regime and the existing system" (Entelis and Arone 1992, 28). While explanations of the FLN's decline and the success of the FIS rooted in the general crisis faced by the Algerian state and the nature of state-society relations in Algeria have much merit, they do not explicitly address why it is that some social groups, especially the middle class, supported the FIS. This chapter argues that an examination of the economic policies pursued by the FLN will provide an explanation for why the small business sector, low-level administrators, and the educated segments of society defected in larger proportions than other groups.

2. A former government minister suggested in 1990 that over the years party officials had garnered more than $26 billion in ill-gotten gains (EIU Country Report 1990, 2:9).

3. See Waterbury 1993 for a prescient analysis of the conditions under which this division can emerge because of public sector reform.

4. In the absence of survey data, it is difficult to discern either the influence of perceptions of the "problem of order" on support for the FIS or which group feels

most disaffected by the "problem of order." In India, groups most likely to perceive "order" as a problem are the educated, urban segments of society (Chhibber, Misra, and Sisson 1992).

5. Apart from these two major parties, a number of smaller parties also contested the election. Among them, the Association Populaire pour l'Unité et l'Action (APUA), the Front des Forces Socialistes (FFS), the Front National du Renouveau (FNR), the Mouvement pour la Démocratie en Algérie (MDA), and the Parti de l'Avant-Garde Socialiste (PAGS) wanted to continue the policy of state intervention and limit private industry. The Mouvement Démocratique pour la Renouveau Algérien (MDRA) and the Parti Social-Democratique (PSD)—centrist parties—were for privatization, but, like the FLN, they wanted to retain a large role for the state. The other Islamic parties—the Parti National Algérien (PNA) and the Parti de Renouveau Algérien (PRA), also advocated a free market system. The Rassemblement pour la Culture et la Démocratie (RCD) represented Berber interests.

6. The data was collected by Dhelia Williamson and is reported in greater detail in Williamson 1993. Election returns were reported in *El Moudjahid*, 19–27 June 1990. The demographic data for 216 Algerian communes were drawn from Algeria 1977.

7. It could be argued that since the electoral data are aggregated at the commune level the analysis suffers from an "ecological fallacy." The ecological fallacy is less troublesome, however, since the attempt is "merely to account for the cross-[commune] variance in voting patterns" (Ames 1994, 100).

8. In a two-party competition, we would expect the signs to reverse. In Algeria, however, not only were other parties contesting the election but there were a large number of independent candidates in the electoral fray as well. The presence of other parties and a low correlation between the number of seats won by the FLN and the FIS make the reversal of the signs a more robust finding.

9. The correlation between levels of education and the other independent variables was around 0.4, not high enough to warrant concerns about multicollinearity.

10. The commercial register controlled large areas of local business life and could be very restrictive (EIU Country Report 1990, 3:21).

11. This should come as no surprise, especially given the authoritarian legacy of Spain. Consequently, concerns about democratic consolidation dominated the political agenda of parties throughout the 1970s and much of the 1980s. Despite a severe economic crisis and the presence of one of the highest degrees of social inequality in Europe, economic decisions were "consensually" postponed in order to consolidate political changes (Maravall 1995). Also, elites among most of the significant national parties adopted catchall electoral strategies.

12. Gunther et al. (1986, 390) assert that the characteristics of the new Spanish party system were the product of six factors: attitudinal predisposition interacting with voters, party's ideological stance, the effects of the electoral law, the strength of each party's organization, the nature of the transition to democracy, the advantages of incumbency, and the politics of consensus.

13. The AP's 1982 electoral program was a very long one, consisting of 198 pages. Economic issues constituted only 15 percent of the total program.

14. Some of the increases in government expenditures may be attributed to investments made for the 1992 Olympic Games and the International Fair in Seville.

References

Government of India Publications

Backward Classes Commission. 1955. *Report of the Backward Classes Commission.* Vol. 1. Delhi: Manager of Publications.
———. 1991. *Reservations for Backward Classes: Mandal Commission Report of the Backward Classes Commission, 1980 along with Introduction.* Delhi: Akalank Publications.
Bureau of Police Research and Development. Various Issues. *Crime in India.* New Delhi: Ministry of Home Affairs.
Committee on the Status of Women in India. 1975. *Toward Equality: Report of the Committee on the Status of Women in India.* New Delhi: Ministry of Education and Social Welfare.
Finance Commission. 1990. Final Report of the Ninth Finance Commission. New Delhi: Finance Commission.
India Commission on Centre-State Relations. 1988. *Commission on Centre-State Relations.* Nasik: Government of India Press.
Lok Sabha Secretariat. 1987. *President's Rule in the States and Union Territories.* New Delhi: Lok Sabha Secretariat.
Ministry of Agriculture, Directorate of Economics and Statistics. Various Issues. *Bulletin on Food Statistics.* Delhi: Controller of Publications.
Ministry of Agriculture and Irrigation. 1976. *Report of the National Commission on Agriculture, 1976.* Part 2. Delhi: Controller of Publications.
Ministry of Finance. 1997. *Government Subsidies in India: Discussion Paper.* New Delhi: Ministry of Finance.
Ministry of Finance, Department of Economic Affairs. Various Issues. *An Economic and Functional Classification of the Central Government Budget.* Delhi: Controller of Publications.
———. Various Issues. *Indian Economic Statistics, Public Finance.* New Delhi: Ministry of Finance.
Ministry of Rural Development. 1991. *Panchayati Raj Institutions in India 1991.* New Delhi: Ministry of Rural Development.
———. 1996. *Annual Report.* New Delhi: Ministry of Rural Development.
Planning Commission. 1957. *Report of the Study Team for Community Development and National Extension Service.* Vol. 1. Delhi: Controller of Publications.
Reserve Bank of India. Various Issues. *Bulletin.* Bombay: Reserve Bank of India.

Newspapers and Serials

Aaj
Amar Ujaala
Asian Recorder
Deccan Herald
Economic Times
El Pais
Hindu
Hindustan Times
India Today
Indian Express
Times of India

Congress Party Documents

All India Congress Committee. Various Issues. *Economic Review.* New Delhi: Indian National Congress.
Indian National Congress. Various Issues. *Report of the General Secretaries.* Allahabad and New Delhi: Indian National Congress.

Books and Articles

Aguero, Felipe. 1995. *Soldiers, Civilians, and Democracy: Post-Franco Spain in Comparative Perspective.* Baltimore: Johns Hopkins University Press.
Ahmad, Imtiaz, and N. C. Saxena. 1994. Caste, Land, and Political Power in Uttar Pradesh. In *Caste and Class in India,* ed. K. L. Sharma. Jaipur: Rawat.
Ahuja, M. L., and Paul Sharda. 1992. *1989–1991 General Elections in India.* New Delhi: Associated Publishing House.
Alavi, Hamza. 1973. The State in Post-Colonial Society. In *Imperialism and Revolution in South Asia,* ed. Kathleen Gough and Hari P. Sharma. New York: Monthly Review Press.
Al-Ahnaf, M., Bernard Botiveau, and Franck Fregosi. 1991. *L'Algerie par ses islamistes.* Paris: Karthala.
Aldrich, John. 1995. *Why Parties? The Origin and Transformation of Political Parties in America.* Chicago: University of Chicago Press.
Alesina, Alberto. 1987. Macroeconomic Policy in a Two-Party System as a Repeated Game. *Quarterly Journal of Economics* 101:651–78.
Alesina, Alberto, Gerald Cohen, and Nouriel Roubini. 1992. Macroeconomic Policy and Elections in OECD Economies. *Economics and Politics* 4:1–30.
Alesina, Alberto, and Nouriel Roubini. 1992. Political Cycles: Evidence from OECD Economies. *Review of Economic Studies* 59:663–88.
Algeria. 1977. Recensement general de la population et de l'habitat, vols. 1–13. Oran: Services des statisques.
Ali, Sadiq. 1959. *The General Elections, 1957: A Survey.* New Delhi: Indian National Congress.

Ames, Barry. 1987. *Political Survival: Politicians and Public Policy in Latin America*. Berkeley. University of California Press.

———. 1994. The Reverse Coattails Effect: Local Party Organization in the 1989 Brazilian Presidential Election. *American Political Science Review* 88 (March): 95–111.

Andersen, Walter K., and S. Damle. 1986. *The Brotherhood in Saffron: The Rashtriya Swayamsevak Sangh and Hindu Revivalism*. Boulder: Westview.

Austin, Granville. 1966. *The Indian Constitution: Cornerstone of a Nation*. Oxford: Clarendon.

Bagchi, Amaresh. 1991. India. In *Economic and Social Commission for Asia and the Pacific. Fiscal Decentralization and the Mobilization and Use of National Resources for Development: Issues, Experience, and Policies in the ESCAP Region*, 97–128. Bangkok: ESCAP.

Bagchi, Amaresh, J. L. Bajaj, and William A. Byrd, eds. 1992. *State Finances in India*. Delhi: Vikas.

Bardhan, Pranab. 1984. *The Political Economy of Development in India*. Oxford: Blackwell.

Barnabas, A. P., and O. P. Bohra. 1995. *Finances of Panchayati Raj Institutions: Case Studies*. New Delhi: National Institute of Public Finance and Policy.

Barnes, S., P. McDonough, and A. López Pina. 1985. The Development of Partisanship in New Democracies: The Case of Spain. *American Journal of Political Science* 29:695–720.

Bartolini, Stefano, and Peter Mair. 1990. *Identity, Competition and Electoral Availability: The Stabilisation of European Electorates, 1885–1985*. Cambridge: Cambridge University Press.

Basu, Amrita. 1990. State Autonomy and Agrarian Transformation in India. *Comparative Politics* 22:483–500.

———. 1992. *Two Faces of Protest*. Berkeley and Los Angeles: University of California Press.

———. 1995. Why Local Riots and Not Simply Local: Collective Violence and the State in Bijnor, India 1988–1993. *Theory and Society* 24 (1): 35–78.

Bates, Robert H. 1981. *Markets and States in Tropical Africa: The Political Basis of Agricultural Policies*. Berkeley and Los Angeles University of California Press.

Bayly, Christopher. 1975. *The Local Roots of Indian Politics: Allahbad, 1880–1920*. Oxford: Clarendon.

Bednar, Jenna, W. N. Eskridge Jr., and J. Ferejohn. 1997. A Political Theory of Federalism. Mimeo.

Bell, David S., and Byron Criddle. 1989. The Decline of the French Communist Party; a review article. *British Journal of Political Science* 19:515–36.

Bennoune, Mahfoud. 1989. *The Making of Contemporary Algeria, 1830–1987: Colonial Upheavals and Post-independence Development*. Cambridge: Cambridge University Press.

Berger, Suzanne, ed. 1981. *Organizing Interests in Western Europe: Pluralism, Corporatism, and the Transformation of Politics*. Cambridge: Cambridge University Press.

Beteille, Andre. 1963. Politics and Social Structure in Tamilnad. *Economic Weekly* 15:1161–67.

———. 1970. Caste and Political Group Formation in Tamilnad. In *Caste in Indian Politics,* ed. Rajni Kothari. New Delhi: Longmans.

Bharatiya Jana Sangh. 1973. *Party Documents.* Vol. 1. New Delhi: Bharatiya Jana Sangh.

Brass, Paul. 1965. *Factional Politics in an Indian State: The Congress Party in Uttar Pradesh.* Berkeley: University of California Press.

———. 1981a. Class, Ethnic Group, and Party in Indian Politics. *World Politics* 43:449–67.

———. 1981b. Congress, the Lok Dal, and the Middle-Peasant Castes: An Analysis of the 1977 and 1980 Parliamentary Elections in Uttar Pradesh. *Pacific Affairs* 54 (1): 5–41.

———. 1983. *Caste, Faction, and Party in Indian Politics.* Vol. 1. Delhi: Chanakya.

———, ed. 1985. *Ethnic Groups and the State.* Totowa, N.J.: Barnes and Noble.

———. 1988a. *Caste, Faction, and Party in Indian Politics.* Vol. 2. Delhi: Chanakya.

———. 1988b. The Punjab Crisis and the Unity of India. In *India's Democracy: An Analysis of Changing State-Society Relations* ed. Atul Kohli. Princeton: Princeton University Press.

———. 1989. Political Parties and Electorial Politics. In *India Briefing, 1989,* ed. Marshall M. Bouton and Philip Oldenburg. London: Westview.

———. 1990. *The Politics of India since Independence.* New York: Cambridge University Press.

———. 1993a. Caste, Class, and Community in the Ninth General Elections for the Lok Sabha in Uttar Pradesh. In *India Votes: Alliance Politics and Minority Governments in the Ninth and Tenth General Elections,* ed. Harold A. Gould and Sumit Ganguly. Boulder: Westview.

———. 1993b. The Rise of the BJP and the Future of Party Politics in Uttar Pradesh. In *India Votes: Alliance Politics and Minority Governments in the Ninth and Tenth General Elections,* ed. Harold A. Gould and Sumit Ganguly. Boulder: Westview.

———. 1997. *Theft of an Idol.* Princeton: Princeton University Press.

Brecher, Michael. 1966. *Nehru's Mantle: The Politics of Succession in India.* New York: Praeger.

Brown, Judith. 1994. *Modern India: The Origins of an Asian Democracy.* Oxford: Oxford University Press.

Butler, David, P. Roy, and A. Lahiri. 1996. *India Decides: Elections, 1952–1995.* Delhi: Living Media Books.

Byres, Terence, ed. 1994. *The State and Development Planning in India.* Delhi and New York: Oxford University Press.

Caciagli, M. 1986. Elecciones y partidos en la transición Española. Madrid: *Centro de Investigaciones Sociologicas and Siglo XXI.*

Calman, Leslie J. 1992. *Toward Empowerment: Women and Movement Politics in India.* Boulder: Westview.

Caporaso, James A. 1995. Research Design, Falsification, and the Qualitative-Quantitative Divide. *American Political Science Review* 89:457–60.

Chakravarty, S. 1987. *Development Planning.* New Delhi: Oxford University Press.

Chandok, H. L, and the Policy Group. 1991. *India Database: The Economy.* Delhi: Living Media Books.

Chatterjee, Partha. 1994. Development Planning and the Indian State. In *The State and Development Planning in India,* ed. Terence J. Byers. Delhi: Oxford University Press.

———. 1996. The Manifold Uses of *Jati.* In *Region, Religion, Caste, Gender, and Culture in Contemporary India,* ed. T. V. Sathyamurthy. Delhi: Oxford University Press.

Chatterji, P. C. 1996. Reservation: Theory and Practice. In *Region, Religion, Caste, Gender, and Culture in Contemporary India,* ed. T .V. Sathyamurthy. Delhi: Oxford University Press.

Chatterji, S., and B. Price. 1991. *Regression Analysis by Example.* 2nd ed. New York: Wiley.

Chhibber, Pradeep. 1995. Political Parties, Electoral Competition, Government Expenditures, and Economic Reform in India. *Journal of Development Studies* 32:74–96.

Chhibber, Pradeep K., and John Petrocik. 1989. The Puzzle of Indian Politics: Social Cleavages and the Indian Party System. *British Journal of Political Science* 19 (2): 191–210.

Chhibber, Pradeep, and Ken Kollman. 1998. Party Aggregation and the Number of Parties in India and the United States. *American Political Science Review* 92:329–42.

Chhibber, Pradeep K., Subhash Misra, and Richard Sisson. 1992. Order and the Indian Electorate: For whom does Shiva Dance? *Asian Survey* 32 (7): 606–16.

Chhibber, Pradeep K., and Richard Sisson. 1990. Electoral Competition and the Rise of the "Personal Party": Evaluations of Congress' Electoral Dominance, 1952–1989. Paper presented at the conference Democracy and Development in South Asia, Tufts University, 20–22 April.

Chhibber, Pradeep, and Mariano Torcal. 1997. Elite Strategy, Social Cleavages, and Party Systems in a New Democracy: Spain. *Comparative Political Studies* 30 (1): 27–54.

Chowdhury, Abdur R. 1993. Political Surfing over Economic Waves: Parliamentary Election Timing in India. *American Journal of Political Science* 37 (4): 1110–18.

Coleman, John H. 1996. *Party Decline in America.* Princeton: Princeton University Press.

Collier, David. 1995. Translating Quantitative Methods for Qualitative Researchers: The Case of Selection Bias. *American Political Science Review* 89:461–66.

Coppedge, Michael. 1994. *Strong Parties and Lame Ducks: Presidential Partyarchy and Factionalism in Venezuela.* Stanford: Stanford University Press.

Cox, Gary. 1997. *Making Votes Count.* Cambridge: Cambridge University Press.

Criddle, Byron, and David S. Bell. 1989. The Decline of the French Communist Party. *British Journal of Political Science* 19 (October): 515–36.

Dalton, Richard J., Scott C. Flanagan, and Paul A. Beck. 1984. Political Forces and Partisan Change. In R. J. Dalton, S. C. Flanagan, and P. A. Beck, eds., *Electoral Change in Advanced Industrial Democracies: Realignment or Dealignment?* 451–76. Princeton: Princeton University Press.

Das Gupta, Jyotindra. 1970. *Language Conflict and National Development: Group Politics and National Language Policy in India.* Berkeley: University of California Press.

———. 1988. Ethnicity, Democracy, and Development in India: Assam in a General Perspective. In *India's Democracy: An Analysis of Changing State-Society Relations,* ed. Atul Kohli. Princeton: Princeton University Press.

Datta, Abhijit. 1993. Institutional Aspects of Urban Governance in India. *Indian Journal of Public Administration* 60:616–32.

Davey, Hampton. 1972. Polarization and Consensus in Indian Party Politics. *Asian Survey* 12:701–16.

Desai, Meghnad. 1995. Economic Reform: Stalled by Politics? In *India Briefing: Staying the Course,* ed. Philip Oldenburg. London: M. E. Sharpe.

Dharma Kumar. 1993. Land and Caste in South India: Agricultural Labour in the Madras Presidency during the Nineteenth Century. *Journal of Economic History* 53 (September): 675–76.

Dillman, Bradford. 1992. Transition to Democracy in Algeria. In *State and Society in Algeria,* ed. John P. Entelis and Phillip C. Naylor. Boulder: Westview.

Dua, Bhagwan D. 1981. India: A Study in the Pathology of a Federal System. *Journal of Commonwealth and Comparative Politics* 19 (3): 257–75.

Dutta, Bhaskar. 1996. Coalition Governments and Fiscal Policies in India. Mimeo.

Echeverri-Ghent, John. 1993. *The State and the Poor: Public Policy and Political Development in India and the United States.* Berkeley: University of California Press.

EIU (Economist Intelligence Unit). Various Issues. *Country Report—Algeria.* London: The Unit.

Eldersveld, Samuel J. 1982. *Political Parties in American Society.* New York: Basic Books.

Eldersveld, Samuel J., and Bashiruddin Ahmed. 1978. *Citizens and Politics: Mass Political Behavior in India.* Chicago: University of Chicago Press.

Engineer, Asghar Ali. 1994. A Perspective on Hindu-Muslim Conflict. In *Democracy in India: A Hollow Shell,* ed. Arthur Bonner. Washington, D.C.: American University Press.

Entelis, John P., and Lisa J. Arone. 1992. Algeria in Turmoil: Islam, Democracy, and the State. *Middle East Policy* 1 (2): 23–35.

Ersson, S., and J-E Lane. 1987. *Politics and Society in Western Europe.* London: Sage.

Esping-Andersen, Gosta. 1985. *Politics against Markets: The Social Democratic Road to Power.* Princeton: Princeton University Press.

———. 1990. Single-Party Dominance in Sweden: The Saga of Social Democracy.

In *Uncommon Democracies: The One-Party Dominant Regimes,* ed. T. J. Pempel. Ithaca: Cornell University Press.

Faath, Sigrid. 1990. *Algerien: Gesellschaftliche Strukturen und politische Reformen zu Beginn der neunziger Jahre.* Hamburg: Deutsche Orient Institut.

Fair, Ray C. 1978. The Effect of Economic Events on Votes for President. *Review of Economic and Statistics* 60 (2): 159–73.

Fickett, Lewis P., Jr. 1993. The Rise and Fall of the Janata Dal. *Asian Survey* 33 (12): 1151–62.

Finegold, Kenneth, and Theda Skocpol. 1995. *State and Party in America's New Deal.* Madison: University of Wisconsin Press.

Fiorina, Morris P. 1991. Elections and the Economy in the 1980s: Short- and Long-Term Effects. In *Politics and Economics in the Eighties,* ed. Alberto Alesina and Geoffrey Carliner. Chicago: University of Chicago Press.

Forrester, Duncan. 1970. Indian State Ministers and Their Roles. *Asian Survey* 10 (6): 472–82.

Franda, Marcus F. 1962. The Organizational Development of India's Congress Party. *Pacific Affairs* 35 (3): 248–60.

Frankel, Francine R. 1978. *India's Political Economy, 1947–1977: The Gradual Revolution.* Princeton: Princeton University Press.

———. 1987. Politics: The Failure to Rebuild Consensus. In *India Briefing, 1987,* ed. Marshall M. Bouton. London: Westview.

———. 1988. Decline of a Social Order. In *Dominance and State Power in Modern India,* ed. Francine R. Frankel and M. S. A. Rao. Vol. 2. Delhi: Oxford University Press.

———. 1989a. Caste, Land, and Dominance in Bihar: Breakdown of the Brahmanical Social Order. In *Dominance and State Power in Modern India: Decline of a Social Order,* ed. Francine R. Frankel and M. S. A. Rao. Vol. 1. Delhi: Oxford University Press.

———. 1989b. Introduction to *Dominance and State Power in Modern India: Decline of a Social Order,* ed. Francine R. Frankel and M.S.A. Rao. Vol. 1. Delhi: Oxford University Press.

Frey, Bruno S,. and Friedrich Schnieder. 1978. A Politico-Economic Model of the United Kingdom. *Economic Journal* 88:243–53.

Gallagher, John. 1973. Congress in Decline: Bengal, 1930 to 1939. In *Locality, Province, and Nation: Essays on Indian Politics, 1870–1949,* ed. John Gallagher, Gordon Johnson, and Anil Seal. Cambridge: Cambridge University Press.

Gallagher, John. Gordon Johnson, and Anil Seal, eds. 1973. *Locality Province and Nation: Essays on Indian Politics 1870–1940.* Cambridge: Cambridge University Press.

Gandhi, Nandita. 1996. *When the Rolling Pins Hit the Streets: Women in the Anti-Price Rise Movement in Maharashtra.* New Delhi: Kali for Women.

Gangas, P. 1994. El Desarrollo organizativo de los partidos políticos nacionales de implantación nacional. Ph.D. diss., Departamento de Ciencia Política y de la Administración, Universidad Autónoma de Madrid.

Gerschenkeron, A. 1962. *Economic Backwardness in Historical Perspective.* Cambridge: Harvard University Press.

Gopal, S. 1976. *Jawaharlal Nehru: A Biography.* Vol. 2. Cambridge: Harvard University Press.

Gould, Harold A. 1963. The Adaptive Functions of Caste in Contemporary Indian Society. *Asian Survey* 3 (9): 426–38.

———. 1980. The Second Coming: The 1980 Elections in India's Hindi-Belt. *Asian Survey* 20:595–616.

Gourevitch, Peter Alexis. 1986. *Politics in Hard Times: Comparative Responses to International Economic Crises.* Ithaca: Cornell University Press.

Goyal, O. P., and Harlan Hahn. 1966. The Nature of Party Competition in Five Indian States. *Asian Survey* 6:580–88.

Graham, B. D. 1970. The Jana Sangh and Party Alliances: 1967–70. *South Asian Review* 4 (1): 9–26.

———. 1973. Congress as a Rally: An Image of Leadership. *South Asian Review* 6 (2): 111–24.

———. 1990. *Hindu Nationalism and Indian Politics: The Origins and Development of the Bharatiya Jana Sangh.* Cambridge: Cambridge University Press.

———. 1993. *Representation and Party Politics.* London: Blackwell.

Gulati, I. S. 1987. Introduction. In *Center-State Budgetary Transfers,* ed. I. S. Gulati. Bombay: Oxford University Press.

Gunther, R. P. 1991. *The Dynamics of Electoral Competition in a Modern Society: Models of Spanish Voting Behavior, 1979 and 1982.* Working Papers, no. 28. Barcelona: Institut de Ciències Polítiques i Socials.

Gunther, R. P., and J. R. Montero. 1994. Los anclajes del partidismo: Un análisis comparado del comportamiento electoral en cuatro democracias del Sur de Europa. In *Comportamiento electoral y político,* ed. P. Del Castillo. Madrid: Centro de Investigaciones Sociológicas.

Gunther, R. P., D. P. Nikiforos, and H.-J. Puhle, eds. 1995. *The Politics of Democratic Consolidation: Southern Europe in Comparative Perspective.* Baltimore and London: Johns Hopkins University Press.

Gunther, R. P., G. Sani, and G. Shabad. 1986. *Spain after Franco: The Making of a Competitive Party System.* Berkeley: University of California Press.

Hall, Peter. 1986. *Governing the Economy: The Politics of State Intervention in Britain and France.* Oxford: Oxford University Press.

Hanson, A. H. 1966. *The Process of Planning: A Study of India's Five Year Plans, 1950–1964.* London: Oxford University Press.

Haragopal, G., and G. Sudarshanam. 1995. Andhra Pradesh. In *Status of Panchayati Raj in the States of India, 1994,* ed. George Matthew. Delhi: Concept.

Hart, Henry C. 1976. *Indira Gandhi's India: A Political System Reappraised.* Boulder: Westview.

Hasan, Zoya. 1989a. *Dominance and Mobilisation: Rural Politics in Western Uttar Pradesh.* New Delhi: Sage.

———. 1989b. Power and Mobilization: Patterns of Resilience and Change in Uttar Pradesh Politics. In *Dominance and State Power in India: Decline of a*

Social Order, vol. 1, ed. Francine Frankel and M. S. A. Rao. Delhi: Oxford University Press.

Herring. Ronald J. 1987. *Land to the Tiller: The Political Economy of Agrarian Reform in South Asia.* New Haven: Yale University Press.

Hibbs, Douglas. 1987. *The Political Economy of Industrial Democracies.* Cambridge: Harvard University Press.

Higley, John, and Richard Gunther, eds. 1992. *Elites and Democratic Consolidation in Latin America and Southern Europe.* Cambridge: Cambridge University Press.

Hirschman, Albert. 1970. *Exit, Voice, and Loyalty.* Cambridge: Harvard University Press.

Hopkin, Jonathan. 1995. Party Development and Party Collapse: The Case of Union de Centro Democratico in Post-Franco Spain. Ph.D. diss., European University Institute, Florence.

Horowitz, D. 1984. *Ethnic Groups in Conflict.* Berkeley: University of California Press.

Hunt, Robert. 1980. Business Associations and the Small Manufacturing Sector in India. *International Journal of Comparative Sociology* 21 (2): 254–67.

Inglehart, Ronald. 1995. Modernization and Postmodernization: Cultural, Economic, and Political Change in 43 Societies. Mimeo.

Institute of Social Sciences. 1995. *Status of Panchayati Raj, 1994.* New Delhi: Concept.

Instituto Nacional de Estadística. 1992. *Boletín de Estadísticas Laborales.* Subdirección General de Estadística. Madrid: Ministerio de Trabajo.

Iratni, Belkacem, and Mohand Salah Tahi. 1991. The Aftermath of Algeria's First Free Local Election. *Government and Opposition* 26:466–79.

Jain, S. P. 1993. Reorganising Grassroots Institutions for Sustainable Development. *Indian Journal of Public Administration* 39 (3): 396–405.

Jaffrelot, Christophe. 1994. The Genesis and Development of Hindu Nationalism in the Punjab: From the Arya Samaj to the Hindu Sabha (1875–1910). *Indo-British Review* 21 (1): 3–39.

———. 1996. *The Hindu Nationalist Movement and Indian Politics, 1925 to the 1990s: Strategies of Identity-Building, Implantation, and Mobilisation (with Special Reference to Central India).* New Delhi: Viking

Jaisingh, Hari. 1989. *India after Indira: The Turbulent Years, 1984–1989.* New Delhi: Allied.

Jalali, Rita. 1993. Movement of the Disadvantaged: The Case of the Scheduled Castes in India. *Ethnic and Racial Studies* 16:95–120.

Jayaprasad, K. 1991. *RSS and Hindu Nationalism: Inroads in a Leftist Stronghold.* New Delhi: Deep and Deep.

Johnson, Chalmers A. 1982. *MITI and the Japanese Miracle: The Growth of Industrial Policy, 1925–1975.* Stanford: Stanford University Press.

Joshi, Ram, and Kirtiv Desai. 1987. Dominance with a Difference: Strains and Challenges. In *Congress in Indian Politics: A Centenary Perspective,* ed. Ram Joshi and R. K. Hebsur. Bombay: Popular Prakashan.

Joshi, Vijay, and I. Little. 1996. *India's Economic Reforms: 1991–2001.* Oxford: Clarendon.

Juergensmeyer, Mark. 1991. *Radhasoami Reality: The Logic of a Modern Faith.* Princeton: Princeton University Press.

Justel, M. 1992. *El Lider como factor de explicación del voto.* Working Papers, no. 51. Barcelona: Institut de Ciències Polítiques i Socials.

Karve, Irawati. 1958. What Is Caste? *Economic Weekly* 10:125–38.

Kaviraj, Sudipta. 1996. Dilemmas of Democratic Development in India. In *Democracy and Development: Theory and Practice,* ed. Adrian Leftwich. Cambridge: Polity.

Kendrick, S., and D. McCrone. 1989. Politics in a Cold Climate: The Conservative Decline in Scotland. *Political Studies* 37 (December): 589–603.

Key, V. O. 1949. *Southern Politics.* New York: Knopf.

Kitschelt, H. 1992. The Formation of Party Systems in East Central Europe. *Politics & Society* 20:7–50.

Knauss, Peter. 1987. *The Persistence of Patriarchy: Class, Gender, and Ideology in Twentieth Century Algeria.* New York: Praeger.

Kochanek, Stanley A. 1968. *The Congress Party of India: The Dynamics of One-Party Democracy.* Princeton: Princeton University Press.

———. 1974. *Business and Politics in India.* Berkeley and Los Angeles: University of California Press.

———. 1976. Mrs. Gandhi's Pyramid: The New Congress. In *Indira Gandhi's India: A Political System Reappraised,* ed. Henry C. Hart. Boulder: Westview.

———. 1987. Briefcase Politics in India: The Congress Party and the Business Elite. *Asian Survey* 27 (12): 1278–1301.

Kohli, Atul. 1987a. The Political Economy of Development Strategies. *Comparative Politics* 19:233–46.

———. 1987b. *The State and Poverty in India: The Politics of Reform.* Cambridge: Cambridge University Press.

———. 1988a. From Elite Activism to Democratic Consolidation: The Rise of Reform Communism in West Bengal. In *Dominance and State Power in Modern India,* ed. Francine R. Frankel and M. S. A. Rao. Vol. 2. Bombay: Oxford University Press.

———. 1988b. Interpreting India's Democracy: A State-Society Framework. In *India's Democracy,* ed. Atul Kohli. Princeton: Princeton University Press.

———.1989. Politics of Economic Liberalization in India. *World Development* 17:305–28.

———. 1990. *Democracy and Discontent: India's Growing Crisis of Governability.* New York: Cambridge University Press.

———. 1994. Centralization and Powerlessness: India's Democracy in a Comparative Perspective. In *State Power and Social Forces: Domination and Transformation in the Third World,* ed. Joel S. Migdal, Atul Kohli, and Vivienne Shue. New York: Cambridge University Press.

Kohno, M., and Y. Nishizawa. 1990. A Study of the Electoral Business Cycle in Japan: Elections and Government Spending on Public Construction. *Comparative Politics* 22:151–66.

Kolenda, Pauline. 1986. Caste in India since Independence. In *Social and Economic Development in India: An Assessment,* ed. Dilip K. Basu and Richard Sisson. New Delhi: Sage.

Kothari, Rajni. 1961a. Form and Substance in Indian Politics II: Union and State Relations. *Economic Weekly,* 6 May.

———. 1961b. Form and Substance in Indian Politics III: Panchayati Raj, A Reassessment. *Economic Weekly,* 13 May.

———. 1961c. Form and Substance in Indian Politics IV: Parliamentary Government, Law, and Usage. *Economic Weekly,* 20 May.

———. 1961d. Form and Substance in Indian Politics V: Party System. *Economic Weekly,* 3 June.

Kothari, Rajni. 1964. The Congress "System" in India. *Asian Survey* 4:1161–73.

Kothari, Rajni, and G. Shah. 1965. Caste Orientation of Political Factions: Modasa Constituency. In *Indian Voting Behaviour: Studies of the 1962 General Elections,* ed. Myron Weiner and Rajni Kothari. Calcutta: K. L. Mukhopadhayay.

Kothari, Rajni. 1970. Introduction to *Caste In Indian Politic,.* ed. Rajni Kothari. Delhi: Orient Longmans.

Krishnaswamy, K. S. 1993. For Panchayats the Dawn Is Not Yet. *Economic and Political Weekly* 28:2183–86.

Kumar, Sushil. 1968. Nomination Politics in the Congress Party: A Case Study in Rajasthan. In *The Fourth General Election in India,* ed. S. P. Varma and Iqbal Narain. Vol. 1. Delhi: Orient Longmans.

Laakso, Markku, and Rein Taagepera. 1979. "Effective" Number of Parties: A Measure with Application to West Europe. *Comparative Political Studies* 12:3–27.

Laitin, David D. 1989. Language Policy and Political Strategy in India. *Policy Sciences* 22:415–36.

Lakdawala, D. T. 1991. Inaugural Address. In *The Ninth Finance Commission: Issues and Recommendations.* New Delhi: National Institute of Public Finance and Policy.

Lakehel, M., ed. 1992. *Algerie: de L'Independance a l'etat d'urgence.* Paris: Larmises et L'Harmattan.

Lamchichi, Abderrahim. 1992. *L'Islamisme en Algerie.* Paris: l'Harmattan.

LaPalombara, Joseph. 1987. *Democracy, Italian Style.* New Haven: Yale University Press.

Laver, Michael. 1989. Party Competition and Party System Change: The Interaction of Coalition Bargaining and Electoral Change. *Journal of Theoretical Politics* 1 (3): 301–24.

Lazreg, Marnia. 1976. *The Emergence of Classes in Algeria: A Study of Colonialism and Socio-Political Change.* Boulder: Westview.

Leca, Jean. 1990. Social Structure and Political Stability: Comparative Evidence from the Algerian, Syrian, and Iraqi Cases. In *The Arab State,* ed. Giacomo Luciani. Berkeley: University of California Press.

Lehmbruch, Gerhard, and Philippe C. Schmitter. 1982. *Patterns of Corporatist Policy-Making.* London: Sage.

Levine, Daniel H. 1973. *Conflict and Political Change in Venezuela.* Princeton: Princeton University Press.

———. 1995. Beyond Exhaustion of the Model: Possibilities for Democratic Survival and Transformation in Venezuela. University of Michigan. Mimeo.

Levine, Daniel, ed. 1986. *Religion and Political Conflict in Latin America.* Chapel Hill: University of North Carolina Press.

Lewis, Bernard. 1985. Islamic Political Movements. *Middle East Review* 17 (1): 23–27.

Lewis-Beck, Michael S. 1988. *Economics and Elections: The Major Western Democracies.* Ann Arbor: University of Michigan Press.

Lieten, G. K. 1994. On Casteism and Communalism in Uttar Pradesh. *Economic and Political Weekly,* 2 April.

Lijphart, Arend. 1994. *Electoral Systems and Party Systems.* New York: Oxford University Press.

———. 1996. The Puzzle of Indian Democracy: A Consociational Interpretation. *American Political Science Review* 90:258–68.

Linz, Juan J., and Jose Ramón Montero, eds. 1986. *Crisis y Cambio: Electores y Partidos en la España de los Ochenta.* Madrid: Centro de Estudios Constitucionales.

Lipset, Seymour M., and Stein Rokkan. 1967. *Party Systems and Voter Alignments.* New York: Free Press.

Low, D. A. 1988. Congress and "Mass Contacts, 1936–1937: Ideology, Interests, and Conflict over the Basis of Party Representation. In *Congress and Indian Nationalism: The Pre-independence Phase,* ed. Richard Sisson and Stanley Wolpert. Berkeley: University of California Press.

Lutz, Donald S. 1995. Towards a Theory of Constitutional Amendment. In *Responding to Imperfection: The Theory and Practice of Constitutional Amendment,* ed. Sanford Levinson. Princeton: Princeton University Press.

Maguire, Maria. 1983. Is There Still Persistence? Electoral Change in Western Europe, 1948–1979. In Hans Daalder and Peter Mair eds., *Western European Party Systems,* 67–94. Beverly Hills: Sage.

Maheshwari, B. 1968. Campaign Techniques and Organization. In *The Fourth General Election in India,* ed. S .P. Varma and Iqbal Narain. Vol. 1. Delhi: Orient Longmans.

Maheshwari, Shriram. 1976. Constituency Linkage of National Legislators in India. *Legislative Studies Quarterly* 1 (3): 331–54.

Mainwaring, Scott, and Timothy R. Scully. 1995. *Building Democratic Institutions: Party Systems in Latin America.* Stanford: Stanford University Press.

Mair, Peter. 1989. The Problem of Party System Change. *Journal of Theoretical Politics* 1 (3): 251–76.

Majumdar, B. B. 1956. Bihar. In *Reports on the Indian General Elections, 1951–1952,* ed. S. V. Kogekar and Richard L. Park. Bombay: Popular Book Depot.

Malik, Yogendra K., and V. B. Singh. 1992. Bharatiya Janata Party. *Asian Survey* 32:318–36.

Manor, James. 1988. Politics: Ambiguity, Disillusionment, and Ferment. In *India Briefing, 1989,* ed. Marshall M. Bouton and Philip Oldenburg. London: Westview.

———. 1989. Karnataka: Caste, Class, Dominance, and Politics in a Cohesive Society. In *Dominance and State Power in Modern India: Decline of a Social Order,* ed. Francine R. Frankel and M. S. A. Rao. Vol. 1. Delhi: Oxford University Press.

———. 1990. How and Why Liberal and Representative Politics Emerged in India. *Political Studies* 38:20–38.

———. 1991. India: The Misconceptions and the Reality. *The World Today,* November.

———. 1993. *Power, Poverty, and Poison.* New Delhi: Sage.

———. 1995. India's Chief Ministers and the Problem of Governability. In *India Briefing: Staying the Course,* ed. Philip Oldenburg. London: M. E. Sharpe.

Maravall, Jose María. *Los resultados de la democracia.* Madrid: Alianza.

Mathur, Kuldeep. 1992. The State and the Use of Coercive Power in India. *Asian Survey* 32:337–49.

Matthew, George, ed. 1995. *Status of Panchayati Raj in the States of India, 1994.* New Delhi: Concept.

Mehta, Pratap Bhanu. 1997. India: Fragmentation amid Consensus. *Journal of Democracy* 8 (1): 56–69.

Meyer, Ralph C., and David S. Malcolm. 1993. Voting in India: Effects of Economic Change and New Party Formation. *Asian Survey* 33:507–19.

Migdal, Joel. 1988. *Strong Societies and Weak States.* Princeton: Princeton University Press.

Migdal, Joel S., Atul Kohli, and Vivienne Shue, eds. 1994. *State Power and Social Forces: Domination and Transformation in the Third World.* New York: Cambridge University Press.

Ministerio de Economía y Hacienda. 1990. Informe sobre las Financiación de las Comunidades Autónomas en 1989. In *Dirección General de Coordinación con las Haciendas Territoriales.* Madrid: Ministerio de Hacienda.

———. 1991. Informe sobre las Financiación de las Comunidades Autónomas en 1990. In *Dirección General de Coordinación con las Haciendas Territoriales.* Madrid: Ministerio de Hacienda.

———. 1992. Informe sobre las Financiación de las Comunidades Autónomas en 1991.In *Dirección General de Coordinación con las Haciendas Territoriales.* Madrid: Ministerio de Hacienda.

———. 1993a. La Descentralización del Gasto Público en España. Periodo 1984–1992. In *Madrid Dirección General de Coordinación con las Haciendas Territoriales.* Madrid: Ministerio de Hacienda.

———. 1993b. Informe sobre las Financiación de las Comunidades Autónomas en 1992. In *Dirección General de Coordinación con las Haciendas Territoriales.* Madrid: Ministerio de Hacienda.

Ministry of Rural Development. 1991. *Panchayati Raj Institutions in India, 1991.* Delhi: Government of India Press.

Mishra, Amaresh. 1995a. Cracks in the Alliance. *Economic and Political Weekly* 30:983–84.

———. 1995b. Limits of OBC-Dalit Politics. *Economic and Political Weekly* 30: 1355–57.

Mitra, Ashok. 1988. Introduction. In *Essays in Federal Financial Relations,* ed. I. S. Gulati and K. K. George. New Delhi. Oxford and IBH.

Mitra, Subrata Kumar. 1978. *Governmental Instability in Indian States: West Bengal, Bihar, Uttar Pradesh, and Punjab.* New Delhi. Ajanta.

———. 1979. Ballot Box and Local Power: Elections in an Indian Village. *Journal of Commonwealth and Comparative Politics* 17:283–99.

———. 1992. *Power, Protest, and Participation: Local Elites and the Politics of Development in India.* London: Routledge.

———. 1993. Desecularising the State: Religion and Politics in India after Independence. *Comparative Studies in Society and History* 33:755–74.

———. 1994. Caste, Democracy, and the Politics of Community Formation in India. In *Contextualising Caste,* ed. Mary Searle-Chatterji, and Ursula Sharma. Cambridge: Blackwell.

Mohapatra, Manindra Kumar. 1971. *Intervention and Non-intervention: A Study of Legislators: Administrative Role Orientation in an Indian State.* Ann Arbor: University Microfilms.

Montero, Jose Ramón. 1994. Religiosidad y Voto en España. *Revista de Estudios Políticos* 83 (January–March): 77–111.

Montero, Jose Ramón, and Mariano 1990. Torcal. Autonomías y Comunidades Autónomas en España: Preferencias, Dimensiones y Orientaciones Políticas. *Revista de Estudios Políticos* 70 (October-November): 33–91.

Morris-Jones, W. H. 1964. Parliament and Dominant Party: The Indian Experience. *Parliamentary Affairs* 17:296–307.

Mortimer, Robert. 1991. Islam and Multiparty Politics in Algeria. *Middle East Journal* 45:575–93.

Mozoomdar, Ajit. 1994. The Rise and Decline of Development Planning in India. In *The State and Development Planning in India,* ed. Terence Byres. Delhi: Oxford University Press.

Muller, Wolfgang C. 1993. The Relevance of the State for Party System Change. *Journal of Theoretical Politics* 5 (4): 419–54.

Namjoshi, M. V., and B. R. Sabade. 1967. *Chambers of Commerce in India.* Bombay: Asia Publishing House

Narain, I., and M. Lal. 1968. Introduction to *Fourth General Election in India,* ed. S. P. Varma and I. Narain. Vol. 1. New Delhi: Orient Longman.

National Council of Applied Economic Research. 1994. *Problems in the Implementation of Economic Reforms at the State Level.* New Delhi: March.

National Institute of Urban Affairs. 1983. *A Study of the Financial Resources of Urban Local Bodies in India and the level of Services Provided.* Part 1. New Delhi: National Institute of Urban Affairs.

Nehru, J. 1985. *Letters to Chief Ministers, 1947–1964.* Vols. 3–4. Delhi: Oxford University Press.

Nicholson, Norman. 1972. Factionalism and the Indian Council of Ministers. *Journal of Commonwealth Political Studies* 10:1979–97.

———. 1975. Integrative Strategies of a National Elite: Career Patterns in the Indian Council of Ministers. *Comparative Politics* 7:533–57.

Omvedt, Gail. 1980. Caste, Agrarian Relations, and Agrarian Conflicts. *Sociological Bulletin* 29:38–56.

———. 1991. The Anti-caste Movement and the Discourse of Power. *Race and Class* 33 (2): 15–28.

Organisation for Economic Co-operation and Development. 1992–93. *OECD Economic Surveys: Spain.* Paris: Organisation of Economic Co-operation and Development.

Panebianco, Angelo. 1988. *Political Parties: Organization and Power.* Cambridge: Cambridge University Press.

Papachristou, G. 1968. The Interplay of Local and State Politics: The Rajasthan Case. In *The Fourth General Election in India,* ed. S. P. Varma and Iqbal Narain.Vol. 1. Delhi: Orient Longmans.

Paranjape, H. K. 1964. *The Planning Commission: A Descriptive Account.* Delhi: Indian Institute of Public Administration.

Parekh, Bhikku, and Upendra Baxi, eds. 1995. *Crisis and Change in Contemporary India.* New Delhi: Sage.

Parikh, Manju. 1993. The Debacle at Ayodhya: Why Militant Hinduism Met with a Weak Response. *Asian Survey* 33:673–84.

Pedersen, Mogens N. 1983. Changing Patterns of Electoral Volatility in European Party Systems; 1948–1977: Explorations in Explanation. In Hans Daalder and Peter Mair, eds., *Western European Party Systems,* 29–66. Beverly Hills: Sage.

Pfiefer, Karen. 1992. Algeria's Implicit Stabilization Program. In *The Political Economy of the Middle East,* ed. Henri Barkey. New York: St. Martin's.

Porteous, Tom. 1991. The Crisis in Algeria: What Chance Democracy? *Middle East Intelligence,* 12 July.

PP 1989. *El Proyecto Popular. Todo lo que el Partido Popular va a Cambiar.* Madrid; Partido Popular.

———. 1993. *Programa de Gobierno para Todos.* Madrid: Partido Popular.

Prasad, Bimal. 1988. Congress versus the Muslim League, 1935–1937. In *Congress and Indian Nationalism: The Pre-independence Phase,* ed. Richard Sisson and Stanley Wolpert. Berkeley: University of California Press.

Prasad, Kamta. 1994. Future Role of Planning under New Perspectives. *Indian Journal of Public Administration* 40:525–36.

Prasad, Nageshwar. 1979. Oligarchy in Indian Parties at the Local Level. *Asian Survey* 19:896–909.

Przeworski, Adam, and John Sprague. 1988. *Paper Stones: A History of Electoral Socialism.* Chicago: University of Chicago Press.

PSOE [Partido Socialista Oberero Español]. 1982. *Programa Electoral, 1982.* Madrid: Elecciones Generaless.

———. *Programa, 1986/1990.* 1990. Madrid: Para Seguir Avanzando por el Buen Camino.

————. *Programa Electoral, 1989.* 1990. Madrid España en Progreso.

————. *Programa Electoral, 1993.* 1993. Madrid: El Programa de la Mayoría.

Puhle, Hans-Jurgen. 1986. El PSOE: Un Partido Predominante y Heterogéneo. In *Crisis y Cambio: Electores y partidos en la Espana de los ochenta.* ed. Juan J. Linz and Jose Montero. Madrid: Centro des Estudios Constitutionales.

Putnam, Robert D. 1993. *Making Democracy Work: Civic Traditions in Modern Italy.* Princeton: Princeton University Press.

Raheja, Gloria Goodwin. 1988. India: Caste, Kingship, and Dominance Reconsidered. *Annual Review of Anthropology* 17:497–522.

Ramachandran, V. 1995. Kerala. In *Status of Panchayati Raj in the States of India, 1994,* ed. George Matthew. Delhi: Concept.

Ramaswamy, E. A. 1988. *Worker Consciousness and Trade Union Response.* Delhi: Oxford University Press.

————. 1995. Organized Labor and Economic Reform. In *India Briefing: Staying the Course,* ed. Philip Oldenburg. London: M. E. Sharpe.

Rao, M. Govinda, and R. J. Chelliah. 1991. *Survey of Research on Fiscal Federalism in India.* National Institute of Public Finance and Policy. New Delhi.

Rao, Govinda M., and V B Tulsidhar. 1991. *Public Expenditure in India: Emerging Trends.* Working Papers, no. 5. New Delhi: National Institute of Public Finance and Policy.

Reiter, Howard L. 1989. Party Decline in the West: A Skeptic's View. *Journal of Theoretical Politics* 1 (3): 325–48.

Richards, Alan, and John Waterbury. 1990. *A Political Economy of the Middle East: State, Class, and Economic Development.* Boulder: Westview.

Roberts, Hugh. 1992. The Algerian State and the Challenge of Democracy. *Government and Opposition* 27:433–54.

Robins, Robert S. 1979. Votes, Seats, and the Critical Indian Election of 1967. *Journal of Commonwealth and Comparative Politics* 17 (3): 247–62.

Rogowski, Ronald. 1995. The Role of Theory and Anomaly in Social-Scientific Inference. *American Political Science Review* 89:467–70.

Roy, Ramashray. 1969. Two Patterns in India's Mid-Term Elections. *Asian Review* 2 (4): 287–302.

Rudolph, Lloyd I, and Susanne H. Rudolph. 1960. The Role of India's Caste Associations. *Pacific Affairs* 33:5–22.

————. 1967.*The Modernity of Tradition.* Chicago: University of Chicago Press.

————. 1980. The Centrist Future of Indian Politics. *Asian Survey* 20:575–94.

————. 1987. *In Pursuit of Lakshmi: The Political Economy of the Indian State.* Chicago: University of Chicago Press.

Rudolph, Lloyd I. 1989. The Faltering Novitate: Rajiv at Home and Abroad in 1988. In *India Briefing, 1989,* ed. Marshall Bouton and Philip Oldenberg. Boulder: Westview.

Rudolph, Susanne Hoeber. 1987. Presidential Address: State Formation in Asia—Prolegomenon to a Comparative Study. *Journal of Asian Studies* 46:731–46.

Rudolph, Susanne Hoeber, and Lloyd I. Rudolph. 1993. Modern Hate. *New Republic,* 22 March.

Ruedy, John. 1992. *Modern Algeria: The Origins and Development of a Nation.* Bloomington: Indiana University Press.

Rummel, Lynette. 1992. Privatization and Democratization in Algeria. In *State and Society in Algeria,* ed. John P. Entelis and Phillip C. Naylor. Boulder: Westview.

Semmoud, Bouziane. 1986. Politique d'habitat et acces au logement en Algerie. L'exemple de L'Oraine. *Annuaire de L'Afrique du Nord* 25:127–39.

Sen, Amartya. 1984. *Resources, Values, and Development.* Cambridge: Harvard University Press.

Shamir, Michal. 1984. Are Western European Party Systems "Frozen"? *Comparative Political Studies* 17:35–79.

Shefter, Martin. 1994. *Political Parties and the State: The American Historical Experience.* Princeton: Princeton University Press.

Shepsle, Kenneth A., and Ronald N. Cohen. 1990. Mulitparty Competition, Entry, and Entry Deterrence in Spatial Models of Elections. In *Advances in the Spatial Theory of Voting,* ed. James. M. Enelow and Melvin J. Hinich. New York: Cambridge University Press.

Shrader, Lawrence L., and Richard Sisson. 1987. Representation and Elites: Legislators in Nation and State. In *Congress in Indian Politics: A Centenary Perspective,* ed. Ram Joshi and R .K. Hebsur. Bombay: Popular Prakashan.

Singh, Hoshiar. 1994. Constitutional Base for Panchayati Raj in India. *Asian Survey* 34:818–27.

Singh, R. S. 1969. Bases and Strategies in Elections: A Study of Voting in Azamgarh Parliamentary Constituency. *Economic and Political Weekly* 4:1601–4.

Singh, Ranbir. 1979. Legislative Elites in Haryana: Representation of Agriculturist Castes. *Indian Journal of Political Science* 4:618–31.

Singh, S. S., and Suresh Mishra. 1991. Panchayati Raj Experiment in Madhya Pradesh. *Indian Journal of Public Administration* 37 (4): 526–58.

Singh, V. B., and Shankar Bose. 1984. *Elections in India: Data Handbook on Lok Sabha Elections, 1952–80.* New Delhi: Sage.

———. 1994. *Elections in India: Data Handbook on Lok Sabha Elections, 1986–1994.* New Delhi: Sage.

Sinha, K. K. 1995. Bihar. In *Status of Panchayati Raj in the States of India, 1994.* Delhi: Concept.

Sisson, Richard. 1972. *The Congress Party in Rajasthan: Political Integration and Institution Building in an Indian State.* Berkeley: University of California Press.

———. 1981. Prime-Ministerial Power and the Selection of Ministers in India: Three Decades of Change. *International Political Science Review* 2:137–57.

———. 1985. The Political Stratification of India's National Governing Class. Paper presented at the meetings of the International Political Science, Paris, 15–20 July.

———. 1990. Dominant Party or Marketing Franchise? The Congress Party in Early Independent India. Mimeo.

Sisson, Richard, and L. L. Shrader. 1972. *Legislative Recruitment and Political*

Integration: Patterns of Political Linkage in an Indian State. Berkeley: Center for South and Southeast Asian Studies, University of California, Berkeley.

Skocpol, Theda. 1995. *Social Policy in the United States: Future Possibilities in Historical Perspective.* Princeton: Princeton University Press.

Smith, Gordon. 1989. A System Perspective on Party System Change. *Journal of Theoretical Politics* 1 (3): 349–63.

Srinivas, M. N. 1958. Caste and Politics. *Economic Weekly* 10:570–72.

Stern, R., and K. L. Kamal. 1974. Class, Status, and Party in Rajasthan. *Journal of Commonwealth and Comparative Politics* 12 (3): 276–96.

Stimson, James A. 1985. Regression in Space and Time: A Statistical Essay. *American Journal of Political Science* 29:914–47.

Strøm, Kaare. 1989. Inter-party Competition in Advanced Democracies. *Journal of Theoretical Politics* 1 (3): 277–300.

Suresh, V. 1996. The Dalit Movement in India. In *Region, Religion, Caste, Gender, and Culture in Contemporary India,* ed T. V. Sathyamurthy. Delhi: Oxford University Press.

Taagpera, Rein. 1989. *Seats and Votes: The Effects and Determinants of Electoral Systems.* New Haven: Yale University Press.

Taagapera, Rein, and Matthew Shugart. 1993. Predicting the Number of Parties: A Quantitative Model of Duverger's Mechanical Effect. *American Political Science Review* 87:455–64.

Tambiah, Stanley. 1990. Presidential Address: Reflections on Communal Violence in South Asia. *Journal of Asian Studies* 49 (4): 741–60.

Tarrow, Sidney G. 1989. *Democracy and Disorder: Protest and Politics in Italy, 1965–1975.* Oxford: Clarendon.

Thakur, Ramesh. 1993. Ayodhya and the Politics of India's Secularism: A Double-Standards Discourse. *Asian Survey* 33:645–64.

Tlemcani, Rachid. 1986. *State and Revolution in Algeria.* Boulder: Westview.

Tsebelis, George. 1990. *Nested Games: Rational Choice in Comparative Politics.* Berkeley: University of California Press.

Tufte, Edward R. 1978. *Political Control of the Economy.* Princeton: Princeton University Press.

Valenzuela, Arturo. 1978. Chile. In *The Breakdown of Democratic Regimes,* ed. Juan J. Linz and Alfred Stepan. Baltimore: Johns Hopkins University Press.

Vallès, Josep Maria. 1987. Quante Spagne Elettorali? Dimensioni Territoriali del Fenomeno Elettorale nella Spagna Odierna. In *Lezioni Regionali e Sistema Politico Nazionale. Italia, Spagne e la Repubblica Federale Tedesca,* ed. Mario Caciagli and Piergiornio Corbeta. Bolonia: Mulino.

Varshney, Ashutosh. 1993. Contested Meanings: India's National Identity, Hindu Nationalism, and the Politics of Anxiety. In *Daedalus* 122:227–61.

———. 1995. *Democracy, Development, and the Countryside: Urban-Rural Struggles in India.* New York: Cambridge University Press.

———. 1997. Postmodernism, Civic Engagement, and Ethnic Conflict: A Passage to India. *Comparative Politics* 30 (1): 1–20.

Wallace, Paul. 1988. Religious and Secular Politics in Punjab: The Sikh Dilemma in Competing Political Systems. In *Political Dynamics and Crisis in Punjab,* ed. Paul Wallace and Surendra Chopra. Amritsar: Guru Nanak Dev University.

Washbrook, David. 1973. Country Politics: Madras, 1880 to 1930. In *Locality Province, and Nation: Essays on Indian Politics, 1870–1940,* ed. John Gallagher, Gordon Johnson, and Anil Seal. Cambridge: Cambridge University Press.

Waterbury, John. 1993. *Exposed to Innumerable Delusions: Public Enterprises and State Power in Egypt, India, Mexico, and Turkey.* New York: Cambridge University Press.

Webster, Neil. 1992. Panchayati Raj in West Bengal: Popular Participation for the People or the Party? *Development and Change* 23 (4): 129–63.

Weiner, Myron. 1957. *Party Politics in India.* Princeton: Princeton University Press.

———. 1959. Some Hypotheses on the Politics of Modernization in India. In *Leadership and Political Institutions in India,* ed. Richard L. Park and Irene Tinker. Princeton: Princeton University Press.

———. 1962a. India's Third General Election. *Asian Survey* 2:3–18.

———. 1962b. Village and Party Factionalism in Andhra Pradesh. *Economic Weekly,* 22 September.

———. 1964. Traditional Role Performance and the Development of Modern Political Parties: The Indian Case. *Journal of Politics* 26:830–49.

———. 1967. *Party Building in a New Nation: The Indian National Congress.* Chicago: University of Chicago Press.

———. 1986. The Political Economy of Industrial Growth in India. *World Politics* 38 (4): 596–610.

———. 1987. Rajiv Gandhi: A Mid-Term Assessment. In *India Briefing, 1987,* ed. Marshall Bouton and Philip Oldenberg. Boulder: Westview.

———. 1989. *The Indian Paradox: Essays in Indian Politics.* Delhi: Sage.

Weiner, Myron, and John Osgood Field, eds. *Electoral Politics in the Indian States.* Vols. 1–4. New Delhi: Manohar Book Service.

Williamson, Dhelia. 1992. Who Voted For the FIS. Masters Thesis. Ohio State University.

Wood, John R., ed. 1984. *State Politics in Contemporary India: Crisis or Continuity?* Boulder: Westview.

Wright, Gillian. 1995. The Decline of Congress: The Rise of Mulayam. *Seminar* 432:19–23.

Wright, Theodore P. 1977. Muslims and the 1977 Indian Elections: A Watershed? *Asian Survey* 17:1207–26.

Wolinetz, Steven B. 1979. The Transformation of Western European Party Systems Revisited. *West European Politics* 2:4–28.

Yadav, Yogendra. 1996. Reconfiguration in Indian Politics: State Assembly Elections, 1993–95. *Economic and Political Weekly* 20:95–104.

Zaidi, A. M. 1985. *A Tryst with Destiny: A Study of Economic Policy Resolutions of the Indian National Congress Passed during the Last 100 Years.* Delhi: Indian Institute of Applied Political Research.

———. 1986. *Promises to Keep: A Study of Election Manifestos of the Indian*

National Congress, 1937–1985. New Delhi: Indian Institute of Applied Political Research.

Zaidi, A. Moin, and Shaheda Zaidi, eds. 1981. *The Encyclopaedia of Indian National Congress.* Vol. 15. New Delhi: S. Chand.

Zelliot, Eleanor. 1992. From *Untouchable to Dalit: Essays on the Ambedkar Movement.* New Delhi: Manohar.

Zoubir, Yahia. 1992. The Painful Transition from Authoritarianism in Algeria. *Arab Studies Quarterly* 15 (3): 83–110.

Index